CANCER FAMILY

The Search for the Cause of **Hereditary Colorectal Cancer**

C. Richard Boland, MD

authorHOUSE®

AuthorHouse™
1663 Liberty Drive
Bloomington, IN 47403
www.authorhouse.com
Phone: 1 (800) 839-8640

Published by AuthorHouse 08/27/2015

ISBN: 978-1-5049-2868-7 (sc)
ISBN: 978-1-5049-2869-4 (hc)
ISBN: 978-1-5049-2867-0 (e)

Library of Congress Control Number: 2015912930

Print information available on the last page.

This book is printed on acid-free paper.

"The Greatest Generation"

The Boland family about 1927, shortly after the death of Thomas N. Boland Sr. Crouching in the front, left to right: Clement, Rita, Alice, Larry and Bob (the youngest). Standing, left to right: Matthew, Mary Gertrude (Thomas, Sr's wife), John, Anna (furthest back), Helen (in the patterned dress), Mary, Margaret, Loretta, and Thomas Jr.

Contents

Prologue (Summer, 1946)

"Keep passing the open windows." (From *Hotel New Hampshire*, John Irving.)

A twenty five year old man with a gaunt and haunted look paced back and as he passed the window in his third floor apartment on over Bonham's Drug Store in Binghamton, New York (*Figure 1*). It was the summer of 1946. He paused and gazed silently out the open window. He turned and walked again, stopping each time at the window, looking down onto Main Street. His belly was wracked with pain, and he knew it was time for another injection. He had been sent home from Europe with a large cancerous mass in his abdomen, and he knew how this would end. He had finished medical school a year earlier, married the first love of his life, and had a one-year old daughter. He looked again as the cars slowly passed below in the summer sun. Occasional people meandered in and out of the drug store onto the sidewalk below. He paused again, looked out, and resumed his pacing.

Behind him, Cathie held Suzanne in her arms, calming her as she fussed. Suzanne finished her bottle, and Cathie put her into the crib in the living room. She looked at her husband from behind as he paced. She was worried about his pacing and pausing before the window. Clement slowly turned towards her. It was "the look" and it made her shudder. The once magnificent face had changed. His temples were sunken. His arms were thin. The loving smile was spent. He was slightly bent over because of his pain. He disappeared into the bedroom. Cathie looked over the edge of the crib as Suzanne's fidgeting stopped and she drifted into sleep. Cathie watched and smiled. She leaned over to smell the fresh scent of her daughter, and wondered what she might become when she grew up.

She heard an unidentifiable sound from Clem and a thud in the bedroom. Cathie rushed through the door, and Clem was on the floor, eyes rolled back, thrashing as a seizure gripped his body. She was terrified and didn't know what to do. His arms and legs gradually stopped moving and he took several deep breaths, sudden desperate gasps, with pauses between each one. His eyes blinked, but seemed not to see.

Cathie began to sob. Her husband of not two years had just finished his internship, was shipped out by the Army to Naples and into northern Yugoslavia. The war was over. He told her he would not be gone long. Just some peacekeeping between the partisans of the Balkans.

"I'll write every day," he promised.

"I love you".

"Just a short while until I get back".

"Don't worry".

Fate was not so kind. A few months into his deployment Clement began to lose weight and the abdominal pain started. He felt a mass in his abdomen, just over his appendix—the appendix that had been removed. Clem knew what it was, but couldn't mention it to the other medics. Cancer was a forbidden word in the Boland family.

"You have an ulcer," they told him.

"You are homesick."

"Drive that ambulance, medic."

Finally, he lost forty pounds and the Army sent him back to the States. The "ulcer" was actually a cancer in his colon. Cathie and her mother spirited him off the Army base, home to upstate New York for surgery. Clem had already seen two sisters die of cancers. His father had died of colon cancer. He knew what was coming. Fate was stalking to collect its dues.

He had a very large tumor. Lymph nodes were involved. Probably fatal. The Army discharged him to die. Six months. Try injecting this new pain medicine. Not addicting like morphine. The pain returned as soon as the medicine wore off. Had to increase the dose. Now a seizure.

This is the story of Clement R. Boland's life, and the life his son had to follow as a consequence.

Figure 1: The apartment over Bonham's Drug Store in Binghamton, New York, where Clement Boland paced on the third floor as he considered his fate in the summer of 1946. (Photo taken in 2014).

Chapter 1

In Medias Res (1969-70)

Ancient epics often began their story in the middle of things—*in medias res*. Actually, the Latin phrase as written implies a more active situation, as the protagonist is thrust *into the midst of things*, and is immediately in motion. He recognizes that he is in a problematic situation, and must take action. To explain the situation, the narrative first must look back, which provides the historical context, and then move forward. So my story begins—in the middle, and into the midst.

In September, 1969, I started Yale Medical School in New Haven, Connecticut, about four hours by car east of Endwell, New York, where I had lived since age four. Endwell was the next town west, just a few miles down the Susquehanna River, from Johnson City, where I was born. I came home for Thanksgiving after my first three months of medical school. It was November, 1969; my first vacation break from this new journey. The sixties were almost gone, a tough time during which the world flipped upside down. I had previously gone to college about seven hundred miles west. Unlike that journey, New Haven to Endwell would mean easy trips home. I was entering the profession of my father; time to get to know him better. That felt good.

The events of the 1960s had a polarizing effect between fathers and sons. However, as a medical student, the edginess of the sixties no longer stood between my father and me. Pursuing my father's profession created a transformation in me. Dad was very excited to hear about what they were teaching in medical school. "What's new? How are you enjoying anatomy (one of the first courses)? Can you stand the smell of the cadaver room?

What are they teaching now?" Very positive exchanges. On the Sunday morning after Thanksgiving, as I readied for my return from upstate New York to Connecticut, and I gave Dad a hug just. He winced with pain.

"What's the matter?" I asked.

"Oh, it's nothing".

Mom interrupted, "This has been going on for some weeks now and he won't see anyone."

I encouraged him to have it evaluated. I left, with school on my mind, not knowing what this portended.

There were about three weeks between the Thanksgiving and Christmas breaks. Yale Medical School was filled with a lot of people just like me. It was fun but competitive, and I loved the course material. Each day was intense but I couldn't get enough of the information. It was not an overload, just a load, and it came effortlessly. I had been back at school about three weeks when my life began to change on Wednesday morning, December 17. I was in a microbiology lab, and we were at the bench discussing how many viruses and bacteria could live on bars of soap. A teaching assistant came to me with a message from the Dean of Students' office: "call home". I found a pay phone, and called. Mom told me that Dad was in the hospital. His pain had worsened, and he couldn't stand up straight. He was evaluated, and they found colon cancer. An operation was scheduled for Friday.

I headed back to upstate New York the next morning. It was a gray morning, as I headed west on Route-17 through the Catskill Mountains. I was totally preoccupied with what was happening at home, and was stopped (with about ten other drivers on a long downhill stretch) for going seventy-five in a seventy zone. I tried to tell the state policeman that I had a special circumstance, but he handed me a clipboard, told me to fill out the form, and dashed to the person stopped behind me. He spent about five seconds with me, collected his fine, and went to the next driver. Never mind. I had just passed through a small-town toll gate.

I got home safely and went directly to Wilson Memorial Hospital in Johnson City, the hospital where my mother and all four of her children had been born. Dad was the Chief of Pediatrics. Mom intercepted me in the hallway outside his room. They found two colon cancers—one at the junction of his small and large intestine, and another further down.

Surgery was planned for the next day. I was confident he would be cured by the operation; that's what we did with modern medicine. The surgeon opened him up, but couldn't remove anything, so he sewed him back up. The tumor appeared to involve the liver. I spent the night after surgery with him. They advised him to go to Roswell Park, the cancer center in Buffalo, New York, for specialized surgery. So, off he and Mom went, and I caught up on the day of the planned surgery. In mid-February, the Roswell Park surgeons also realized that the cancer was too advanced, and after eight hours of surgery, that operation was also aborted. He was sent home to die for the second time in his forty-nine years. He died on July 26, 1970, leaving me with a medical mystery to solve.

Chapter 2

CANCER IN THE FAMILY (1970)

There had been occasional, quiet talk in the family about Dad's "illness" during his time in the Army. That discussion was not specifically suppressed, but there was never a lot said about cancer in the family. I knew from family reunions—mostly funerals and weddings—that discussions of health were carried out privately. All other matters could be vigorously discussed in groups: political discussions, opinions, grand family legends, and recollections. But when we were with Dad's family, it would have been easier to bring a live rattlesnake into the room to perform tricks than to openly ask who in the family had died of cancer.

One of the unspoken reasons for fearing any discussion of a familial predisposition to cancer was the nasty history of eugenics that contaminated Western science from the late Victorian era until the end of the Nazi political experiment in 1945. Darwin's explanation for the generation of species in the biological world was a polarizing concept, one that pitted the scientific world against traditionalists and the religious world. Some extrapolated these concepts from the biological into the social realm. The term "eugenics" was coined by Francis Galton, a polymath cousin of Darwin. He extended Darwin's concepts and proposed that it would be possible to improve the human condition by encouraging the breeding of the "best" of the human race and by discouraging breeding among the "less gifted" among us. Essentially, he thought humankind should use the same breeding techniques that were used in agriculture and animal husbandry to produce better corn, more milk, or tastier beef. From the late nineteenth century through the first half of the twentieth century, research studies were published suggesting that the breeding of bad human "stock" gave rise to murderers, alcoholics, rapists, and morons—terms used by eugenicists to describe what they needed to eliminate from the gene pool. (This is reviewed in detail in a monograph entitled *DNA* by James Watson, published in 2003)

In the United States, programs of sterilization of a variety of unwanted classes of people were undertaken, driven by multiple statutes passed by individual states as well as the federal government. Immigrants were particularly targeted, supported by a body of odiously inept research studies. The Nazis took this much further. Within three years of the passage of eugenically driven laws in 1933, 225,000 people were sterilized in the name of protecting the German race. Of course, the Holocaust represented the absolute depths of the concept. This type of thinking became unpopular, and largely declined after the end of World War II for obvious reasons. However, during the first half of the twentieth century, anyone who feared the social consequences of a possible genetic defect did so on the basis of solid evidence.

Not long after Dad's death, I was on a short trip with my mother and maternal grandmother. They were in the front seats of the car; I was in the back. That was the first time I had heard about Mom and my grandmother going to the army hospital near New York City to bring Dad back to Johnson City after his repatriation from Italy. He was on a stretcher, as if he had been a wounded soldier. He had lost so much weight that my mother couldn't recognize her husband. He tried calling to her as she passed by but was too weak to be heard. They eventually found him, and horrified, took him away without official permission. Mom mentioned that Dad's next older sister, Alice, was ill with cancer at that same time, and died of cancer shortly after Dad's operation in 1946. She knew that Dad's father had also died of cancer when Dad was just five. There were other cancers as well. I realized it was time to find out what was actually happening in the family.

It took some digging, but when family members knew I was serious about this, they opened up and began talking to me. I visited the Boland family homestead in Reading, Pennsylvania, visited several of the local hospitals, and took notes from medical records there. Gradually, a coherent picture began to emerge.

Dad was one of thirteen siblings (*Figure 2*). By 1970 when I first started to contemplate this problem as a first-year medical student, seven of the siblings had either died of cancer or had been operated on for a tumor in the colon or uterus. Everyone had developed his or her first cancer by age forty-five. Five had developed a cancer before age forty. Some had more than one cancer. Dad's father—my grandfather—had developed colon cancer at age twenty-seven in 1907, which he survived with a partial colon resection. He later died of a second cancer in lower portion of his colon or rectum at age forty-six. His father—my great grandfather—had also died of colon cancer. As far back as I could trace, every one of my male ancestors had died of colon cancer, and not one had reached the age of fifty. Moreover, as I gathered the medical records on these cancers, all of the initial cancers had developed in the proximal colon, the upper part that is attached to the small intestine. Ordinarily, one expected that only a quarter to a third of all colorectal cancers would occur in that region. Also, the women had been very susceptible to uterine cancers. When I got those medical records, all had involved the endometrium (the inner lining of the uterus), and none of them were cervical cancers, which would have been more common during that era.

I sought help from the professors at my medical school, and they told me that there was no form of hereditary colorectal cancer except for a rare disease called familial adenomatous polyposis. That was a different problem, and the records indicated that no one in the family had it. I had to make a "deep dive" to figure out what was happening. I searched back in time as far as I could, and collected medical records and family recollections to make sense of what was happening. I realized that this was not going to be an armchair exercise.

Chapter 3

The Boland Family (1870-1926)

The Bolands are a classic American immigrant family. I traced my earliest ancestor, John Boland, Sr. to a small town, Feakle, in County Clare Ireland, where he lived and died in the mid-nineteenth century. Yes, the village is pronounced "fecal". I have no details about his life or his family.

First generation American-born Bolands

His son, my great-grandfather John Boland, Jr., was born in Feakle, Ireland in 1854, and immigrated to the US in 1870 at age sixteen, as a consequence of one of several famines in Ireland. He entered the country through Hoboken, New Jersey and made his way to Harrisburg, Pennsylvania where he worked for the Pennsylvania Railroad, presumably as a physical laborer. In 1876, he married Margaret Kenny, born in 1853, who had also immigrated to Pennsylvania from County Clare, Ireland. They had known one another in Feakle, and corresponded until she arrived in America to marry. John, Jr. died in 1895 at age forty-one following a failed operation for colon cancer in a Philadelphia hospital. He had seven children—six boys and one girl (*Figure 2*).

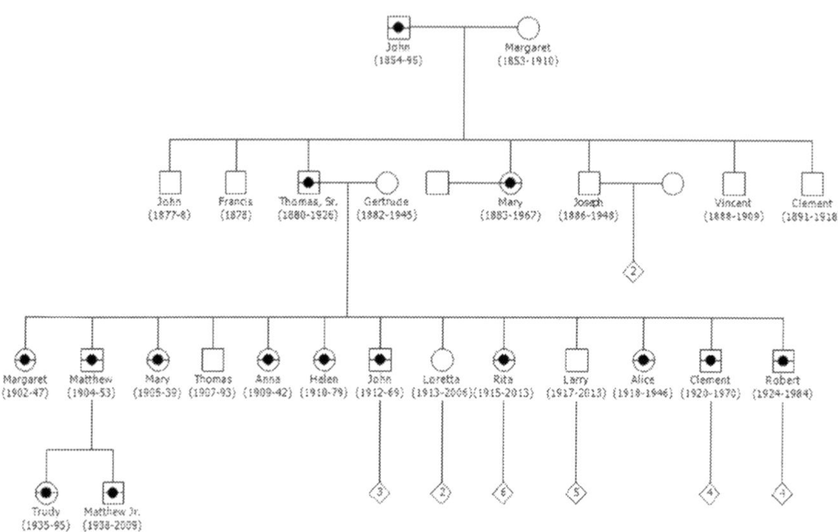

Figure 2: Pedigree of the offspring of John Boland Jr, who emigrated from Ireland to Pennsylvania in 1870. Males are square and females round. Circles and squares containing black dots indicate those who developed cancer. The initial immigrating member of the family (John) died of colorectal cancer at age forty-one. Of his seven children, five reached adulthood, and two died of cancer. Thomas Sr had a colon cancer treated surgically at age twenty-seven, but died of a second tumor at age forty-five. He had thirteen children, ten of whom developed cancers. Margaret died of an endometrial (uterine) cancer at forty-five; Matthew died of a lung cancer at forty-nine; Mary died of an endometrial cancer at thirty-three; Anna died of a colon cancer at thirty-three; Helen suffered sequentially from cancers of the endometrium, ovary, colon and brain, which she survived, but finally died at age sixty-eight of gastric cancer; John had a colon cancer removed at age fifty, which he survived, and died of a heart attack at age fifty-seven; Rita had two colon cancers found and successfully removed at age sixty-five, and died of "old age" at age ninety-seven; Alice died of colon cancer at age twenty-eight; Clement had his first colon cancer at twenty-five, and died of a second colon cancer at age forty-nine; Robert developed gastric cancer at age fifty-two, and died of a recurrence at age sixty. Only those members of the fourth generation (i.e., the generation of Trudy and Matthew, Jr) who have died are indicated there, and the living mutation carriers are not indicated for privacy. Trudy developed an endometrial cancer in her fifties, which was successfully treated, but she died of gastric cancer at age fifty-nine. She was the person from whom the mutation in the family was isolated. Her brother Matthew developed two colon cancers, and died of the second one at age seventy-one.

The first two died in childhood. The third-born was my grandfather, Thomas Nicholas Boland, Sr. He was born in 1880 and lived until 1926. He developed a colon cancer in 1907 at age twenty-seven, had half of his colon removed, and lived nineteen more years. He then developed a second cancer in the lower colon or rectum, and died in 1926 at age forty-five of metastatic cancer, leaving thirteen children.

The youngest child of John Boland, Jr. was Clement Boland (my great-uncle), who was born in 1891 and died fighting in France just prior to the armistice of World War I, in November, 1918, and just shy of his twenty-seventh birthday. There are a couple of family legends surrounding his death – from being gassed in the trenches to being murdered by the Germans for not providing them with military information. I will never know. Most notably, my father was the next male born in the Boland family, and he was given Clement's name by my grandparents to commemorate his death in battle (*Figure 3*).

Figure 3. Clement Boland, born 1891, died in 1918 in World War I and namesake of Clement R. Boland Sr and C. Richard Boland Jr.

Second Generation American-born Bolands

My grandfather, Thomas Nicholas Boland, Sr lived a life of successful upward mobility in an America that rose up on the backs of its immigrants. He married Mary Gertrude Flanagan, of Harrisburg, Pennsylvania, who was born in 1882. Her family called her "Gert" or "Gertie". She apparently hated the name. Thomas and Gertie had thirteen children. He worked in a pig iron factory in the tiny town of Robesonia, Pennsylvania starting about 1903 at age twenty-three. The factory was called "The Furnace", and was situated between a railroad line (for coal and ore) and Furnace Creek.

Thomas was hard-working, and clever enough to be given the task of monitoring the chemical properties of the pig iron, measuring the content of iron, carbon and other elements. He became the factory foreman, and was called "the chemist" of The Furnace. He was a highly respected man, which was hard to come by as the Bolands were among the only Catholics in this staunchly German-Lutheran part of "Pennsylvania Dutch" country. Apparently, some degree of competence and geniality trumped prejudice. However, one of my aunt's strongest recollections had to do with bigotry that the family occasionally faced. Thomas served on the borough council of Robesonia, an elected position, and eventually served as council president, reflecting his stature in the borough.

The Chemist

I once found a picture of my grandfather sitting on the front steps of the furnace in Robesonia (*Figure 4*), and recalling that he had been a chemist, asked my Uncle Tom "What college did Grandpa go to?"

He looked at me askance and said "He didn't go to college. No one went to college in those days." (Tom had incidentally become editor of the *Reading Eagle*, the local paper, without a college education.) "They called him the chemist because he did the analyses of the pig iron before they sold it." So, a chemist he was.

Figure 4: Thomas N. Boland Sr, "the chemist", sitting in front of "the furnace" near his home in Robesonia, Pennsylvania.

One of the benefits Thomas gained through his position as foreman and chemist at the furnace was the privilege of living in the Taylor Mansion, just a short walk from the factory. Apparently, the superintendent of that era chose not to live in the mansion. So, the Boland family moved in, and eventually there were as many as fifteen in the house—which easily accommodated them—as well as a second family. It was a beautiful large house surrounded by a lawn and wrought-iron fence (*Figure 5*). However, when Thomas developed his second cancer and died in 1926, his wife Gertie had to move with ten of her thirteen children to the small borough of Mount Penn, about eighteen miles east of Robesonia and essentially in Reading, Pennsylvania. One of my aunts said that she remembers with bitter tears first losing her father, and then having to leave the mansion for cramped quarters in Mount Penn. This was a sad time for everyone. The family was essentially evicted from the home (after all, it was 1926), and some of the local residents were upset at the insensitivity of that act. They informed anyone interested in moving into the mansion of this point, and the house sat empty for many years.

Figure 5. The Taylor Mansion, which was the home of Thomas N. Boland Sr, and his thirteen children, near "the furnace" in Robesonia, a large mansion that comfortably accommodated Thomas' large family. They were evicted from the house after the untimely death of Thomas in 1926.

Thomas' thirteen children

Thomas Nicholas Boland had seven daughters and six sons. The earliest photo available of the entire family was taken in about 1927, shortly after the death of Thomas (*Figure 6*). The family became strongly matriarchal after Thomas' death, and Gertrude was worshipped and obeyed by her children (*Figure 7*). In spite of the obvious hardships and the economic times, the older siblings brought their earnings home to mother; all of the children eventually became educated and successful.

Figure 6: The family of Thomas Nicholas Boland Sr, after his death, about 1932. Sitting in the front (left to right): Thomas Jr, Gertrude, Clement, Bobby, Matt, Alice, and Anna. Standing in the back: Larry, John, Margaret, Loretta, Rita, Mary and Helen.

Figure 7: Mary Gertrude (Gertie) Flanagan Boland, wife of Thomas N. Boland Sr. Date uncertain, early 1930s.

The family tree was shown as a pedigree in *Figure 2*. The first child was Margaret, born in 1902. She had no children, and died at age forty-five in 1947, of endometrial cancer. The second was Matthew, born in 1904. He went to medical school, and became a surgeon in Reading. He had two children. His daughter was Gertrude Ann, called Trudy, born in 1935, who was to become a critical link in solving the mystery of the family illness in 2001. His son was Matthew, Jr., born in 1938. Matthew, Sr. developed lung cancer and died of this at age forty-nine. Trudy developed endometrial cancer in her fifties, which she survived; but later she developed gastric cancer, of which she died in 1995 at age fifty-nine. I only met her once, in 1994, and she gave me a sample of blood at that time for research purposes. Matthew, Jr. developed colon cancer—twice—and died of this in 2009 at age seventy-one. Matthew Sr's successful medical practice may have provided much of the financial support for Gertrude's brood after her husband's death, but everyone was expected to sacrifice and contribute to the family's well-being. No one complained, either.

The third child, Mary, was born in 1905, and died in 1939 of endometrial cancer at age thirty-three. The fourth was Thomas, Jr, born in 1907, and the first of his siblings not to develop cancer. Tom became the family patriarch after his father's death, and everyone's behavior had to meet his exacting standards. Tom didn't attend college, but wanted to work as a newspaper reporter. He applied for a job at the *Reading Eagle*, the main paper in the region. He confessed to them that he hadn't gotten an "A" in English ("no Catholic boys did", he explained), so he was given a job sweeping floors at the newspaper, by his description. He worked his way up the ranks, first as Obituary Editor, then Sports Editor, and eventually Managing Editor. He retired from the *Eagle* at age seventy-five, having served as Managing Editor for many decades. He was not happy to leave his position, but he showed me with pride the manual typewriter he used for many years, generously given to him by the *Eagle*. Tom contributed his earnings to the family, and helped them make it through the grim economic times of the 1930s. He died in 1993, at age eighty-five. He was a giant of the family, and for the Bolands, it was like burying a Pope when he died.

The fifth child was Anna, who died of colon cancer at age thirty-three in 1942, without children. The sixth born was Helen, who got the worst of the family disease. She had an operation for an ovarian tumor at age thirty-seven; at that time, her uterus was removed and there was evidence of early endometrial cancer. She lived in good health for a number of years, developed colon cancer and survived surgery for this at age sixty-four. She then developed a tumor mass in her midbrain, underwent irradiation, and the symptoms abated. It is not clear that this was a cancer. She then developed a gastric cancer and died of this at age sixty-eight. So, Helen may have had as many as five cancers, and survived four of them. Interestingly, she survived these tumors before the institution of a single preventive or even early diagnostic measure. In a way, she was pretty lucky.

The seventh child was John, who developed a cancer in his mid-colon at age fifty, and enjoyed a durable cure after surgical removal of the tumor, only to die of a heart attack in 1969 at age fifty-seven. He was the first of my uncles for whom I clearly remember the death and funeral, and the first of his siblings to die of anything other than cancer. The eighth born was Loretta, who enjoyed a long life, never developed cancer, and died at age ninety-two. Ironically, her daughter Mary Anne died of colon cancer at age sixty, and her son Ed (Jr.) has survived two cancers. The ninth born was Rita, who lived to age ninety-seven. Curiously, she was found to have two cancers in her colon and rectum in 1980, at age sixty-five, and she had curative surgery for these, living another thirty-three years. None of her children has developed any type of cancer. The basis of her tumors was a conundrum as we were trying to solve the genetic basis of the family's disease, but was finally resolved in the laboratory. Her cancers represented the occurrence of tumors in a family at risk for that type of tumor, but not caused by the familial predisposition. This is called a "phenocopy", and was one of the confounding issues when we were trying to unravel the mystery of the Boland family disease. At this point, I understand that the "Boland" familial colorectal cancer gene was definitely not the reason she developed her tumors, but I don't understand why this happened. I have a working hypothesis.

The tenth child was Lawrence. He had a large polyp removed from his mid-colon in his forties, but never had any type of cancer. Like Tom and Rita, he lived to a ripe old age, dying at ninety-three. The eleventh was Alice, who died of colon cancer at age twenty-eight in 1946, while her younger brother was suffering with his colon cancer. The twelfth born was Clement (my father). He was born in 1920, and being the first male born after the death of his Uncle Clement in World War I, he received that name. He had no middle name at birth, but spontaneously adopted the middle name, Michael. His mother insisted that Michael was not his middle name, and forbade him from using it. When it came time for his confirmation (age thirteen), in the Catholic tradition the child chooses a "confirmation name". Of course, Clement wanted Michael, but for unknown reasons, his obstinate mother refused this, so he chose Richard. Thereafter he was Clement Richard Boland. He was just five when his father died and the family relocated from Robesonia to Mount Penn. He went to Albright College in Reading on an athletic scholarship, and finished medical school in three years on the GI Bill, as the government needed physicians for the war effort. He later became a pediatrician and practiced in Endwell, New York. He was the fifth of his siblings and the only brother to leave Reading, and he settled in upstate New York—initially Johnson City. Clement developed his first colon cancer while in the Army in Italy in 1946, at age twenty-five. He had a successful operation removing this tumor, but later developed a second colon cancer in 1969 at age forty-eight, and died of this in the summer of 1970 before his fiftieth birthday. He had four children, and I am the second of them.

The thirteenth and final child was Robert, who was just two when his father died; he never knew him. At age fifty-two he developed a cancer in his stomach, and had a curative operation. However, after seven quiescent years, he developed a second cancer in the region of his surgical anastomosis, and died of gastric cancer at age sixty in 1984. He was very close to his brother Clement, and his death was the hardest for me to accept, as I knew him better than any of the others who had developed cancers.

The Boland culture

The Bolands of this generation were tight-knit, highly supportive, and sacrificed personal gains for the good of the family (*Figures 8a, 8b, 8c*). To some degree, they were bound together as minority Irish-Catholics, but most of them married outside of that clan—five of the twelve married Protestants. That was apparently not a serious social barrier. All remained church-attending faithful, and were typically involved in their local parishes. Six of them had no children. If any of them considered not having children because of familial cancer, it was never discussed. I will never know what they thought about this risk in their private moments.

Figure 8a: Thomas Nicholas Boland Sr and his family, in late 1919 or early 1920. The photos include Thomas and Gertrude in a family photo with eleven children. In the back, left to right: Margaret, Mary, Thomas Sr, Gertrude—holding Alice, and Matthew. Sitting in the front: Helen, Larry, Thomas Jr, John, Rita, Loretta, and Anna. Clement and Robert were yet to be born.

Figure 8b: A family portrait after Thomas Sr's death, about 1932. The youngest three, Alice, Clement and Bobby are in the front, and all were to die of cancer.

Figure 8c: The six Boland boys, about 1932. Left to right: Matthew, Thomas Jr., Clement (eyes closed), Larry, Bobby, and John. Four of the six carried a lethal cancer-predisposing mutation.

When they got together, there was a lot of talking, laughing, singing and obvious love and affection for one another. The males were excellent athletes, and their accomplishments frequently made it into the *Reading Eagle,* facilitated by Thomas, Jr's inside position as editor. There were many reminiscences of these accomplishments. They were particularly good sprinters, giving rise to the term "the flying Bolands", but also excelled at basketball and baseball. They were outstanding students, which might not have been the expectation for what was essentially a second-generation immigrant family. Tom became the Managing Editor of the local paper, Matt and Clem became physicians, John and Bob became lawyers, and Larry was a prominent metallurgist and businessman. The women of the time were not expected to seek professions, but they became teachers, nurses, businesswomen, and mothers. Even though six of the thirteen had no children, the other seven had twenty-seven among them. They were apparently evenly split as Republicans and Democrats, and had lively discussions and debates about politics. I experienced a deep sense of warmth and openness when we visited, and even though one or two years may have passed between visits, it was as if we had always been there. Although there must have been some, I never witnessed a family fight or felt that there were any of the siblings who didn't get along. Of course, they all shared a common enemy—cancer—so why waste the effort? The conversations were lively, and there was no reluctance to sing, especially when it came to Irish ballads. The one issue that was not easily discussed was cancer. A look came over the faces, one of fear; cancer might not have been a forbidden topic, but it was a dangerous one. I remember the looks when the health issues of a deceased sibling were raised. Many years later, when I gathered a group of them to obtain blood for research, most were open, and wished me luck to solve the problem. However, one uncle and two cousins refused to give me blood for research. Fear is a difficult emotion to control. There might even have been sound reasons to fear the answers to the problem what I was stalking. Who could predict how this would turn out? Why take the risk to determine if you have a disease if there would be no way to control it? At that time, we didn't know if we would ever know how the disease occurred, and it was an even bigger stretch to imagine that we would one day control it. Better to let the sleeping dogs lie.

Chapter 4

Clement Richard Boland, Sr: from Robesonia to Endwell (1926-1970)

The idyllic life of the Bolands in Robesonia underwent an abrupt change in July, 1926. Thomas N. Boland, Sr. had been an attentive father, a strong role model, and provided for a family of fifteen. In 1907, at age twenty-seven, he had developed a cancer in the proximal (right side of the) colon, and underwent a successful, curative surgical procedure to remove this. The current family has no recollections of his illness, and there is no oral history available about how this diagnosis was reached, or what he was told by his physicians. In all of the notes I gathered on the family history, the story of this illness was excised as cleanly as the tumor itself. In 1907, x-ray was a new modality, and there were no clinically useful imaging techniques—such as a barium enema—to provide any insight into what was making him ill. A surgeon probably had to perform an exploratory operation based upon his clinical suspicion, found the tumor, and took it out. It is difficult to guess what the surgeons thought about the presence of a cancer in a twenty-seven year old man whose father died of the same disease. He came home to his wife and three children, and carried on. My guess is that very few people were told that he had been ill, and that the word "cancer" was probably not spoken out loud.

Thomas then rose to the position of foreman and chemist at the furnace, was a leader in his community and his church, and had another ten children. Unbeknownst to him, there was a problem lurking that was to return nineteen years later. There were no screening or surveillance tests available. Even if his exact situation had been appreciated, there were no interventions that were likely to alter the outcome. His father had died of colon cancer at age forty-one, and if someone had made a connection between these two events, none of that discussion survives. Thomas fell ill a second time with a cancer in the lower part of his colon or rectum and underwent a second operation that left him with a colostomy. It has not been recorded whether there had been an attempt to resect the tumor, or whether he experienced a bowel obstruction and had a palliative operation.

In July, 1926, Thomas Boland, Sr. died. The oldest three children were out of the home, and the Boland family, consisting of Gertrude and her ten children, were asked to leave their homestead in Robesonia for Mount Penn. Clement was just five, and his younger brother Bobby was only two.

Life in Mount Penn, Pennsylvania

Clement had few recollections of Robesonia. He was next to the youngest, and whatever he remembered was rarely mentioned. Boland family tales I heard as a youth all came from Mount Penn. The family moved into a tow family semi-detached duplex home on Perkiomen Avenue. As a curious coincidence, if one drove east from Robesonia to Reading, the main highway became Penn Avenue, and then Perkiomen Avenue continuing eastward. But this was much more than a move down the road. There were no pensions or social safety nets in 1927. The Boland family was on its own. Thomas N. Boland, Jr, became the *de facto* father and brought his earnings home, as did his siblings, for family support. The eldest three were out of the house. Margaret had married a college professor and moved to Lancaster, Pennsylvania. Mary had married a doctor, and moved to Virginia. Matthew was just finishing medical school, and would become a surgeon in Reading. Thomas started working for the newspaper. All the rest got as much education as they could, and contributed to the survival of the family, which was the most important issue.

The family had to be run efficiently, given its size. A daily chart was hung on the wall in the kitchen with each child's name on it. You were expected to check the box next to your name when you left the house, and cross your name off each day when you got home. The last one in was instructed to "lock the doors and extinguish the lights". The family had meals together. After dinner, Gertrude would assign some to do the dishes and others to scrub the floor. There was a parlor or sitting room, into which she would retire with a cup of tea, and shut the door. The family respected her quiet and private time until she finished her tea and came back to the kitchen. She would announce "I am going to shut the door, and no one is to disturb me until I come out."

As previously stated, the Boland children were both excellent scholars and athletes. The six boys were close enough in age that some overlapped in school, and even ran on the same track team relays. As Thomas, Jr. was Sports Editor for the *Reading Eagle* at one time, the boys received plenty of attention in the local news.

Clement Boland, Sr. and his younger brother Bobby received particular attention from the rest of the family because they were so young at the time of their father's death. Clement was very close to his brothers. One of my favorite pictures is a grainy, wrinkled photo of Clement and his next older brother, Larry, proudly showing the two fish they had caught (*Figure 9*).

Figure 9: Clement and his brother Larry Boland, showing off the day's catch, about 1928. The younger brother appears a bit more proud of his fish, whereas the elder seems less sanguine about how many mouths might be fed with his.

Clement was initially sent to a Catholic elementary school. He noted that there was a minor degree of harassment of Catholics from a few of the students in the public schools. He also mentioned that these issues were sorted out with a brief fight, and perhaps a bloody nose or torn shirt would resolve the issue. The family was not fixated on this, and harbored no long-term hostilities or sense of being victims. It was simply the way the world was at that time. Standing up physically was the required response. These episodes were recalled with a slight smile, shrug of the shoulders, and a suppressed look of satisfaction. I do not remember a single episode where another ethnic group was slighted or called out for these past episodes by the family. There were bigger challenges to face.

Clement matured early and was a very good student and athlete (*Figure 10*). Family lore is uncertain on this point, but Clem reported that he skipped grades in elementary school. Moreover, there was confusion for years in our family whether he was born in 1920 or 1921. His driver's license said 1921, but his family says it was 1920. If the latter is true, he probably skipped no grades, and he may have made this up for effect. The issue was that the Bolands were expected to be exceptional students, and his children would have to pass muster accordingly. If the facts weren't sufficiently impressive, then embellishment might have been required. Clem was a highly accomplished individual, but it was sometimes hard to know where the simple truth ended and the tales developed additional height.

Figure 10: Clement Richard Boland Sr, about 1932.

After the elementary years, Clem went to Mount Penn High School, which was the public school, where he excelled as a student, on the soccer field, basketball court and track team. He was six feet tall before he was sixteen, and jumped center for the basketball team, a critical job when there was a center jump after every basket. The game was slow and deliberate in those days. He said that if someone took a jump shot from the top of the key, he might have been pulled out of the game by the coach for "bombing". In his high school yearbook, one of the basketball games final score was 20-10 (for the entire game!). Clem once set a county scoring record with twenty points in one game. There were many tales about the vagaries of the gyms in the small high schools where they competed. One had a supporting post in the center of the court, which prompted novel dribbling strategies, and a monster "pick" if used cleverly. Another gym had guy-wires on either side of the backboard, and if touched (or surreptitiously kicked) just enough at a critical time during a free throw, there would be a slight movement of the basket, greatly enhancing the difficulty of the shot. He would have been an ideal candidate for the football team, but his mother refused to let him play. He was big, strong, and fast. But when the head football coach came to the Boland household to convince Gertrude to let her son play the game, she was ever the protective mother, and said she didn't want anyone to hurt Clem. It probably was safer for the opponents that he was kept off the football field.

The communities were divided along ethnic lines in those times, especially because of the strong German-Lutheran influence of the region. The family noted it, but didn't complain. The family had no political or financial power. The mantra was to defend the family. One of my father's lessons was, if someone was hurting a family member, you "protect the family (fight) first and ask questions later". He mentioned this issue more than once, and surely thought it was important. But as I grew up, ethnic tensions (at least among the European-based tribes in upstate New York) were only a minor issue, and this strategy seemed very foreign to me. I took note, but never felt that I had to raise fists to defend my family.

Albright College

In the 1930s, there was no expectation that a high school graduate would necessarily enter college—let alone one from a financially strapped family like the Bolands in the mid-1930s. Clement was the twelfth of thirteen, and the family pooled its resources for a house and food—and there was not much left for higher education, even though that was highly valued. As Clement recalled it, in spite of his accomplishments in high school, he hadn't applied to college by the end of his senior year. However, he was the star quarter miler on the track team, which competed in the spring, at the end of the academic year. He had been winning races while running on poor-quality cinder tracks, getting some notoriety for his achievements, and his quarter mile times were in the low fifty-second range. With this time, he qualified for the state track meet, probably the only one in his school. His coach took him to the state meet, and told him "if you win, you will go to college". He looked over the stadium, and for the first time ever, he saw a pristine track, rolled and groomed. He used starting blocks for the first time in his life, and they ran the quarter mile (440 yards) "out of the chute", which meant starting on the back straightaway of the track, running around just one corner (two turns) instead of the usual two corners/four turns, and finishing down a final straightaway, as if it were a 220 yard race, for a side-by-side finish. This was going to be a fast race, and Clement was particularly motivated. He had his day in the sun, won the race, broke fifty seconds, and was the state champion in 1938.

After he got home, he was offered an athletic scholarship by Albright College, in Reading (*Figure 11a*). This allowed him to live at home and take the trolley to school. He was recruited to play basketball and run track, but, as the world circumstances careened towards World War II, many of the competitions were suspended. This wasn't a particular problem for Clement; it permitted him to become more committed to academic studies. He was elected president of his senior class, and graduated in 1942 (*Figure 11b*).

Figure 11a: Clement R. Boland Sr, running on a track while a student at Albright College (about 1938).

Figure 11b: Clement R. Boland Sr, college graduation photo, about 1941.

Georgetown Medical School (1942)

Clement had been a sufficiently good student that he qualified for medical school. He was encouraged by his family to pursue such studies, not least by his eldest brother, Matthew, who was by now an established surgeon in Reading. However, Clement still had another brother behind him, and his siblings continued to give their earnings to Gertrude to run the household. Money for more post-graduate schooling was another issue. However, at the time of his college graduation, the United States had declared war on Japan and Germany, and the Army needed physicians to care for those wounded in battle. It was Clement's good fortune that Congress passed a bill that paid for medical school education, and accelerated it to a year-round, three-year curriculum. Clement entered Georgetown Medical School in 1942, and suddenly, the young man from financially challenging circumstances found himself on the path to becoming a physician. For the first time in his life, at age twenty-two, he left home for Washington, DC.

Catherine Jane Armstrong (1944)

Clement was a handsome Irishman, now on his way through medical school. Each of his sisters had picked out the woman she thought he should marry. However, for the first time, he was experiencing life on his own in Washington, outside of the scrutiny and supervision of his family. One evening, he was at a party, and his eyes met those of Catherine Jane Armstrong, from Johnson City, New York. She was born in 1923 (*Figure 12*), the daughter of Frank Slade Armstrong, a middle-class traveling meat salesman who worked for the Armour meat company, and Blanche Van Dusen, who was born in the Catskill mountains and moved to Binghamton to become a nurse. Frank (known as "Army") was born in 1884, had moved to upstate New York from Virginia, and his family were "Scots-Irish", Protestants from Belfast, Ireland. For some reason, we have virtually no information about his family. Blanche was born in 1896 in Harpursville, New York, in the foothills of the Catskills, coincidentally, also on the banks of the Susquehanna River, which winds through the mountains to Binghamton. Blanche was the product of Dutch and English ancestry—classic New York State settlers. Army and Blanche lived in a modest but well-kept house on Floral Avenue in Johnson City (*Figure 13*)

Figure 12: Catherine Jane Armstrong: childhood photo (about 1928).

Figure 13: Home of Army and Blanche Armstrong, parents of Catherine Jane, on Floral Avenue, Johnson City, New York, where Clem and Cathie lived early in their marriage, when Clem was convalescing after his first cancer. (Photo taken in 2014.)

By the time she graduated from Johnson City High School, Cathie was an attractive and vivacious blonde, who had no trouble catching the eye of men. She was called Jane by her family, but when she joined the military service (*Figure 14*), they called her Catherine or Cathie.

Figure 14: Catherine Jane Armstrong, Navy photo (1944).

Her maternal grandfather was the founder of an inn in the Catskills called the Maple Farm Inn, in Stamford, New York, which was agricultural and had dairy farms and sugar maples in abundance. This was a summer inn, which permitted visitors, many from the New York City area, to get away, breathe fresh air, and experience the peace and quiet of the Catskills. The farm changed hands due to multiple deaths in the family from tuberculosis, and was not passed to Cathie's mother, Blanche. Cathie had spent many summers at Maple Farm Inn, and had warm memories of her interactions with her father and mother "in the country", and the farm hands. Actually, Catherine had a long-standing dream that she would one day become an innkeeper, and get Maple Farm Inn back.

Cathie was a good enough student and wanted to attend the School of Hotel Management at Cornell University in Ithaca, New York. I never knew for sure whether she applied or was offered a position at the school, but her father refused to send his daughter to college, as these were dens of evil. Cathie said that her father told her that she would only learn how to drink, smoke, and 'something else' (she demurred on this, sometimes said "swearing" was the final sin, but we always knew better), and he would have none of it. Cathy was determined to get out of the house and see the world.

After she graduated from Johnson City High School and was forbidden a chance to get a college education, she joined the WAVES, which was the Women Accepted for Volunteer Emergency Service, or essentially, the women's Navy Corps, shortly after this was commissioned by the government in the summer of 1942. As a coincidental issue, Cathie suffered from otosclerosis, a disorder that leads to ossification of the joints connecting the three bones of the middle ear, and this led to her progressive deafness. By the time she graduated from Johnson City High, she was nearly deaf, but was a very proficient lip reader. She hid her deafness, and simply watched people when they spoke, or batted her eyelashes and politely asked the speaker to repeat what they said. She had to pass an audiology test to enter the WAVES, in which the tester would speak in an ordinary tone on each side of the person being tested—not very sophisticated. The tester was a man, and did not object when she looked right at him, read his lips and passed the test. She had learned very well how to use all of the talents given to her.

Cathie was proud of her service to her country during the War. As a child, I asked her where she went to college, and she responded, "Oklahoma State". I later found that she had been sent by the WAVES to Oklahoma State for training in typing, shorthand and other secretarial skills. After that, she was sent to Washington, DC for her deployment, where she worked in an office with other women. One fateful evening, she went to a party and her eyes met Clement Boland's from across the room. According to both, it was love at first sight, and the first real love for both of them. Clem was about half-way through Georgetown Medical School. Against all advice, the two lovers got married.

Unfortunately, marrying a woman who was in the WAVES, not a Catholic, and unknown to the Boland family was met with disapproval at home. Similarly, Frank Armstrong warned his daughter against marrying someone who was not only Catholic but also Irish. Catholics kept weapons in the basement awaiting instructions from the Pope for insurrection, and he would be a "wife-beater". None the less, they made their plans, and went ahead with the wedding. The Armstrongs made their peace with Cathie's decision to marry the Irish Catholic; eventually the Boland family did too. Clem and Cathie went to the Maple Farm Inn and had a Catholic wedding in September, 1944 (*Figure 15*). One of Clem's Georgetown classmates, George Rutherford, stood with Clem as best man. George's wife June stood up with Cathie. Cathie converted to Catholicism, perhaps to the dismay of her parents, but, they recognized a good man, and were happy with Clem as a son-in-law. If they had major misgivings, I never heard them.

Figure 15: Marriage of Clement Richard Boland to Catherine Jane Armstrong, September 25, 1944, at the Maple Farm Inn, in Stamford, New York.

The wedding was partially an elopement, in that the Boland side of the family had no knowledge of their marriage in September, 1944. I was visiting my Aunt Rita about 1990 and she was showing me a scrapbook that contained many family pictures and press clippings. As she turned a page, a small piece of paper slipped out and to the floor. She looked at it quizzically, recognized what it was, and read it to me. It was the telegram from my mother (Cathie) to Rita (Clem's sister) informing her that:

"Clem and I are married and very happy. Please tell Mother. Cathie." (Full stop.)

I was unable to get a report on Gertrude's response to her prodigal son's decision. Unfortunately, she died of a stroke shortly thereafter, in February, 1945, just before Clem finished medical school. She was idolized as much as her husband, Thomas. A saint was buried that day. When the family discussed "mother" it was done with a reverence reserved for no one else.

Johnson City, New York, and first child (1945)

Clem and Cathie returned to Washington for his last year of the three year medical curriculum. They had planned to use birth control— since there was insufficient income between them to raise a family— but the mechanical birth control devices that my mother described (which I could never quite visualize, and still have no idea what she was talking about) were difficult to use, would "spring across the room." She admitted that in the heat of passion, the devices weren't used at times. Consequently, just one month after the wedding, Cathie became pregnant. Right after graduation, Clem and George Rutherford went to Wilson Memorial Hospital in Johnson City, New York for their internships. The hospital was just a few blocks from the home of Frank and Blanche Armstrong—which is where they lived during the internship. Internships provided no pay, but gave the interns a place to stay (in the hospital—which is why they called them "internships"), some meals, and washed their white uniforms. They would spend most of their time in the hospital, and get occasional evenings off to pursue whatever outside life they thought they had.

On August 23, 1945, just under eleven months after the wedding, Cathie gave birth to Suzanne Jane. Clem was in and out of the labor area—on call as an intern at the hospital—but at that time, fathers weren't invited into the delivery rooms. Cathie had the support of her mother and father, just eight blocks from Wilson Hospital. The world was giving Clem and Cathie everything—for now.

Into the army, and Europe

At the end of the internship year in mid-1946, all of the newly minted physicians who had been trained at the expense of the US government were called into active military duty. Clem was sent to basic training in Texas for a few weeks. He was given a rifle, but claimed he had no training in its use, and never fired it. He told me once—in jest—that if he were attacked, his best move would have been to grab his rifle by the barrel and use it as a bat.

He was then shipped off to Naples, Italy, joining the forces there to preserve the post-war peace. He was shipped across Italy, north and east to Yugoslavia. He claimed that no one was sure exactly where they were. He was given the job of driving an ambulance through a valley that had combatants and partisans on each of the hillsides. Occasional shots were fired, but no one knew by whom or what the targets might have been. The best strategy was to lay low and hope that hostilities did not escalate.

Clement's first cancer (1946)

Once in Europe, Clem began to lose weight. The food was different, he was in an uneasy semi-war zone, and away from his wife and child. There were lots of reasons why this might have been occurring. He spoke to one of the other medical officers about what might be going on. He was told that he probably had an ulcer. I think he understood the implications of the fact that his father had died of colon cancer, and had experienced his first tumor at age twenty-seven. Clem was just twenty-five and a few months old at that time.

He must have been terrified by what had been happening in his family. His father died in 1927 of his second cancer, and had his first "episode" at age twenty-seven. Clem's sister Mary had died of endometrial cancer at age thirty-three in 1939. His sister Anna had died of colon cancer at age thirty-three in 1942. Alice—who was just two years older than Clem and his closest sister—was ill with colon cancer at that time, and died of this in December, 1946.

Clem knew what was happening, but could only fear the truth, and wouldn't speak to anyone about it. He felt a large mass in the lower right side of his abdomen, and immediately suspected (or knew) that this was a tumor. He eventually lost forty pounds in Italy. He was already a trim and fit athlete, and had no fat to shed. He was losing muscle and healthy tissue.

He finally told his commanding officer about the mass. They looked him over and knew something was wrong. But this was the Army, and they had seen worse. Send him home. They'll figure it out.

Back to Johnson City for surgery

So, back to Naples, and back across the ocean to New York City. It was still the summer of 1946. He had told Cathie that he would be returning, but did not give full details of his condition. Cathie and her mother Blanche drove from Johnson City to the military base to find him. He had been placed on a medical stretcher with a large number of other returning soldiers. Cathie and Blanche walked up and down the aisles of stretchers looking for Clem. They actually walked past him, but didn't recognize him because of the weight loss. He tried to call out, but was weak and his voice too soft to get their attention. Eventually, they found him, and were horrified. Cathie and Blanche made a quick decision to get him out of the Army base, and take him back to Wilson Memorial Hospital in Johnson City.

They contacted a surgeon, Dr. Frank Moore. They had a short discussion, and Moore knew what to do. He operated immediately, and removed a large cancer in the cecum (the first portion of the colon which is attached to the small intestine in the lower right side of the abdomen). There was cancer in the lymph nodes (which made it a Stage III tumor by later staging systems). The prognosis was not good, and it was more likely than not he would die from the cancer. To deal with the post-operative pain, he was given a "new" medicine—"like morphine, but not addicting" he was told. The drug was meperidine, or Demerol, and it was just as addicting as morphine. He returned to the Army base in New York with his surgical records. They did a quick review and discharged him from the Army. The record of his discharge hearing said:

"Lieutenant Boland, what is your diagnosis?"

His reply: "Adenocarcinoma of the colon—with metastasis to the lymph nodes."

"What is the prognosis?"

"Six months."

Discharged.

After returning to Johnson City, Clem, Cathie and Suzanne moved into an apartment over Bonham's Drugs, at 110 Main Street, in Binghamton, a few blocks east of the border with Johnson City, and still just a short trip to Wilson Memorial Hospital. Cathie's younger sister Pat (just ten years old at the time) helped take care of Suzanne, and took her on outings to the nearby park. She recalled her thrill at being able to help that summer, but also the confusion about what was going on with her older brother-in-law. She was so young, and the concept of cancer was impossible to comprehend. Clem was fifteen years older than Pat, and was actually a father figure to her. It was never explained to her that everyone assumed Clem was dying.

The new non-addicting drug for pain

Clem descended into the lowest depths of life. As the effects of the injections for pain wore off—and the effect of the Demerol was only good for about three hours—pain returned to his abdomen. Clem knew this must be the cancer, so he would take another injection. If that didn't help, he would draw up a little more. After all, he was a doctor, and could make these decisions. The doses got higher, but the pain was relentless. He experienced hallucinations when the doses got high. He paced across the front room of their apartment, looking out the window onto Main Street below. He felt he was on the same path to death that his sisters had taken. The once strapping athlete had been reduced to skin and bones—and despair.

Years later Dad commented to me that Dr. Moore said he had never operated on someone with so little body fat. One incision through the skin, and he was down to the muscle. Ironically, Dad interpreted that observation as a compliment, and boasted that he had been in such terrific shape leading up to his operation—rather than the reality that he was wasting away from his cancer. He never completely acknowledged what the cancer had done to his body. The descriptions all came from Mom. As he paced by the window, Cathie saw "the look" on his face—the weight loss, the depression, the fear. She worried that he might try to take his life by jumping out the window of the apartment. He suffered a seizure one day in front of Cathie. In less than two years, their perfect lives were replaced with fear and uncertainty. Cathie worried that she would lose her beloved husband, and be left as a single mother of Suzanne.

Clem returned to Dr. Moore and told him of the recurrent abdominal pains, the timing of the pains, and his use of the "non-addicting" Demerol. Moore looked straight at him and said: "that tumor isn't going to kill you, this medicine is." So, Clem stopped the injections, went through withdrawal in Cathie's arms, and decided to wait and see when the tumor would return and kill him.

The myth of radiation-induced sterility

Clem was told that he should take radiation treatments to his abdomen to slow down the growth of his tumor. At the time there was no scientifically legitimate data indicating that this would help—and we now know that it would have caused considerable toxicity and provide no benefit in his situation. He decided on his own not to take the treatments, but told Cathie that he was getting them. As he slowly recovered from the Demerol addiction, the pains abated, he began to get his appetite back, gain weight, and regain energy. The tumor had been successfully removed. And, he still had the loves of his life—Cathie and Suzanne.

His romantic interests recovered along with his strength. He told Cathie that it was not necessary to use birth control, as the radiation treatments (that he was not taking) had made him sterile. This was a particularly good decision for which I shall be forever grateful. In January, 1947, Cathie became pregnant from her "sterile" husband, and in October, I was born—and became the third Clement Boland in the family. During Cathie's pregnancy during 1947, Clem recovered his health, lost "the look", and began to make plans to resume his life, miraculously given back to him.

During the depths of his illness in the summer and fall of 1946, Clem had what he called "a vision" or a "visitation" from the Blessed Virgin Mary. Mary was a particularly favored saint among Irish-Catholics, and it fit well with Clem's adoration of his mother and the role she played in the successes of the Boland family. During his "vision", which may or may not have been associated with a very high dose of Demerol, he felt that she had come to save him from cancer. He was grateful, and made the following agreement:

"Let me live another twenty-five years, see my children graduate from college, and I will become a dedicated pediatrician."

So, the deal was struck. As the worst of his illness began to fade into the distance, Clem made his plans for the future. He always kept a statue of Mary on his dresser and a medal of her image on a chain around his neck.

Training in pediatrics

There were no pediatrics training programs at the hospital in Johnson City, or anywhere in the region. So, he sought pediatrics training at Mary Drexel Children's Hospital in Philadelphia. However, there was no salary paid for this residency program, and since Cathie and Clem had no money, Cathie and Suzanne stayed on Floral Avenue in Johnson City with her parents, and Clem took a series of trains and buses to Philadelphia on Sunday nights, stayed at the hospital for two weeks at a time, and then took trains and buses back to Johnson City for a few hours of time with his family on the weekend. He did this even knowing that his longevity was uncertain. After a year of this, he decided he had had enough of the buses and trains, and he decided to stay at home and practice pediatrics. Moreover, he now had two children. It would have taken another year of pediatrics training to become fully certified in the specialty. But, it was 1948, he was feeling more positively about the future, he had a family whom he desperately missed, and he was ready to get to work.

The E-J company doctor

Having no money to set up a practice, Clem went to work as a pediatrician for the Endicott-Johnson (E-J) Shoe Company. Besides being the largest shoe factory in the world under one roof at that time, it ran on an enlightened business model, considering the era. The company employed a large number of immigrant workers, many from the poorest parts of the nations most affected by World Wars I and II. There were workers from Italy, Yugoslavia, Russia, Ukraine, Czechoslovakia, and other parts of Central Europe—anyone who could get out of the political messes that occurred in the early twentieth century. Starting in the final decade of the 1800s, Henry B. Endicott and George F. Johnson came to the "Triple Cities" (Binghamton, Johnson City and Endicott, New York) founded the eponymously named shoe company, offered jobs to the resident and immigrant labor, built houses for the workers, provided discounts on the shoes, and free health care. The Triple Cities were located sequentially along the north shore of the Susquehanna River (*Figure 16*).

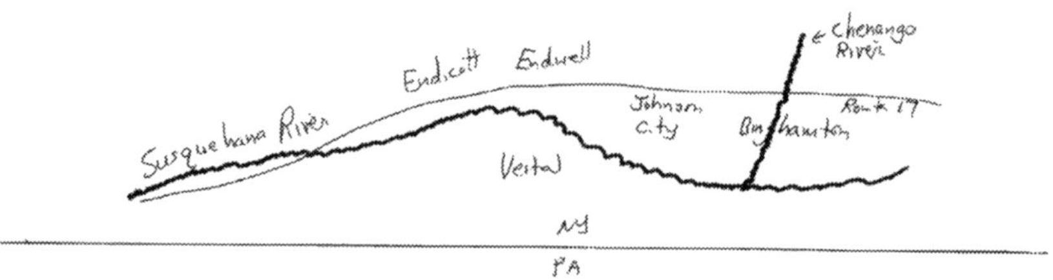

Figure 16: Schematic map of the Triple Cities. Clem and Cathie initially lived over Bonham's Drug Store in Binghamton in 1946, then on Floral Avenue and Massachusetts Avenue in Johnson City, and finally, in Endwell. They never lived more than a mile from the Susquehanna River, and between 1946 and 1961, sequentially moved a few miles "downstream" from Binghamton, Johnson City, to Endwell.

So, Clem went to work for the E-J medical clinic in Endicott, which was another one of the river towns supporting factories along the Susquehanna River. Although he had taken just one year of specialized training in Pediatrics, he was the most trained caretaker for children they had, and he became the company pediatrician. He regained his pre-illness form, was extremely kind and dedicated, had the Blessed Virgin Mary on his shoulder, and his good looks were popular with the mothers. Now employed, in the late 1940s, Clem and Cathie bought their first house on Massachusetts Avenue in Johnson City for $9,999 (*Figure 17*), were just a few blocks from Cathie's parents on Floral Avenue, and a short drive to Wilson Memorial Hospital. He had some initial difficulty obtaining a loan, since he was such a recent cancer patient, so they were very pleased when this was approved and they became home-owners and their family continued to grow.

Figure 17: The house on Massachusetts Avenue, Johnson City, the first house purchased by Clement and Cathie, in 1949, after Clem's first cancer surgery. (Photo taken in 2014.)

Setting up a pediatric practice

After a few years, he became confident of his ability to set up a private practice. As time accumulated between him and his cancer surgery, it became a little easier to borrow money. He rented an office in Endicott, not far from the shoe factory, behind the commercial district on Washington Avenue, and opened a one-man practice. Endicott was a prototype of the small American post-war town. Most men had a job, no one was rich, and no one thought they were particularly poor, even if they may have been by some objective measure. He was a "solo practitioner", which meant that he had no partners, and had to be available for his patients every hour of every day of every week. No breaks. The phone rang constantly when he was home. He visited two or three hospitals every day, had office hours six days a week (full load on Saturday, of course) and did house calls on the way home from the office. Most people could pay for their office visits (which ranged from two to five dollars), and those who could not, did not, and the bill was forgiven. Clem remembered what hard times meant. The Blessed Virgin Mary did her part, Clem did his.

The family grows

By 1951, several significant milestones passed. First, it had been five years since Clem's cancer surgery. That was considered the time one could start to "exhale", and begin to accept that the surgery may have been curative. Reports of Clem's sterility were seriously exaggerated, as Cathie gave birth to Alice Patricia in 1949 (named after Clem's sister, who died of colon cancer in December 1946), and James Armstrong, born in 1951. Cathie was determined not to challenge her mother-in-law's fecundity, and had a tubal ligation shortly after Jim's birth. They had now outgrown the house in Johnson City, and were able to get a loan to buy a stately modest-sized colonial home on a one-acre lot on River Road (literally on the Susquehanna River) in Endwell, a small bedroom community surrounding the highway between Johnson City and Endicott. The house was purchased for $21,000, had four bedrooms, and forthwith, Clem and Cathie became full-fledged members of the American post-war middle class. More importantly, after Clem's brother Matt died of lung cancer in 1953, there were no more cancer deaths in the family for a period of seventeen years. Bad luck took a break from the Boland family.

To Endwell, New York

In the late 1950s, Clem's practice grew sufficiently that he was able to build his own office, this time in Endwell, between the hospitals in Endicott and Johnson City. He became one of just two pediatricians in the western half of Broome County, which included Endwell, Endicott, and the surrounding hamlets. Endwell was a town of fewer than 10,000 people, and was essentially a bedroom community nestled between Johnson City and Endicott, two of the three Triple Cities. The town allegedly got its name from a model of shoe produced by E-J called the "Endwell". Their ad proclaimed that if one wore the Endwell shoe, your day would "end well". Endwell had no specific commercial district, a few tiny strip malls and gas stations, and a few markets and diners. Endwell was more or less an appendage of Endicott, the village to the west, and there was no geographical boundary between them. Just a road sign that said you had entered Endwell or left Endicott.

The E-J Shoe Company began to contract in the 1950s, and was essentially dying by 1960. Gradually, the old factories (tanneries and shoe manufacturing) were torn down. Fortunately, while this was taking place, a new industry came to town—IBM. This new industry built its primary production plant in close proximity to the old shoe factories, and the community morphed from a blue collar town of shoe makers into an engineer-driven white collar town. When I was in primary and elementary school, nearly half of the families had working ties to IBM. Unfortunately, as there were no technical universities in the region, most of the workers had relocated to the Triple Cities to work for IBM, and among those of us who had spent our entire childhoods there, IBM meant "I've Been Moved". Families came and went. However, since the end of World War II brought so many fathers back home, a very large number of children were born, there was a furious building of new schools, and a need for pediatricians in the region. Life was good. Clem became a pillar of the community, continued to work every hour of every day, complete with an open phone line from 7 AM-8 AM every morning. The phone rang so frequently at that time, Clem's four children learned not to hear the phone ring. Dad would answer the phone, provide advice for a routine childhood illness, hang it up, and it would ring again. He had to take the phone off the hook for ten minutes to shower and shave. He was on the road by eight in the morning for hospital rounds prior to seeing patients in his office. He never seemed tired, and never complained. He got home by seven or eight in the evening, sometimes later, depending upon the hospital situation. On Tuesdays, he got home by about five o'clock, took a short nap, had dinner with the family (at six, sharp), and then returned for evening office hours from 6:30 until nine or ten. He took a two week family vacation in the summer, and he and Cathie took a one or two week winter vacation without the kids. He almost never attended medical meetings, and essentially took no other time off. I cannot remember his taking a sick day. He also never took a partner and remained a member of the old-fashioned "solo practitioner" club. He would arrange coverage with the one other pediatrician in western Broome County if there was a family event on Sunday (never on Saturday, which was a full work day), and that was his life.

The house on the river (*Figure 18*)

As mentioned, in the spring of 1951, the family moved to River Road, Endwell, into a house that had been built in 1921 on an acre of semi-rural land. The Susquehanna River flooded in 1925, and there was a mark visible in the lathe-and-plaster walls all around the first floor representing the high water mark that year. The river was the southern border of the property, just across the road, and was a "no exploring zone", a restriction we all obeyed. The northern boundary in the back was a chain-link fence, and a drive-in movie theater was on the other side. You could see the movies from two of the bedrooms of the house, but couldn't hear them. There was an old chicken coop at the very back of the yard that we could sit upon, and almost hear the movies. But, they didn't start the movies until dark, and we didn't watch them except on rare occasions. The back yard had very rich soil (because of the proximity to the river, periodic flooding, and the heavy summer rains), and we had a garden that provided a variety of tomatoes, cucumbers and other vegetables through the summer. The back yard was also an apple orchard that produced many more apples than we could eat. We harvested the apples for an annual trip to the Cider Mill in Endicott, and would return with many gallons of cider. The children would drink the cider for a couple of days (producing plenty of belly-aches), and then the cider began to turn and the jugs would disappear. I am not sure who took the remaining jugs, but I assume someone had expertise in fermenting hard cider. Cathie would make apple pies, applesauce, and anything else one could make with apples, and would make many jars of tomato sauce that would be stored in the "fruit cellar" for dinners through the long winters. It was an idyllic time.

Figure 18: The House on River Road, Endwell, where Clem and Cathie and four children lived from 1951-1961. The house was facing the Susquehanna River, and was less than 100 yards from the river bank. (Photo taken about 2000.)

However, the river exacted a predictable toll. The spring thaw would melt the snowy mountains of the Catskills, and the river would swell and overflow its banks. We never had the river flood over its northern banks into the house while we lived there (although it got very close). None the less, the water would flow to the lowland behind the house, and we were periodically surrounded by water for a few hours at the crest of the flood. Moreover, the ground became super-saturated with water, and water would spurt through cracks in the concrete floor of the cellar. We owned three sump pumps, and when the water began to fill the basement, the pumps were brought in from the garage to pump the water up and out the cellar windows. The flooding usually lasted only a day or two, but it was hectic. As mentioned, there were occasions when the house was completely surrounded by the flooding river, and it was not possible to get out without a boat. That never lasted long and was not a critical issue. I found these times rather exciting, but as I look back, it was harrowing for Clem and Cathie, and they worried about the inevitable catastrophic flood.

After suffering recurring floods over a ten year period, the family decided to move to higher grounds in Endwell in the spring of 1961. Clem and Cathie sold the River Road house, and we moved to the higher ground on Alpine Drive in Endwell, just about two miles north. Some forty years later, because of the inevitable floods over the banks of the river, the last family to live in the River Road house moved out, and the structure was leveled. The last time I visited, one could not tell that a house had ever stood there. Totally gone. I was quite upset when I saw it.

Clem continued his faithful service to the community. He was elected Chief of the Department of Pediatrics at Wilson Memorial Hospital, something that he was very proud of, and he continued in that position until his death. He was a regular attendee at the local Catholic Church with his four children. He also attended Mass each day during Lent. Cathie attended church for a while after their marriage, but quietly had her concerns about many of the attitudes of the Church, not the least being its approach to women. One Sunday in the late 1950s—on Mother's Day no less—the pastor, Father Aylesworth, delivered a sermon that was a misogynistic rant against women that started with the premise that Eve was mainly responsible for the problems in Eden, and it went downhill from there. She was furious, and rarely attended Church thereafter. The four children continued to go to Church with Dad, then went with him to the hospitals for his "rounds", waiting in the car or somewhere in the lobby of the hospital, playing games of some sort. As time went by, I realized this was Mom's "time off". Clem remained faithful to the end, and I never heard a cynical word from him about his or anyone's religion, although any discussion of the pastor and the sermon in question made for an uncomfortable dinner conversation.

The 1960s in Endwell

Clem and Cathie remained in Endwell until his death in 1970, while all of Clem's living siblings except Rita remained in Reading, Pennsylvania. We visited Reading with some regularity, and also, for about ten summers, vacationed on the New Jersey shore in Stone Harbor, where some of the Boland clan would also vacation. It was there that we got to know Loretta and Ed Kuhn (the funeral director) family best. The Kuhns had two children, Ed, Jr and Mary Anne, who were just a little older than our family, and we had an extra bond from staying at the Funeral Home in

Reading and because of our time at the Jersey shore. Also, Clem's brothers John and Bob would often visit the shore for vacation up.

Clem was always happy to see his siblings, and there was just one cancer death among his siblings between 1948-1970. Clem's brother John died of a heart attack in August 1969. Then came December, 1969, when Clem was found to have two cancers of the colon, one of which had metastasized to his liver. He died the next summer, on July 26, 1970. He was the sixth of his sibship to die of cancer. Two more—sister Helen and brother Bob—would follow in 1979 and 1984. They all thought they were at risk of cancer, but none would talk about it. The problem was that some of them had concerns that weighed heavily on their minds, but actually were at no increased risk for cancer. Others carried a gene that conferred a dangerous risk for cancer—but didn't know for sure they had it, or what needed to be done to mitigate their risk of dying of cancer. Help was on the way, but had to wait a few years.

Chapter 5

C. Richard Boland, Jr., Endwell, New York (1947-1965)

I was born in October, 1947, just over a year after my father assumed he would die of cancer. I was born in the same hospital where my mother was born, by the same obstetrician, Dr. Topping. My birth was partly due to the ruse my Dad used on my Mom that he was sterile because of his radiation treatments. I suppose the history of my life has been going through cycles of good luck and bad luck. I don't know how to explain the occurrence of random variations in fortune. Some things happen in life because of certain skill sets or the exercise of good judgment. Others occur for no apparent reason and certainly no exercise of skill, so I call it luck. Good luck and bad luck; no telling what's coming your way. Clearly I had nothing to do with my own birth, but it appeared to occur as a bit of good luck.

The early years in Johnson City

By the time I was born, Dad was over his first bout with cancer. He had regained his weight, had gone back to work, and was making plans for life instead of death. By 1947, he and Cathie had moved out of her parents' home on Floral Avenue in Johnson City, and had moved a few blocks away, close to both Cathie's parents and the hospital. My very first memory, and this is crystal clear to me, was sitting at the table having breakfast at the house in Johnson City. I was just three and a half years old, and it was April, 1951. I was eating Cheerios with milk at the breakfast table. I finished (leaving a few Cheerios and milk behind), got up, and walked out the front door to play with friends. There was a tree stump between the sidewalk and the curb, and I sat on it to talk with the neighbor friends. On my way out of the kitchen towards the front door, I looked to my left down the side door at our "ice box" (an insulated non-powered refrigerator-like cabinet that took a large block of ice in the bottom to keep milk and other items cold). We also had a small electrical refrigerator in the kitchen. The ice box sat on a small landing in the stairway to the cellar, immediately next to an outside door on the side of the house. There, the milkman and iceman would walk up the sidewalk along the house and use the side door for their deliveries. People did not necessarily lock their doors at this time, in this place. It was the spring of 1951, Americans were happy to be prospering after the war. There was enough for everyone. There were few rich people in this community (except for the Johnsons and Endicotts, who owned the factories), and the poor people weren't that much worse off than the working and middle classes; so, house burglary was not common. Cars were usually left unlocked when parked in front of stores, and it wouldn't be unusual to see the car keys dangling inside the empty cars. Times were good.

I am certain about the date that I have my first conscious memory because shortly thereafter my younger brother, Jim was brought home from the hospital in early May, 1951. He was placed in a crib in the living room. I peered over the edge of the crib and looked in. I didn't know what to think about this particular addition to the family, and I couldn't imagine what a great friend he would eventually become. After looking briefly at baby Jim, I went outside, and looked at the casement window where coal was delivered at one time. We had a new television set in the living room, next to the crib. We were a truly prosperous family with our new television set. It was small, had a round picture tube with a black and white image, and we got one grainy local station, received through a "rabbit ears" antenna. There wasn't much to watch actually, and we didn't use it much initially. For entertainment, we first would use a large stand-up radio, taller than I was, in a beautiful wooden cabinet, sitting in the living room. The only radio show I can remember was "Big John and Sparky". When you turned on the radio, it took several minutes for the vacuum tubes to heat up and the sound to begin. There was a huge radial dial to tune in the stations. The sound was magnificent. For some reason, these recollections of living in Johnson City are particularly clear.

Endwell, New York

In June, 1951, three important events occurred in the family, all in just a few months. First, brother Jim was born on May 2. Almost immediately after that, we moved from Johnson City to River Road in Endwell, a distance of about four miles, into the colonial-style house with four bedrooms (*Figure 18*). More importantly, in June, my grandfather 'Army' died of a heart attack at age sixty-seven while getting prepared for a fishing trip. I have few recollections of Army, and of course, never knew either grandparent on the Boland side, as both had died before I was born. What I recall of Grandpa Armstrong was his sense of humor. Like any competent grandfather, he could pull eggs and coins out of my ears. After his death, when I was about eight, I stood on a chair to explore the upper shelf of my bedroom closet, and found a box containing a very small New York Yankees uniform. I asked my mother what that was. She got a little misty-eyed, and recalled that her father had brought home the baseball uniform for his newborn grandson. By the time I found it, I was too big to wear it. We lived about ten minutes from Grandma (Armstrong) and Cathie's much younger sister, Pat. That was our extended family in town, and we enjoyed many Sunday and holiday dinners together.

On River Road in Endwell, we had a life that was somewhat isolated, but quiet and pleasant. We lived along the river, but about half a mile from any population density. We had the drive-in movie theater in the back on the northern border of the property, a field in which corn and other vegetables were grown immediately to the east, the river a few feet across the road to the south, and an open field of tall weeds to the west. Just beyond the weed field was a miniature golf course, which had bright lights, as well as music and people's voices, for the two summer months. Outside of the summer, when there was drive-in movie and miniature gold activity, the neighborhood was quiet with few passers-by. Some creeks ran through the neighborhood to the River, draining the hills to the north, and there were plenty of open fields and stands of trees to explore. There was an old cemetery a few hundred yards east on River Road that was excellent for exploration and reading the tombstones. It was a little scary for us, I must admit. I wasn't exactly sure what it was about death and cemeteries, but either one would make me a bit anxious as a child. My parents were fulfilled in their lives, no one complained, and my three siblings and I got along well. There were no familial divisions. We were happy there, and grew up in an innocent, friendly and predictable atmosphere (*Figure 19*).

Figure 19: Boland family photo on River Road, 1959. From the left: Sue, Cathie, Alice, Jim, Clem (Clement R. Boland, Sr), and Rick (C. Richard Boland, Jr).

I particularly enjoyed the plants and animals in this semi-rural setting. Every animal I encountered was fair game for my curiosity. When the floods came in the spring, the rodent burrows filled with water, forcing the animals to higher ground. A next-door neighbor (David) on the other side of the miniature golf course and I once took an animal cage with us and explored the fields just beyond the edge of the swollen spring River—a long way from its natural banks. Nearly every time we turned over a rock or board, we found mice huddling beneath that were easily captured and put in the cage. I hate to mention it, but on one occasion, we put a mouse on a little raft into the water. The mice were not avid swimmers, and since we were typical boys, there were targets for rocks or David's sling shot. This happened only once, and I regret it still. However, during one of these outings, we encountered a very large "river rat". He was a good swimmer, and when he surfaced and looked at us, we beat a hasty retreat. Rats had a different reputation than mice. For that day, this was his part of the river.

The microscope and the dissecting kit

I declared from age five that I wanted to be a doctor like my father. He was my hero, and I didn't have a complicated approach to this desire. In the morning while he was dressing, he gave me lessons and quizzes on simple issues of medicine. One of the earliest lessons he gave me was about the diseases caused by vitamin deficiencies. I learned everything he gave me, and loved pleasing him. The one Christmas I remember most vividly and fondly was when I was eleven, and my parents gave me two gifts: a dissecting kit and a microscope. I was in heaven, and realized that I could now look *inside* the animals. I took a large metal lid from an empty pretzel can, inverted it, and melted several candles in it to create a circular wax plate. This was to become my dissection platform, and any animal who died in the yard was likely to become one of my study subjects.

When I reached the eighth grade, my interest became such that my mother took me to the Humane Society, and I picked up a freshly euthanized cat. I brought it home, dissected it, and saved the critical internal organs—in formaldehyde, which could be purchased at the local pharmacy for some reason. The cat had been pregnant, which was a surprise addition to this anatomy lesson. I boiled the carcass (outdoors, over an open fire that I built in a pit in the ground) to get all of the muscle off the bones. I had found one of my father's college books, called *The Anatomy of the Cat* (which prompted my interest in the cat), and used it to guide a reassembly of the bones. This won first prize at Endwell Junior High School Science Fair, and later another prize at the Broome County Science Fair. I found that I could take a coat hanger and thread the vertebral bones on it like a string of pearls, which also permitted me to configure the cat's posture however I wanted. The skeleton lasted in the bedroom that Jim and I shared until my mother moved out of the house in 1971. I never found out how much she got for selling it.

Animal house

About that same time, I was interested in having animals as pets at home. I liked to put frogs or fish into a bucket in the back yard, but the "animal angel" always visited after I had gone to bed, and the animals were gone by morning. Once, I bought a chameleon at the pet store, and brought it home. I wasn't sure that my parents would approve, so I put it into my desk drawer in our bedroom. Jim didn't mind. Although the family had cats and a dog, this was my first foray into personal animal husbandry. I foolishly thought my desk would be a good place to keep this pet. After one day, it disappeared, and I never knew where it went. No one complained about finding a live or dead lizard in the house, so I was never busted. This taught me that my interest in a pet was not always mutually shared by the animal. Chameleons were not like dogs or cats.

Hamsters, however, were another story. A friend named Johnny O'Brien and I decided to get one hamster each. Somehow, Johnny came up with three cages, one purchased and others homemade—I assume by someone's father and passed around. The hamsters were escape artists, the cages not very secure, and they were constantly getting loose in the house. One time, Johnny's family went on vacation for a few days, so I agreed to take care of his hamster for that period. We thought we had two female hamsters, but our veterinary skills were weak. After repeated escapes, I put the two hamsters in the most secure cage for a day or two while I tried to repair the leaky cage. After a short period of time, my hamster delivered a litter of pups, belying our assessment of hamster gender. For over a year thereafter, I had an abundance of hamsters at home.

The first place I kept the hamster cage was in my bedroom (the same place where the lizard previously escaped). It took only a couple of days before the first hamster escape occurred. I didn't immediately mention this to my parents, knowing this would endanger my rodent-raising aspirations, but I hunted for it all over the house. The children's bedrooms had hardwood floors, but my parent's room had a wall-to-wall carpet that went all the way into a walk-in closet. They had two rows of bars for hanging clothes, with shoes below, so, one had to get on hands and knees to get under the shirts, suits and dresses to crawl back and completely search the floor of the closet. In the far back corner of the closet, the feral hamster had gathered a large fuzz ball of carpet fibers and created a nest. I extracted the hamster from the corner, disposed of the nest, and returned her to the cage. However, the escape act was a recurring problem, and when my parents realized that the hamster always returned to their closet, the hamster was banished to the basement.

As mentioned, one hamster became many, biology being what it is. There were times when I was not even sure how many I had, as they continued to have additional litters—and escape—complicating an accurate census. The washing machine was also in the basement, adjacent to the hamster cages. My mother nearly had a heart attack when she picked up a sheet to put into the washer, and a hamster jumped out. She was no rodent lover. This created difficulties for me and I was forced to improve the security of the cages.

When the spring floods came, the casement windows were opened for the hoses from the sump pumps, the basement got cold, and hamster mortality rates increased, which was disturbing to me. However, this provided dissection opportunities. There was a Saturday night when one of the hamsters was put on a death watch. Its breathing was labored and it stopped moving. My parents were out for the evening, older sister Sue was babysitting, and my younger sister Alice and brother Jim were with me in the basement, with the hamsters. Alice was actually saying prayers for the benefit of the dying hamster, but I knew that the hamster was not going to live much longer. I convinced them that this would be an opportunity to see what the inside of the hamster looked like. They were not as enthusiastic as I about this, but their curiosity won out. I usually dissected animals that had been dead for a while, so I looked forward to this one, as it would be a little "fresher". Finally, the animal stopped breathing, and did not respond to any stimuli. So, out came the wax plate, the animal was pinned down, and I opened the animal to begin the "autopsy" for Alice and Jim to see. Unfortunately, when I opened the hamster's chest cavity, the heart was still beating. (I just about croaked.) I had to feign some degree of comfort and familiarity with the situation, and quickly removed the heart and lungs (putting an end to the life-or-death confusion), explaining that the heart continued to beat for some time after death. I learned a lesson. One maxim that I have come to live by is "keep making *new* mistakes". When we moved away from that house after ten years, I found several carcasses of escaped animals who set up nests beneath the stairs to the cellar, where we stored old newspapers.

Experimental chemistry

I had somewhat more impressive misadventures a few years later with my chemistry lab. By age fourteen, several of my school friends were accumulating a variety of chemicals and glassware and mixing them creatively. One could get just about anything either from the local drug store or ordering by mail from the scientific supply company, Fisher Scientific. We exchanged formulas for what would make the most impressive "glom" (made by mixing glycerin and alcohol), or how to make gunpowder or explosives that would flash different colors. We made gunpowder by mixing potassium nitrate with powdered sulfur and carbon (extracted from left-over bags of charcoal briquettes, and pulverized with a mortar and pestle). We varied the amounts of the ingredients, added different compounds to create interesting colors, and tried to figure out how to package and ignite our new mixtures.

One evening, just before dinner, I had created a new explosive mix, and packed it into an empty cardboard shotgun shell I had found while out walking in the woods. The question I was dealing with was how firmly to pack the gunpowder, and how to (safely) ignite it. I took a piece of string I had soaked in gunpowder, then dried, and inserted it alongside the powder in the shell. My chemistry lab was in the cellar next to an outside door which led to concrete steps, where I could test the explosives. I stood the shell straight up on one of the steps and cautiously lit the fuse, which came over the top, and hung on the side. The fuse burned and quickly disappeared into the shell—but nothing happened. I waited a minute or so. Nothing. So, I slowly leaned directly over the upright shell and looked down into it—just as it exploded in my face and mouth. The time was exactly six PM, and it was Tuesday, when we always had dinner with Dad at six PM sharp. I ran to the cellar sink and flushed my face and mouth with cold water. The flame had shot into my mouth, and it tasted terrible. Fortunately, I wore glasses, which protected my eyes, but I had partially burned off my eyebrows, as well as the hair on the front of my head, but there was no serious burn on my face. Just as I was dealing with this minor disaster, Alice called down the cellar steps for me to come up to dinner. Of course, if I openly admitted what a foolish thing I had done in front of Dad and Mom, I might have had my chemistry laboratory dismantled. So, I cleaned up as best I could, went up the stairs, sat at the table, and said nothing. It was a challenge to put food in my mouth. I was sitting quietly next to Alice, trying to act as if nothing had happened. Alice sniffed the air, looked around and innocently asked:

"Does anyone smell something burning?"

I shook my head and said nothing.

My other chemical misadventure was noisier, and cost me a lot of chemicals. I had gotten an alcohol lamp and some glass tubing in the mail from Fisher Scientific. The alcohol lamp flame was hot enough to permit the bending of glass tubes, and I had concocted a gas generator from the pictures in my father's college chemistry book. This consisted of a large Erlenmeyer flask with a two-holed cork in it. One hole held a long thistle tube with a funnel at the top that permitted you to pour acid that would be delivered to the bottom of the flask. The second hole in the stopper had a glass tube that just reached the inside of the flask, and on the outside was attached to a rubber outlet hose with a finely crafted glass nozzle at the end. (All homemade.) If you put some type of metal catalyst into the bottom of the flask (I was using zinc) and then added concentrated hydrochloric acid through the thistle tube, you would generate hydrogen gas. You could also do it with sulfuric or nitric acids, which I also had on the shelf. Again, these chemicals were all fully available at the local drug store—and no one ever asked why I was buying this stuff. The hydrogen gas would come out the rubber hose, which you could direct wherever you wanted through the glass nozzle. Incidentally, hydrogen gas is the lightest gas, making it useful for balloons. But it is also explosive, which was certainly why it was so attractive to make.

An out of town friend, Billy Hamilton, was visiting for a week, and I told him that we could do something that was cool on a Saturday morning. We made hydrogen gas. You could just barely blow up a small balloon (hard to generate much pressure with the apparatus), which would just barely float in the air. Alternatively, you could collect the hydrogen by water displacement in a beaker or flask inverted in a water tank. Once collected, you could put a flame into the beaker and light the gas, which would explode with a sudden pop.

So, we did those things. However, we did something that could be characterized as a perfect storm. Initially, the acid had given up all of its hydrogen gas, so I gurgled more down the thistle tube. Billy was new to this activity, and I didn't see what he was about to do. He decided to put the glass nozzle directly into the alcohol lamp flame just as I added the acid. The gas generator pumped out a large belch of gas, which was ignited by the alcohol lamp, and the flame quickly burned back inside the gas generator. This resulted in a loud explosion heard all over the house. Worse, acid sprayed all over Billy and me, and shot straight up to the wooden rafters and joists that made up the ceiling over the chemistry lab. Mom was doing laundry at the time, and there was a tub next to the washer filled with soapy water, which we splashed all over ourselves, washing most of the acid off our face and arms. We then ran up to the shower, doused ourselves, and kept the burns to a minimum, although our shirts and jeans developed huge holes where the acid sprayed us. Mom was furious, and while we were in the shower, she took all of my bottles of acid and poured them, one after the other, down the sink. This was probably more dangerous than what we had just done, as the pipes were iron, and she probably generated way more hydrogen than Billy and I did. Fortunately, there were no more explosions that day. (The sinks drained very quickly for a while thereafter, I believe.) Mom wasn't interested in my protests that her draining of the acids was almost as bad as what Billy and I had done. That was one of the last experiments I did involving strong acids.

Family life in the 1950s

Biology and chemistry misadventures aside, my childhood took place in a loving and supportive family setting. There were few discussions about cancer in the family. I knew that Dad had suffered some illness while he was in the service, and that it was cancer, and I had heard some of the details about the Demerol problem and his recovery when I was older. But that didn't really mean anything specific to me or my siblings. I had no anxiety about any excessive risk of cancer for myself. That did not make it into the consciousness of any of us when we were young. I think that Dad just didn't know what to say, so he said nothing.

The expectation was that each child would be an excellent student, and certainly excel. We had spelling bees and "name the national or state capital" quiz with dinner, always led by Dad. He called all the shots—or so it seemed. Actually, Mom ran the household during all the hours that Dad was not there, which was most of the time. It was much later that I began to realize that the household was run like an Anglo-Saxon protestant house during the week, and an Irish-catholic one on Sunday. Something for everyone. Sue, Alice, Jim and I got along well, and there were no particular triangular relationships with one person out. There were the two girls and the two boys. Jim and I shared a room, and many secrets.

When I was thirteen, I was confirmed into the Catholic faith, and like my father before me, had an opportunity to choose a confirmation name. We were sent to religious instruction at the Church from school, and the priest who was involved in our instruction asked us to choose a name and write an essay about why we chose that name. I chose Thomas, which had a strong tradition in the family. I then did a library search of the various Thomases in the Church, and what I found was just right. Thomas the Apostle was not present when Jesus appeared to the others after his crucifixion, and Thomas doubted their story about his resurrection. He finally believed only when he was present and could examine the evidence that Jesus had returned using his own eyes and hands. Thus he was called "doubting Thomas", and that was what my essay addressed. I knew at age thirteen that I was an empiricist, and needed evidence. Whatever the gene humans have for believing in the absence of evidence, I didn't get it.

One curious aspect to our household, especially in light of my adult preferences, was the absence of books. Dad had his medical books, and Mom read her novels, but we were rarely read to as children. I have often wondered if Mom suffered from a reading disability. I never knew for sure. But I had something that would probably be called a form of dyslexia today, and it tortured me.

Endwell Junior High School

I was a very good elementary school student, but by the time I finished sixth grade and more independent reading was demanded, I realized I was in trouble. I was a good auditory learner, and had the capacity to remember a very large amount of what I heard. I also could remember most of what I read, but I just couldn't read very quickly. My eyes scanned across the page, returning over and over to the same spot. It was almost impossible to read a novel or long essay. I had to develop all sorts of "work-arounds" to deal with this. Meanwhile, whenever we were given standardized tests, I scored very high—typically in the ninety-ninth percentile on many of them, certainly for all of the math-based tests, because not much reading was required. So, no one suspected that I was having a reading problem.

In the seventh grade, everyone in the class was given some type of IQ test, and the highest dozen or so in the class were put into a special reading class in which we were expected to read one new book a week. We met once a week with the English teacher, and once every other week in the evening with an English professor from the local university (the State University of New York at Binghamton). I could not finish a single book. To cope with this, I began to learn tricks like reading the notes in the beginning of the book, reading selected chapters, and listening to what others said, but it created a considerable bit of anxiety to think that I couldn't do a simple thing like reading a book. No one else seemed to have this problem. I genuinely wanted to read, and somehow I interpreted that some part of my brain was lazy, which was why I couldn't finish these tasks. I felt guilty as if I had done something wrong by not finishing these books. But, I couldn't do it.

Meanwhile, math and science came easily. Math was something that seemed so intuitive that the teacher was simply reminding us of what we were already programmed to know. I couldn't figure out why those disciplines were so easy, and why reading was so hard. As far as I could tell, none of my siblings had the same problem, but I was afraid to bring it up. For one, they probably would not have believed that I was having trouble. I just gave up trying to convince anyone that this was true. My mother never queried me about this, adding to my later questioning whether she may have been similarly affected when she was my age.

Just as difficult as the reading issue was the problem of maturing later than your peers. I was small, and for a boy, that is a problem. Entering the seventh grade, I felt a little smaller than the others, but I had company. I was already dealing with the fact that, for no understandable reason, I couldn't read. Then, as we moved through junior high school (grades seven to nine), the other boys grew larger, hit puberty, and I felt left behind. By the time I was in the ninth grade, I was exactly five feet tall, weighed ninety-five pounds, was nearsighted and wore glasses. As every boy knows, there is a lot of jostling in the herd for primacy, and the smaller boys get pushed around a bit. I didn't feel specifically targeted or bullied—just getting what I have earned with my late maturation. At the school dances, there were only a few girls short enough that I felt comfortable asking to dance. Being small can also make it difficult to compete effectively in sports. In the late 1950s, the main sports for boys included basketball, baseball and football. Being short was a problem for basketball, and because of the myopia and glasses, my visual impairment made hitting a baseball difficult. All of this was made worse because I was aware that my father had been an outstanding student, athlete, and had reached his full six feet by age sixteen. So, at the age when I was just pushing over five feet, my father had been six feet tall. How could he understand how I felt about that? It would have been as hard for me to discuss this with my father as it was for him to tell me about his cancer.

The beginning of junior high school was probably the most difficult period of my life in terms of feeling out of the mainstream and inadequate. I began to wonder if I would *ever* catch up. School work seemed harder than it had been earlier. Finally, in the ninth grade, I started to feel that a few things were starting to turn my way. I had a Latin teacher who was an outstanding scholar and I really respected—John P. Maher. Latin became a subject that came easily. There wasn't a lot of reading, and I could usually remember all of the vocabulary after seeing it once. Maher made what should have been a deadly dull subject interesting to me. He was very bright, knew several languages. When I showed interest in Latin, he gave me a book and gave me a few lessons in Greek as well. At the time, he seemed to be the smartest person I had ever met. He taught us funny Latin phrases, and we learned the Latin declensions by singing songs that I can still recite today. He had been in the Army in Europe, and returned with a German bride. He had seen the aftermath of the war in Germany, and constantly reminded us that we were lucky to be living in the United States, and not rebuilding a devastated continent. He was a very strict disciplinarian, and only stayed at the Endwell Junior High School for one year, which was a serious loss. I fear that he may have been banished from the school district for whacking a student on the butt with a wooden stick after he refused to refrain from being disruptive. Corporal punishment was on the way out, but I was present when this episode happened. Two students were the objects of Maher's wrath. One student bent over and took the swat, which was mostly symbolic, and sat down. There was no attempt to hurt him; just to make him feel a bit embarrassed. A second, more defiant student refused to take his swat, and stormed out of the classroom to report the incident to the principal. I believe he would have been a better person if he had just taken the whack. I think that there was a discussion of the fact that whacking students' butts was not acceptable, and Maher had to leave. So it goes.

There were 250 students in my junior high school class. After finishing ninth grade, we would merge from students throughout the consolidated school district that combined suburban Endwell with rural areas. There was a ritual graduation for the ninth graders, and they read aloud the names and grade averages for the top ten students. We all knew that there was one boy-genius in the class, Richard Rein, and he was a substantially better student than the rest of us. The night before that graduation, Dad asked me if my name was going to be read the next day. I had no clue, and told him that I didn't think so. Confidence was not my strong suit at that time. I had gotten a very high grade in Latin—although I am not sure how many of the others were actually trying—which gave me a boost. None the less, being in the top group was not my expectation. We all sat down in the auditorium for the event, and they read off the names. Top average, Richard Rein, of course. There was an applause, and he went forward to pick up his award. They then said: "other high averages were…", and there it was, "…Clement Boland". Second place, but a long way from Rein. This totally took me by surprise. I thought I had misheard the principal. It was most important since Dad was there. I didn't want to disappoint him. Maybe there was hope in life after all. If only my body would start to grow.

Maine-Endwell High School, and the 1960s

So, off to high school. By being born in 1947, there too many students, and never enough schools for us. We were the large rock moving through the snake. During sixth grade, we went to three different venues, one of which was the local fire station. My high school class in tenth grade was bigger than the eleventh and twelfth grade classes combined. After all, there weren't that many children born in 1945. But as the fathers returned from the European and Pacific war fronts, the baby boom began in 1946-7. There was a recurring theme in education that we heard over and over: there won't be enough slots in the colleges for all of you. This mantra was repeated by every guidance counsellor we had. Better have some backup plans, because there are too many of you trying to go to the same place at the same time.

I was a classic product of the 1960s. I started ninth grade in 1961 and graduated from college in 1969. A lot happened in that decade, and I was totally immersed in it. In 1962, my class moved into a brand new high school building, and had a school-full of new teachers at the just-opened Maine-Endwell High School. Some of the teachers were brought up from the junior high school, and many had not taught high school before. In any event, everyone was new to this school.

This was an especially big problem for the administration. The principal of the high school was a man named Charles Miller. This was his first job as a principal, and it was never clear what education and training qualified him to run a high school. He appeared to be preoccupied with controlling student behavior, and seemed less interested in developing academic programs. I ended up running into this buzz saw, and was suspended from school, twice, for trivial transgressions. The first was truly a youthful mistake of my own doing. Just into the tenth grade, someone brought a screwdriver to school, and passed it around from one friend to another. Some took the liberty of removing signs from the walls as "souvenirs." Unfortunately, I was one of them. Once the first student was caught, he had to tell of the next student to prevent being suspended from school. Charlie Miller came to my house—over the Christmas break of tenth grade—and told me how shocked and disappointed he was that I had taken the "boys room" sign off the wall. All would be forgiven, he said, if I gave him back the sign (I did) and gave him the name of another transgressor. I didn't know anyone, so, I was busted. This was not a big deal, since if you are suspended and reinstated over Christmas break, not much happens.

Scott Davis and the science project

Later that spring of tenth grade in 1963, my best friend at the time, Scott Davis, and I started a science project. We were very fond of our biology teacher, Tom Jones. Jones was smart, knew his biology, and connected brilliantly and energetically with the students. I wanted to know everything, and he could dish it out. He taught us about evolution, furiously sketched extensive biochemistry cycles on the blackboard, and when completed, he would turn around with a grand smile of accomplishment—and his pants were usually covered with chalk dust. In fact, I am sure that Tom

Jones was the single best teacher I had at any level of my many years of education—high school, college or medical school. He was the best both in content and delivery, and after my father, he was my greatest inspiration to succeed in science. I took biology in the tenth grade, and then advanced placement with him again in the twelfth grade, right after he had returned from a year of graduate work in biochemistry.

So, Scott and I wanted to do a science project. We were friends for many reasons, but were also bonded because both of our fathers returned sick from World War II. Scott's father was in the infantry and landed at Omaha Beach on the morning of D-day. Their company had so many casualties coming ashore that they just assigned the ones who survived to new units. They faced heavy fighting breaking out of Normandy. Sometime in July or early August, 1944, he was assigned scout duty and told that his life expectancy was about two weeks. He spent much of the time hence in the countryside with the second scout, living off what the French farmers would give them. He was the lead scout for the lead division for Patton's army (whom he hated for sacrificing many lives needlessly). As such, he was probably one of the first people—maybe *the* first—where he was in the drive across France. Near the German border he was ambushed by a tank and narrowly escaped with shrapnel in his shoulder. Their unit was surrounded on three sides and pinned against a river. They asked to retreat back across the river, but were denied as another unit was building a floating bridge further up the river and his unit would delay the Germans. In the calculus of war, they were expendable. When the few survivors returned after three days, he had to push his best friend to his death as they swam across the river. The friend was drowning, grabbing Scott's Dad, and bringing him down. Back at the field hospital, he could not recall his name, but said that it was on his dog tags. "The only thing I can tell you", he said, "is that I come from a town where they make shoes". Many years later, he suffered terrible survivor's guilt and deep remorse for the people he had killed. Most of our fathers at that time had served in the war and there were probably many more untold stories. I just knew this one. Those who faced the horrors of war rarely spoke and never boasted of their experiences.

After the war, Scott's father became a pharmacist. I knew that my father had been treated with Demerol after his surgery, and Scott and I discussed this and speculated on how that happened. Scott's father had a drug store and access to drugs. Tom Jones bought us a few rats. There was a biology laboratory in the school, beckoning us to explore. So, we consulted Scott's dad, and came up with a plan to inject our rats with Demerol, giving them ascending doses, and then we would stop one group cold, and taper the drug in the second group. We would observe them, look at their pupils, look for abnormal behavior, nothing very sophisticated, and finally stop the drugs abruptly to see if one group showed worse signs of withdrawal. In the end, we didn't see any differences because we weighed the rats when we first got them (little guys, about fifty grams each), and Scott's dad calculated the drug doses based upon those weights. But by the time we started the injections, they had grown and weighed about two hundred grams, and we didn't use enough of the narcotic. So, inexperience has its consequences. However, by having a narcotic in the lab, the administration had to know about this, and we stored our drugs in a safe in the principal's office. Each time we got the drug (which was every day), we had to interact with the office. This was a reasonable precaution.

About this time, there was a chemistry teacher named Bernard Brunza, but he was transitioning into a job as vice-principal, which was what he did during our senior year of high school. Scott and I were in the lab on a Saturday morning in March or April of 1963 (while tenth graders), tending to our rats. We went to the office for the drugs, and got them from Brunza. For some reason, he then chose to listen to us as we worked in the lab. Every room in the school had a loudspeaker for announcements. Unbeknownst to us, they were two-way microphones, and someone in the principal's office could use it as a listening device. That morning, Brunza chose to eavesdrop on us in the laboratory. He probably wondered if we were misusing the drugs—but he never made such an accusation. As we (innocently) went about our business, suddenly his voice came across the loudspeaker, and he ordered us back to the office. He asked no particular questions or suggested any wrong-doing in the lab. However, Scott had also been involved in the sign-swiping crime spree the prior winter, and Brunza told us that he had decided (that morning, apparently) that he was going to serve up our punishment at this belated date. He took us to the high school auditorium, told us to get the janitor's vacuum cleaners, strap them to our backs, and clean the auditorium for him. We had no idea how this punishment was determined, and I am pretty sure we were the only ones of the group of sign-swipers who got this particular treatment. It only took about an hour or so (which including quite a bit of fooling around, and the discovery of a case of soft drink in the back of the stage that demanded sampling), and we were none the worse for this "punishment". However, this was the beginning of a progression where Scott and I—and I dare speculate, some other students—began to lose trust in some of the authority figures in our lives.

The next year, in the eleventh grade, Brunza was my chemistry teacher. I am not sure how much background he had in the subject, but even though I loved the material almost as much as biology, Brunza's approach to teaching it was uninspired. I was one of those students who genuinely wanted to understand the periodic table and how chemical reactions worked. I had no specific reason for this; just a preference, like vanilla vs chocolate. This particular teacher did not seem happy to be there, and I suspect he had been forced to teach it. The pinnacle occurred at 1:30 PM on November 22, 1963 when we got the announcement over the loudspeaker that President Kennedy had been shot, and about thirty minutes later, that he was dead. We were told to stay in our classes, and not to move to the next period. That put us in chemistry for about ninety minutes, and predictably, there was one student who was a little too energetic to sit that long, and he did something to get Brunza's attention. Brunza glared at him and told him to be quiet and sit still—because the stock market was going to fall due to the assassination. That was his explicit concern. Even at my tender and naïve age, I knew a cynical remark when I heard it.

Up on the roof

Unfortunately, this was not my last brush with arbitrary justice in high school. In the winter of twelfth grade, my growth spurt finally kicked in, and I was getting somewhat close to my classmates in size and strength. After bringing up the rear of most cross country races, track meets, and swimming meets, I was finally getting competitive at swimming. By senior year, I was one of the two starters in the 100-yard and 200-yard freestyle events on the varsity team. I even won two races—at the only swim meet Dad ever attended. That was the best day of my inauspicious athletic life.

The baby boom continued unabated for twenty years. In the winter term of 1965, we had the junior high students coming up behind us, their new school wasn't finished yet, and we had to share the high school swimming pool with them for practice after school. On certain days, we had to kill about forty-five minutes after our last class until swim practice began. I had a good friend on the swim team, David Clark, who was the starter in the 50-yard and 400-yard freestyle events. We were both seniors, and hung out together after school. Having a little extra time like this is probably a good way to ensure that something slightly aberrant will happen. One afternoon in March, Clark and I wandered into the auditorium—for no particular reason. We were interested in the projection booth, never having been there before, and there was no one in the auditorium at the time. So, we climbed the stairs and looked around. We had no malevolent intentions. There was not much to see in the projection booth, but there was a window that led out to the roof over the second floor. So, we opened the window and stepped onto the flat roof to see the view. After about thirty seconds, Clark noted that someone had seen us from the next building over; it was one of the janitors. We hadn't done anything seriously wrong, but we hastened back into the school, and went to swim practice.

The next morning, I went to my "home room", and the teacher told me I was wanted in the principal's office. When I arrived, Clark was sitting in a chair in the lobby. We looked at each other, and one of us smirked and said "the roof"?

Brunza was lurking nearby, and said "So, you think this is funny? You are now on the 'restricted list'". We had never heard of the restricted list; I understood it better many years later in the context of 'double secret probation'. To this day, I suspect that the list may have been created for us, maybe even at that moment. Since this was new to us, we had to ask what the implications were: off the school grounds five minutes after our last class, kicked out of all organizations and clubs, and both of us were kicked off the swim team. We were pretty angry about this, and felt that the punishment was out of proportion to the misdeed, if thirty seconds on the roof qualifies as a misdeed.

At lunch that noon, our friends heard about this. There was a general sense of anger, but actually, we were getting accustomed to arbitrary justice from the administration. There was one ring-leader named Danny Springer, who said that someone should send a letter to the janitor and tell him that he had screwed up. I didn't think he was serious. Actually, it seemed unreal, and both Clark and I assumed that this was a venting exercise, and that no note would ever be delivered. I was carrying a legal-length pad of yellow note paper for an essay I was writing in English class (on evolution). A piece of my paper was used for a note. Danny or someone in the group drew a cartoon of an arm holding a knife. Actually, I don't recall what was written, but someone in the group wrote a few (cartoonish) phrases, although it was not something that would have been construed as a genuine threat. At one point, I was goaded into writing on it, and in the upper left corner, I wrote the tiny phrase, literally in Latin, "*cade sis mortuus*". This was one of the phrases that Mr. Maher had taught me. I was taking my fourth year of Latin, and figured I might be one of a very small number in the school who could translate that. (It means, "drop dead".) My little joke. I assumed the yellow paper note would be discarded. We had had our fun.

So, as we finished lunch, Clark and I we went about the rest of our day, preparing to be banished from the school grounds at three PM. However, at two PM, I was then called out of biology class (being taught by the beloved Tom Jones), back to the principal's office. This time the vice principal, Brunza, served as the prosecutor, and the principal, Miller, was the judge and jury, as if it were a criminal trial. Brunza had searched each of our lockers, and had gone to my English teacher for a sample of my handwriting.

"What do you have?" says Miller.

"A threatening letter was slipped under the door of the janitor's room," says Brunza.

Clark and I swallowed hard. (Who did this?)

"Who wrote it?"

"It's on Boland's paper. I have this essay from his English teacher. Same paper. And here is his handwriting from the English paper that matches his writing in the upper corner of the note."

"What does it mean?" (Neither of them apparently knew any Latin.) Both looked at me.

"Drop dead. It's Latin," I confessed.

"This is very bad. Are there any other charges?" said Miller.

Brunza had an ace in hole now. "Yes, theft."

"Theft?"

Brunza had a library book hidden behind his back. "I found this in Mr. Clark's locker."

He put the book on Miller's desk, and started to read a memo from the librarian, Mr. Marr.

"The following books are missing from the library. They have not been checked out, and I assume they are stolen." The book in Clark's locker was on the list.

Miller and Brunza look at us with disgust.

"You two really disappoint me, and you are hereby suspended from school." (What, again?) "Call your parents."

We had to tell our parents that we were suspended as Miller and Brunza watched. As I was leaving, Brunza delivers a parting shot.

"Boland, you will never finish college."

So, we called our parents and told them of our latest crimes and misdemeanors. If there had been a genuine or credible threat, it would have been a serious matter. But the janitor who turned us in never saw the note. I wrote a Latin phrase, I don't think Clark wrote anything, and we had nothing to do with its delivery. I went home, and to my surprise, both parents agreed with me that this was a relatively minor issue, blown out of proportion. I was still furious. As I had taken two languages in tenth and eleventh grades in addition to a regular load of classes, I had enough credits to graduate after my junior year. All I needed to graduate from high school in New York State was my fourth year of English. I had already been accepted to college.

I told my parents that I didn't want to go back and finish, since what interested me most was the swim team, and that was gone. They told me to think about it, and we would discuss it in the morning. As luck would have it, a family friend called my mother, and mentioned that she planned to drive to Bucknell College the next day to pick up her daughter for spring break. This was a two and a half hour drive, and this friend had a problem with alcohol abuse. Mom thought it would be safer if she had a driving partner, so she would not drink. This issue was not specifically mentioned; it was simply assumed. Therefore, Mom asked if I would accompany her the next day, and I agreed. When we arrived Bucknell, I was surprised to see students sunning themselves—on the roof of the school. Strange irony, duly noted.

That day, as I was driving through northern Pennsylvania, the principal called our home, and asked my mother why I hadn't come to school that day. She reminded him that they had restricted and suspended me, that the essence of the misdeed was a short walk on the roof, and that I had little to do with the "threatening letter". To me, the most ironic part was that none of them could translate or interpret the small phrase I had written in the first place. She said that I had decided to drop out, take English in summer school, and not bother finishing at Maine-Endwell High School. Unexpectedly, Miller acknowledged that he "may have over-reacted", and offered to take us back, reinstate us to the swimming team, and there would be no restrictions. I was informed of the reprieve upon my return from the road trip. (Easy go, easy come.)

I went back to the school, but it was not the same. I was angry, and my distrust of authority was getting worse. I lost interest in trying to finish any of my work effectively. My friends and I were all becoming distrustful of those in authority. The times were a-changing. In August of 1963, between my tenth and eleventh grades, there was a march on Washington, punctuated by Martin Luther King's "I have a dream" speech. That fall there were violent episodes in Montgomery and Birmingham, Alabama, and Medgar Evers was killed because of his efforts to integrate the University of Mississippi. Fracture lines were developing within the country, and it was gradually becoming apparent that not all authority figures were believable. That fall, President Kennedy was assassinated, for no apparent political reason. Random violence was mixed in with political events, and is was not always obvious what logic was driving the times. Among my friends, our most heroic figures were not the President or sports celebrities like Joe DiMaggio or Mickey Mantle. We favored Bob Dylan and Cassius Clay. Counterculture had begun. Before long, we adopted phrases like "don't trust anyone over thirty". Over the next few years, we would find ourselves stuck in an unpopular war, with the young people clashing against the established culture. We began to expect that the President and others in government would lie about everything. Somehow, they didn't think we would notice.

In spite of what was happening, once I left high school, although regularly seething with resentment at the world I lived in, I never had another run-in with any authorities at any university, and never had a conflict with the legal system. I generally kept my head down—and in spite of the prediction, I actually finished college. David Clark also has had a successful life. Scott and I remain close friends, and whenever I need good advice, he is the person I reach to. He is a school teacher in upstate New York, and ran the math department in his school for many years. He is still very enthusiastic about the value of being a teacher. And, we are still distrustful of the abuse of authority.

Chapter 6

Notre Dame to Yale Medical School (1965-69)

Applying to college

I must have been a difficult student to size up for college application. I had excellent science and math grades, only fair in English and History, and a 130 point gap between my verbal and math SAT scores. I left the biology achievement test with the feeling that I hadn't missed a single question. However, I couldn't figure out what a poem was trying to say to me, or write about it coherently. I didn't talk about it, and didn't know anyone in the same predicament.

Our guidance counselors were all new to the business of sending students to college, and no college had more than one year's experience with our high school. I had decided that I was going to be a doctor since a very early age, and had complete—if inappropriate—confidence that I would make it. I told Howard Barnes, my assigned guidance counselor, that I was planning on eventually going to medical school. He took a booklet off his shelf, opened it to the section on medical schools, and wrote down a list of them for me. I looked at it for a few seconds and said, "I think you have to go to college before you can go to medical school."

He paused, apparently not having had a discussion like this before and replied, "If they have a medical school, they probably teach pre-med too." This issue was also new to both parents. Looking at and applying to universities on a national level was novel for the family.

I ended up applying to four schools. Three accepted me (Duke, Notre Dame and Bucknell), and one put me on a waiting list (Cornell). The logic for my applications was naïve and simple. My sister Sue's boyfriend was attending Duke. My father's medical school roommate's (George Rutherford, also his best man) son went to Notre Dame. As mentioned, a friend of the family was at Bucknell. Cornell was the closest major university. That was it. Neither of my parents had gone through a college search. Who knew how to do it?

In the spring of 1965, I had to make my choice. After one day, I announced that I would go to Duke. Dad said that was a nice thought, but I should think it over a bit. A day later, I said, yes, it will be Duke. Dad had the same answer. My sister Alice confided to me that she heard Dad say "if Ricky wants to go to Duke, he will have to pay his own tuition." The next day I announced "Notre Dame", and Dad decided I had thought it over just long enough. Off to the Midwest.

My parents both took me to South Bend, Indiana, and dropped me off for my freshman year. I was jumping out of my skin with excitement. My mother later told me that my father cried when they left the campus. I am certain that he feared that I would drift away from the church if I had not gone to a Catholic school. I attended mass just once after I got to Notre Dame. By the time I finished four years, none of my friends had any interest in Catholicism, and no one attended mass. It had little to do with the school; there was no attempt to force religion on anyone. It was just that the times they were a'changing.

Notre Dame (1965-69)

It probably didn't matter where I had gone. I became a better college student than I had been a high school student. College meant leaving the family, reassembling the peer group, getting an education, and learning how to interact with the world. When I got to Notre Dame, I was probably one of the only students in the freshman class who was disinterested in the football team. I had no idea that they had nearly won the national championship in 1964, losing their last game in the final two minutes of the prior season. What was most comforting was to find myself surrounded by a large number of students with similar academic accomplishments and a similar respect for scholarship. That was exhilarating. Also, my body grew up. At high school graduation, I was 5'8" tall, and weighed 135 pounds. A few months into college, I was 5'9", 145 pounds. I entered the intramural swimming meet—and won two medals. I entered the intramural wrestling meet and won the gold medal in my weight class for the group that hadn't wrestled on their varsity high school teams. My freshman roommate, Dick Caldwell, was an excellent high school wrestler, and he taught me enough to pin all three of the opponents I faced. By the beginning of my sophomore year, I was 5'10" and 155 pounds. Finally, my body got it together. Although it was disappointing that it all came late, but I was happy that it happened at all. I was now normal.

College was for me a great experience because of the new peer group, and all of the rules changed. I embraced the new challenges. Every other student had been as successful as I had been in high school, the talent pool was newly balanced, and we were all competing for success against one another. Importantly, I arrived at Notre Dame with a certainty that I would do well. However, the first two tests suggested that I was in for some surprises. Every freshman in the College of Science took introductory chemistry from the legendary professor Emil T. Hofman. He gave a seven question, ten minute quiz at the beginning of class on each of the thirteen Fridays in the semester. On the final Friday, the quiz counted for double points, and there was one additional bonus question, for a total of one hundred points. If you got ninety-three points, you got an A. So, one could miss no more than seven questions through the semester to get an "A". I loved chemistry, but missed two questions on the first quiz. Yikes.

Second, every Notre Dame freshman had to take the entry level religion course. Most of the time, I had no idea what the professor was talking about, although most of the other students seemed to get it. I had received considerably less instruction in Catholicism than about ninety percent of the class. To top it off, I purchased the wrong text book (which I never could have finished reading, anyway). We had our first major exam, and I was beaten by sixty-three of the sixty-five students in the class. That was essentially, a "low" F. Not even close to a D. Yow! Never saw one of those before. I met with that professor, who was a layman, for some remediation. I think he was puzzled how I could be on such a different wavelength in terms of my knowledge of religion. Then I met with my freshman guidance counsellor, Professor Boyle. He asked about my plans. I told him medical school; that had always been my plan. He said that I should develop a backup plan, since coming from New York, it would be very competitive. It appeared that this wasn't going to be as easy as I thought. I soon realized that I wasn't in Endwell any more.

I struggled my way through the first semester, got A's in chemistry and calculus, squeaked through with B's in English and religion, but got a C in sociology—by a single question on the final exam (in which I answered that a college professor had a higher social status than a doctor!). This wasn't going according to plan. But, I got over the first semester adjustments, and settled in for the second semester, getting more A's, including sociology. This was one of those classes of over sixty students, and we were permitted to call the professor to get our grades at semester's end before we left for the summer. I think that a few of my classmates were surprised at the outcome; maybe he misread my grade. A few years later, I took another sociology course from the same professor, Bob Hassenger, PhD. He recalled to me that the next several phone calls came in with requests for their grades, followed by "and how did Boland do?" I probably got the A by the same margin that I had missed the B last term. One of those random things. Random tends to even out over time.

Each subsequent semester, it got a little easier. All of the 300 pre-meds, as well as the biology majors, took Biology-15 in the sophomore year. It was a diluted form of what Tom Jones had taught us in high school, didn't even have a lab (which surprised me). Even though I should have placed out of this course on the basis of advanced placement credit, they would not give credit for Biology-15, which was required for all of the science students—so I had to repeat it. Two more A's, which were given out very sparingly. (On the first of three exams that semester, there were only twelve A's given to 220 students.) Organic chemistry was quite interesting to me, which permitted me to start accumulating good grades, and wipe out the stumble of my first term. Curiously, both the biology and organic chemistry professors seemed hostile to pre-med students, so after one visit to each one, I never went back for any help.

The problem was that I still couldn't read, and I was a terrible writer. So, at the beginning of my junior year, I transferred from the College of Science (where I was getting mostly A's) into the college of Arts and Letters (where I was not). I knew it was a risk, but I had to fix my reading and writing problem. I reasoned that, if I went into a science-based career such as medicine, this was my last chance to improve my language skills. One of the first courses I took after the switch was "Collegiate Seminar", the typical great-books reading class. We had to read one or two books a week, which was a challenge again. I was getting by with my "work-arounds", and once I figured out what the issues were in that week's book, I had no problem forming my opinions and discussing them in the small group seminar. This wasn't like science and math where you needed to master one discipline to go on to the next. The professor of this course, Richard Stevens, also ran the remedial reading program. I spoke with him after seminar one day and told him I couldn't read, and wanted to take his remedial reading program, but he refused to listen. He told me I read just fine. He had no idea I was faking it.

College and the war

As we worked our way through the four years of college, the Vietnam War grew out of control, and caused the gap between the young and the old in the US to widen. How could World War II veterans understand the opposition to fighting for your country? To them, communism in Southeast Asia in the 1960s was the same as fascism in central Europe in the 1930s and 1940s. Students discussed this issue constantly, and we became progressively more alienated from "the establishment". Some of our professors were sympathetic, others antagonistic. We actually discussed actions of extreme social disruption, as the government and most of the figures of authority seemed unredeemable. We knew that President Johnson and his administration were lying to us. We developed our own jargon, our own music, and our own way of thinking. We carried this theme with us for decades, and to some degree, it continues in some of the old "lefties" from the sixties.

My roommate during senior year—Mike Barr—and I were quite close. We shared an off-campus apartment. He was much more politically radicalized than I, and we shook our heads in disgust as we watched the evening television news each night as our involvement in the war worsened. In the fall of 1968, Mike was involved in canvassing for Eugene McCarthy, and I was for Bobby Kennedy, but not particularly involved with any political activity. After Bobby Kennedy's assassination, I gave up hope for the 1968 election. The Democratic National Convention in Chicago was an unmitigated disaster, and the electoral process was caught in an inexorable maelstrom. We watched the voting results in November, 1968 as they were tallied on the television election coverage. Mike and I both voted for Dick Gregory, an outsider with no chance of winning, and he got about sixty votes in St. Joseph County, where we voted. When the vote tally clicked up by two, we nodded, "those were our votes".

When it was over, we weren't sure what our priorities might be. Mike was an engineer, but never pursued that profession after college. He did some community organizing, and eventually was a teacher. I had a goal that never changed, and thought I would find some hope for the future in medicine. One highlight of our senior year was running onto the field at half-time of a nationally televised football game, when the students were tacitly allowed to show banners of various sorts. Mike and I slipped into the crowd, ran onto the field, and unfurled the banner we had painted on our front porch that morning: "Stop the War".

By going to medical school, I was following a life-long dream. It was a way to do something productive and useful for society, and coincidentally, it prevented me from being drafted at that time. Other graduate students weren't deferred. Mike dreaded the decision he would have to make. He was so opposed to the war he would have left the country rather than join the military. He got a draft notice, and stayed up all night, smoked cigarettes, drank coffee, and did what he could to "mess himself up". He was as anxious as could be. On the morning of his draft physical, his blood pressure was so high that he was refused induction. Funny how things work out.

As an example of how focused we were on global rather than personal issues, it was probably ten years after graduation, and I was visiting Mike who was working in Rhode Island as a teacher. We were discussing family dynamics. I asked Mike:

"Is your family Irish?"

He said "Yes." What was so odd was that this discussion had never come up before. It was also the least important aspect about Mike, and we remain soul mates.

Applying to medical school

By the beginning of my senior year, I had accumulated excellent grades, and from my transcript of the first three years, it wasn't entirely obvious that I had transferred out of the College of Science. All medical school applicants had to take a comprehensive entrance exam called the medical college achievement test—the MCAT. A group of pre-med friends got together the night before the exam, and decided to "study" for the MCAT by reviewing a box of vocabulary cards that someone had gotten. We drank a few beers and threw the cards around the room. As far as I knew, there were no preparatory classes or other ways to prepare for this test, so, there was an even playing field. It just came down to who could remember the most and who was skilled at this particular type of test, which was fine with me. Actually, the playing field was seriously stacked in favor of a person who had a knack for taking standardized tests. As far as I can tell, I did better on that test than any other test I had ever taken. When I showed up for an interview for medical school, the interviewing professor looked at my transcript and said "How did you do this?" I dared not to mention that reading well seemed not to have been required.

Armed with top grades and MCATs, I started to look for medical schools. The usual routine was to ask where some of our slightly older friends had gone—sort of like when I applied to college. There were no ground rules here. George Rutherford's son (who preceded me by two years at Notre Dame) was the valedictorian of Notre Dame two years earlier, and had gone to medical school at Duke. OK, put Duke on the list. Another friend, Fritz Haines, had a brother two years older, and he was happily studying at Georgetown. Someone else's brother was at Cornell—OK, there is one more. Fortunately, I went to the pre-med office for some professional advice, and listened to the counsellor there, Professor Lawrence Baldinger, who had counselled thousands of pre-med students over the years. He was somewhat more experienced than my high school counsellor. He looked at my transcript, and handed me a small blue catalogue for Yale Medical School. "You should apply here," he declared. I read the catalogue, and it sounded interesting. Yale had a thesis requirement, and at this point, I wanted to take on a research project with a little more complexity than giving Demerol to rats. Moreover, the "Yale system" had no tests. Just learn what you need, and learn how to keep learning. This was for me. By September, 1968, I had applications filled out to Yale and Georgetown, and was thinking about Cornell and Duke. There were no standard deadlines for any of these places, and no centralized system of application. You got an application form, filled it out (usually by hand), asked your college to send your transcript, and waited for a letter inviting you for an interview.

A stroke of luck saves the day

Shortly after submitting my application to Georgetown, I was granted an interview in mid-September, which was where the interviewer made the comment about my MCAT scores. Two weeks later, they sent me an acceptance letter, and it was just September of my senior year. I didn't mention it to anyone, as that might have triggered an adverse reaction. I had gotten my application off to Yale in the summer, and they granted me an interview—in Indianapolis, which is about two and a half hours from South Bend. I was asked to go to the office of Dr. Robert Lempke, a surgeon at the Indianapolis Veterans Administration (VA) Hospital, who was a Yale Medical School grad. I planned my visit, not having any assumptions of what might be asked, and rehearsed nothing. I was quite unschooled in the art of guile.

I headed south on Route-91, which runs straight from South Bend to Indianapolis. A road map indicated this would be no problem. I had a 1 PM interview, figured the trip would be uncomplicated, so I left at 10 AM and gave myself three hours to get there. I have mentioned before that if you have good luck, you can overcome all manner of other deficiencies. On this day in September, 1968, luck overcame my inadequate planning. I was about halfway to Indianapolis, making good time, and the radio announcer reported that it was 12:30 PM, but my watch said it was 11:30 AM. I drove past a school, and the clock on the front of the building confirmed that it was 12:30 PM. Only then did I recall that Indiana was split into two time zones. This had been an issue of some irony, because the Indiana State Legislature was exercising civil disobedience to federal law by doing this—and yet they objected to students protesting what we thought was an unjustified war. It was OK to disobey over something foolish like a time zone, but you had better not express your ethical opinion about a war, which involved issues of life and death.

This was not a time to think about the problem of Indiana being split into two time zones. Even though Indianapolis is directly south of South Bend, it was in the Eastern Time zone, and I had left the Central zone, and lost an hour. I had a serious time problem, and worse yet, didn't actually know where the Indianapolis VA was located. Maps were crude, I hadn't bothered planning that part, and had planned to pull into a gas station and ask directions once I got to Indianapolis. Now what? I started to panic.

I drove into the northern outskirts of Indianapolis a little after 1 PM—the time of my appointment. Just by chance, the VA hospital was well-marked, and located off the first exit from the highway at the north end of the city. I held my breath, and almost immediately found Dr. Lempke's building and office. I ran into his office, probably sweating and hyperventilating, and figured that it would be hard to make a worse impression than to show up twenty minutes late for your medical school interview looking frazzled. I did my best to settle down, hide my anxiety, and introduced myself to his secretary. She smiled sweetly, told me to take a seat, and then apologized that Dr. Lempke had been delayed in surgery. I didn't have to mention the time zone issue, and had a few minutes to collect myself. There is no substitute for timely good luck. By the time he arrived, I was relaxed, he was apologetic for being late, and we went to his office for a chat. No difficult questions. He asked what I thought about research. I told him I looked forward to it. He couldn't have been more cordial. Thirty minutes later I was on my way back to Notre Dame. Two weeks later, I got an acceptance letter from Yale. I didn't even know where New Haven was! It was not even the second week in October, and I didn't need to send out any more applications. I mentioned (quietly) to a couple of pre-med friends that I was done applying to medical schools, and based upon their response, I didn't mention it to anyone else. (My non-premed friends were a bit more congratulatory.)

So, it was time to call Dad and make another academic decision. I was asking for a second four year free ride in school, my sister Alice was half way through Syracuse University, and brother Jim was about to start at Cornell the next fall. So, this was not a simple decision. The tuition at Georgetown was $1,650 per year, and at Yale, it was $2,200 per year. Anyone looking at these numbers today will assume these are typographical errors, but those were the published tuitions for that year. It's just that incomes were proportionately lower, and the federal government was giving "capitation" support to medical schools—something that ended in the next decade. When I was accepted by Georgetown, Dad asked if I wanted to go there.

I told him I had a couple of other applications to finish. This time, I told him I had an offer to go to Yale.

He said: "Georgetown's a good school".

I agreed but asked, "Can I go to Yale?"

He said yes, and that was it. For some reason, there were five Notre Dame students in my class of eighty-six at Yale. One classmate later suggested that Yale must have had a Catholic affirmative action program. Who knows? Only Yale College had more students in the Yale Medical School class of 1973 than Notre Dame.

Yale Medical School

I spent my last summer at home in Endwell in 1969. Social activism in the United States was heating up. We were enmeshed in an unpopular war in Vietnam. The Civil Rights movement could no longer be suppressed, and was building momentum. The cities were exploding with riots for the third straight summer. Students were being drafted out of college if they were in the bottom half of their class, and few students were permitted to pursue a graduate degree after college. Medical students were among the only ones exempted. We were special, but we had to be careful to avoid hostility from students not so fortunate.

Each summer I worked for a masonry construction company as a laborer, and made two dollars an hour. Actually, that was a relatively generous amount, as the alternative (which I had to do whenever there was a strike, which occurred almost every summer) was packing groceries for a $1.25 an hour. It was a challenge to save much money, but after getting tuition, room and board from home, it was not considered appropriate in my household to ask for more. That summer, the Woodstock Rock and Roll Festival took place just two hours down Route-17 from Endwell. I didn't see that coming, and missed it, but it had a massive impact on the youth culture. The hair kept getting longer. There was widespread marijuana use, and more. It took some doing to explain to my leftist friends why I wanted to go to medical school. "To make money?" "To be important?" How do you explain that this is what I had planned to do since I was five, to be like my father? It was in my DNA. I never had a back-up plan.

After a politically stormy summer, September arrived and I drove to New Haven on a drizzly September morning. The map told me how to get from Endwell to New Haven. Take Route-17 to the Hudson River and take Interstate-95 to the New Haven exit. I got to New Haven, exited, rolled down my window, and asked a pedestrian where the medical school was. He pointed, and I got there. I parked the car, looked around, and knew this would be a good place for me. I could feel the traditions. I liked the smell of the old books in the library. I was so excited to be there, and had few anxieties about the upcoming challenges.

I took care of registration, and moved into my room on the fourth floor of the Harkness dormitory, where most of the medical students lived. Each first year student was given a "mug sheet", which had a picture of all eighty-six medical students, their names and the colleges they came from. From across the hall, the first classmate I met was David Adler, who came from Westchester County, New York, and had gone to the University of Rochester. He was determined from the first day of medical school that he would become a psychiatrist. He did.

"Did you notice that the class is about one third Catholic, one third Protestant and one third Jewish?" David commented, waving the mug sheet.

How would he know this, or care? "No, I hadn't noticed."

"Yep," he calmly replied.

He was thinking "that's a lot of Catholics." Personally, coming from upstate New York by way of Notre Dame, I didn't think that was so many Catholics, and was wondering where all the Jews had come from. David's father had wanted to be a medical student, but when he applied, in the late 1940s, anti-Semitism was standard policy in many American universities. He was refused admission and chose to go to Europe to get a PhD degree. So, David was quite sensitive to the ethnic and religious make-up of the class, which was less problematic in 1969 than it had been twenty years previously. We quickly became good friends, and part of a cadaver-dissecting quartet. David introduced me to many aspects of Jewish culture that had previously escaped my notice, and he warned me not to ask for a glass of milk with a corned beef sandwich at the Jewish deli. It was a good time, and I was learning a lot more than medicine.

Once again when taking a path like this, each step forward reflects another round of selection that integrates you into a new group of people a lot like yourself, all of whom had been successful in their last setting.

Everyone had a story of accomplishment, and no one was shy about telling it. It was initially intimidating, until I realized that we all had good stories to tell. Fortunately, the Yale system had no tests. Essentially, a full curriculum was scheduled, but the professors paid no attention to attendance. There were no tests, no papers to write, and no assigned books to read—just occasional lists of recommended reading. You had to be a self-starter, and if you were, it was an ideal setting. Each student did what he or she needed to do to learn (the class of 1973 had only eight women when we started), and the emphasis was on how to use the academic resources to teach yourself medicine. Each student had to pass Part I of the national board exam to move from the preclinical years to the clinical years, and then pass Part II of the national boards to graduate. Satisfactory reports were required on the clinical rotations (called "clerkships"), and you had to submit a research thesis in your last year. That was it. The system helped control what would have been a competitive atmosphere, and it also permitted everyone to find one's own best methods to learn. I was very happy with the system. However, by December, fate was about to deal me with a huge piece of terrible news that would change and dictate the rest of my life.

Chapter 7

LIFE-CHANGING EVENTS (1969-1970)

"The times, they are a-changin'". Bob Dylan, 1964

Back to *in medias res,* from the first chapter. September to November of 1969 flew by. I was among kindred spirits with my classmates. However, there was a cultural gap between the members of the first year class and the three classes ahead of us. I had not noticed this in college; it was probably the smaller size of the medical school that made this more obvious. The difference was progressively greater with each older class. The first year class was politically more aware, more liberal, we were more antagonistic towards the government, and we had a very negative attitude about our involvement in the Vietnam War. My class had a sense of saving the world, which was of course naïve, and we clashed during ordinary conversations with our more cynical upper-classmates, who were more interested in material accomplishments. You could almost determine what class a student was in by the length of the hair. By May of 1970, there was a cataclysmic series of political misadventures in the US, including the announcement by the Nixon administration that the War had expanded into Cambodia and Laos. Four students were shot and killed by the National Guard at Kent State, Ohio; just eleven days later, two students suffered the same fate at Jackson State College in Mississippi. Our class went on strike and shut down Yale Medical School. We used that time to visit other medical schools and encouraged them to do the same. We were involved in other political activities as well. May, 1969 was chaotic in the extreme. We never finished the coursework in the last month of my first year of medical school.

Second cancer surgery

For me, everything was interrupted in December, 1969, when my mother called and told me to get home, as Dad was about to undergo cancer surgery. My focus converged on something entirely different than medical school or politics. Upon my return home, Dad was already in the hospital. His tumor had been growing and he had been experiencing pain and other symptoms for several months. He knew about his personal and family history risks—but did nothing of a preventive nature. He didn't want to know, and the preventive measures available for him were not highly effective. The techniques of the 1940s-1960s probably would not have been able to detect an early tumor because of its location. He may or may not have understood those limitations, but the simple fact is that he did nothing by way of prevention since his first tumor was removed twenty-three years earlier.

I got home in the early afternoon of Thursday, December 18, 1969. Dad was in Wilson Memorial Hospital in Johnson City, New York, and was being prepared for surgery the next day by his surgeon and good friend, Charlie Steenburg, MD. After visiting Dad in the hospital, I went home for the evening, and came back the next morning. The surgery was not successful, as the tumor occurred at the junction of his remaining colon (the transverse colon) and his small intestine. The initial surgical anastomosis was contiguous with his liver, and they couldn't tell whether the tumor had directly grown into the liver, or whether there were metastases through the blood to the liver. In any event, they couldn't remove the cancer. He had another tumor in his rectum, but this was not a problem. I stayed in his room with him that night, and he was able to go home after a few days. The surgeons referred him to the Roswell Park Cancer Institute in Buffalo, to be evaluated for more extensive surgery involving the liver. I was not knowledgeable about cancer surgery, and remained inappropriately optimistic that someone at Roswell Park could completely remove his tumor. When Dad came home for Christmas, he looked sick, and was privately worried that this was incurable. We all had an unspoken awareness that he might be dying of this cancer. His children were 23, 21, 19 and 17. We were too old to be fooled, but too young to really understand.

Last hope at Roswell Park

Dad got to Buffalo in early February, 1970, and the lead surgeon was Arnold Mittleman, MD, an experienced and well-known cancer surgeon. Dad was in the hospital for about four days getting tests and being prepped for his surgery. They didn't feed him for the last two days leading up to the surgery, which was postponed twice. I drove to Buffalo for the operation. Finally he was taken to the operating room, where they had him open for about eight hours as they tried to ascertain whether the tumor could be removed. They finally decided that they could not remove the tumor, and sewed him back up. We were crushed that he was no better off for the second surgery, which he barely survived. It took longer to recover from this operation. There were some shaky moments in the post-operative period, but he made it back home. I met Dr. Mittleman by coincidence in the 1980s on a professional basis at a colon cancer research meeting. I had recalled the name—although I had not met him personally in Buffalo. I mentioned that he had operated on my father. He asked me how he was. Unfortunately, I told him, not so well.

At this point, we all knew that Dad was dying of his cancer. I made it back to school, tried to focus on my education, but I was distracted. Once I knew about his cancer, I began to gather more detailed information about his earlier cancer and other cancers in the family. What had been a loose story started to become clear—and very scary. Dad definitely had cancer in 1946. His "illness" was no longer vague, and I insisted upon talking about it and making some sense of it. What had been a mystical curse to my father's generation was now a medical and scientific challenge to me.

By 1969, five of Dad's twelve siblings had died of some sort of cancer, and two more had survived cancer surgery. Dad's father and grandfather had died of colon cancer. There were three in the family who had colon cancers in their mid-twenties (my grandfather, my father, and his sister Alice). I didn't like the looks of this, and knew that my siblings and I were in the cross-hairs of some deadly problem. However, my medical textbooks had no disease that met this description. I found a single line in a two-volume pathology textbook indicating that there had been a family with a cluster of colon and uterine cancers. That was all I could find in the textbooks.

Meanwhile, I had medical school to deal with. Going to classes and seminars was very enjoyable to me. I knew that I had picked the one field of work that would interest me for the rest of my life. Nothing seemed tangential. Everything related to everything else. Medical school was a great distraction from what was going on at home. I got home as often as I could, but Dad was gradually getting worse, losing weight, and very low on hope. He had been unable to return to work since December. He had someone else take over the care of the children in his practice. It crushed him not to be there. There was a slow train coming down the track, and we had nothing with which to stop it.

First trip to the Indian Health Service

After the first year at Yale Medical School, the students were told to leave the medical center for the summer, and tackle a less academic, more clinical experience. There was a collaborative program between Yale and the US Indian Health Service, in which small stipends were offered for twelve medical students to spend eight weeks on the Navajo Indian Reservation in New Mexico and Arizona. There were four different sites available. Several of us found this to be an attractive option for our summer clinical experience. I had been accepted into the program in the winter months, but as we got closer to the start of the program in June, Dad was failing. The medical school liaison for the Indian Health Service (IHS) program was a professor of Psychiatry named Chase Kimball, MD. He was very supportive. I told him of my dilemma, and that I was worried that my father might die when I was in the Southwest. He advised me to carry on with my professional training, and take the chance that he would survive until I returned. So in June, twelve Yale medical students from our class drove out to the Navajo reservation for the summer. I was one of six who went to the Gallup Indian Medical Center in Gallup, New Mexico, near the Arizona border. Three of us lived in a ramshackle house from which we literally had to scrape dried-up dog shit from the floor to move in. (Who was going to rent to three scruffy-looking, long-haired medical students for two months, except a guy with a house full of dog shit?) We had our first exposure to clinical medicine, and our learning curves were very steep. We had the opportunity to explore the Navajo reservation on the weekends, which was quite an experience for all of us.

The little three room house we rented had no phone, and of course, cell phones were a few decades away. I tried to call home as often as possible, and mainly communicated with my sister Sue a couple of times a week through pay phones or phones at the hospital. On Friday July 10, several of us planned to head in the direction of Albuquerque for the weekend. I thought that I should call home first, since we would not be in communication for several days. I got hold of Sue, and she told me that Dad had slipped into a coma, and was in the hospital. So, my colleagues dropped me off at the airport instead, and I got a flight to Kennedy Airport in New York. I arrived in New York at about ten PM. A very nice person sat next to me on the flight, heard my story, and offered to drive me from the airport to my girlfriend's apartment in Mamaroneck, New York.

Patricia Sweeney

My girlfriend was Patricia Ellen Sweeney. We had been dating for about three years, and were very much in love. I was sure she was the one. (She was.) It seemed an inevitability that Pat and I would meet, but the way it happened involved a bit of good luck. Pat was a year behind me in school, and we both lived in Endwell—about a half mile apart. Against all odds, we never met while we were in school. I went to the public schools, whereas Pat and her five siblings all attended the Catholic schools. Pat was an outstanding student, and one of the family jokes is that we never would have gotten along if we had gone to the same school. She was the valedictorian of her high school and college classes. We met, indirectly, because her father had built a summer cottage on Forest Lake, a small lake just over the Pennsylvania border, about twenty minutes from Endwell. As luck would have it, the cottage was immediately next door to the cottage of my friend Scott. There were five Sweeney girls. I saw them periodically while visiting, but I never got to know any of them very well.

But Pat was attractive, which I noticed, and closest to me in age. We both went to the same New Year's Eve party (with different dates) on December 31, 1966. She was a freshman at D'Youville College in Buffalo, and I was a sophomore at Notre Dame. The party was at the apartment of her sister, Sue. The next summer, I asked Pat out on a date. We dated that summer, communicated over the next school year, and she visited Notre Dame during the 1967-68 year. The romance heated up over the 1968-69 year, and we were both sure that we had found our life-long partner, but we had no specific plans for marriage. I had plans for medical school, and she had plans for a career in public health nursing. In fact, it was one of my tenets that I would not marry before age thirty. After graduating in May, 1970, she moved to Mamaroneck in Westchester County, New York, as she had gotten a New York State scholarship for Public Health, and was obligated to take a public health nursing job in New York. That was close enough to New Haven.

So, at about eleven PM on Friday evening, July 10, the helpful fellow traveler dropped me off and I knocked at the door to Pat's apartment. No one was home. She and her roommate (her sister Kathy) had gone back to Endwell for the weekend. There was no way to reach her. So, I walked to the closest freeway ramp, and stuck out my thumb to hitchhike the final 200 miles to Endwell. I got a couple of rides pretty quickly, was finally dropped off about two miles from my home, at about four AM, and walked over the final hill. My mother heard me come in, and told me that Dad had awakened from his coma, which was apparently due to a near overdose of Demerol. (Again!) He was still in the hospital, but seemed better. No one knew how long he had.

I got to the hospital and visited with Dad. Later, I found out that Pat was at Forest Lake with her family. I knew that Dad was extremely fond of Pat, and he was going to die soon. That Saturday, July 11, I asked Pat to marry me, which had been a foregone conclusion to us, but we still had no idea of when to do this. Dad's illness was forcing the timing. We decided to tell Dad of our plans to marry, but we didn't actually have a specific plan to do it. So, we went to the hospital and told Dad that Pat and I had decided to get married. He was delighted, but, for a dying man everything has time value, and he immediately asked "When?" We said we didn't know yet, but perhaps at Thanksgiving or soon thereafter. Also, for now, this was a secret.

At the same time, my mother's step-father, called "Grandpa Earl," was in the same hospital with what was to be a minor illness. Dad insisted that we tell Grandpa Earl of our plans. So, we went to his room, and told him of our marital plans, but that it was a secret. We got home, and didn't mention this to anyone. However, the next day, we returned to the hospital, and when we visited Grandpa's room, his roommate loudly congratulated "the happy couple" on our upcoming marriage. So much for the secret plan.

The next day, on Sunday afternoon July 12, we went to the Sweeney cottage, as I thought I should properly ask for permission to marry Pat from her father, John. All the Sweeney family was present—the usual happy crowd, and I asked John Sweeney for his "daughter's hand in marriage". He had a big belly laugh, said "Sure", and then added "What took you so long?" I was twenty-two, Pat was twenty-one, we looked like teenagers, and John wondered what we were dithering over. We informed the rest of my family, but again, we didn't say or know when. My mother's sister Pat Jones (who had been a teenager when Clem and Cathie married) was visiting in Endwell from California to be with her sister while Clem was dying. We sat around the kitchen table discussing the issue of whether to set a date for the wedding. Pat Jones suggested that we set a date that Dad could realistically look forward to. After some discussion, we set a tentative date for Labor Day weekend, which was about seven weeks away. Would that do it? Dad was delighted to hear a specific date, and had one positive and happy thought for his future.

Dad stabilized, came home, and I needed to get back to New Mexico, since there were no reliable predictions of Dad's course. One of the last days at home, and the last time I saw Dad alive, he was quite weak, and Mom and I helped him move from room to room in the house. When we reached my bedroom, a Beatles record was playing, and Paul McCartney was singing *Yesterday*. Whenever I hear that song and the phrase "… all my troubles seemed so far away, now it looks as though they're here to stay, oh I believe in yesterday…", I am transported to that last sad moment with Dad.

After those few days at home, I returned to New Mexico on July 19, and still had a month to go with my summer clerkship. I was constantly worried that things weren't going well at home. I called on Sunday July 26, and got my sister Sue on the phone. Again, she had been trying to reach me through the hospital, but no one had a way of reaching us. Dad had just died. Get home. So, I returned that day.

At the funeral, I felt saddest for my younger siblings, Alice and Jim. Sue was married, and I had my plans, but Alice and Jim needed more time with their father. Alice was half-way through Syracuse University. Jim was about to start his freshman year at Cornell. Jim was particularly close to Dad; moreover, they were temperamentally the most similar. Like Dad, Jim was a superior student, got his full adult growth early, and was an outstanding athlete. He went to the New York State High School Championships in swimming and track, and held the Maine-Endwell pool record in the 100-yard backstroke for an astounding twenty-five years. Records don't usually last that long in swimming. He was the last one left at home as each of us went off to college one by one, and Jim shared the breakfast table with Dad in a special way. They would eat their breakfast, and exchange sections of the newspaper as necessary, with a minimum of dialogue. They silently understood one another. There would be discussions of the fortunes of the local high school or regional professional sports teams. Not much discussion of politics. Dad was very proud of his son, and got to see some spectacular performances and a lot of victorious races from Jim. Now, Jim would be going to college, but without his greatest supporter. It hit him hard. I knew that would be the case, but didn't know how to manage it. We have stayed very close over the years.

The wedding

After the funeral, Pat and I decided almost on a lark that we would go ahead with the wedding, on the Friday before Labor Day, September 4, at her family's cottage at Forest Lake. I went back to Gallup for my final week. The three students who had driven west eight weeks earlier drove back east together. Pat and I went to a store and bought a pair of wedding rings—ten bucks each, or about 20% of our combined checking accounts. We called a few friends and family members, but wanted the occasion to have a low profile. It was impossible to be celebratory so soon after the funeral, but after Dad's six month decline, there was some sense of relief that he was now out of pain. Pat and I found an apartment in New Haven a short walk from the medical school, and rounded up a few items for the new nest.

On the morning of September 4, 1970, I woke up at home, drove about a mile to pick up Pat, who was staying at the home of a family friend in Endwell. John Sweeney was an IBM engineer, and his job had been transferred to Huntsville, Alabama in early 1970, so they were back in town, staying at Forest Lake. Pat and I picked up a cake and a gallon tub of her favorite flavor of ice cream from Pat Mitchell's Ice Cream Parlor—our favorite place for a date over the past two years. We drove to Forest Lake through a drizzling rain, but at about noon, the rain stopped, the sun magically came out, and we prepared for our nuptials. We had just barely gotten a priest to marry us. Apparently, we seemed not sufficiently serious or religious for some priests, and we wanted to have our ceremony outdoors, which most refused. On the night before, we got a Catholic priest from Pat's high school to marry us—a wonderful fellow named John Quinn. Our friends came in all manner of dress, including one in a tie-died psychedelic jacket. We wrote our own ceremony with Father Quinn's blessing, accompanied by guitars and folk songs. We probably had no more than thirty people on hand, mostly family, and a few close friends (including Scott Davis, who was next door). Everyone went swimming after the ceremony. Father Quinn took off his Roman collar to join in the swim.

We were finally sent away at about eight PM, and told everyone we were going to drive the full four hours to New Haven. They all encouraged us to stop at a hotel on the way, but we had a no money for this—having sprung for the wedding rings. So, a hat was passed to collect some money for us. They gave me the hat (a wrinkled, blue and white seersucker model), and it had forty-two dollars in it. So, we drove less than an hour, and stopped at a minor lake resort just off the highway. We came in at about nine PM with no reservation, no baggage, and carried the remnants of the chocolate ice cream—and two tooth brushes. I asked the clerk for a room for one night. He looked at us for a while, and somehow decided that we were not runaway teenagers. One night was nineteen bucks. No problem, I reported, as I pulled wadded one and five dollar bills out of my pocket, flattened them on the counter, and added up nineteen. He gave us another strange look, and pushed the room key across the counter. In spite of it, our marriage is now in its fifth decade. Some predictions are more difficult to make than others. The next day, we made our way to New Haven, to start the rest of our lives together.

I hadn't always made excellent decisions before, but Pat was the best decision of my life. She kept me grounded, has been my beacon, and continually reminded me of what things were most important. She never asked for anything material, and gave me permission to pursue my passions professionally. Without her, my story might have been very different.

Chapter 8

LEARNING TO BE A DOCTOR (1970-1977)

"You can't always get what you want…. But if you try sometimes, you just might find, you get what you need". The Rolling Stones, 1969

Pat and I got an apartment in New Haven not far from the medical school in one direction, and a short walk to the train station for Pat in the other. The members of the Yale Medical School class of 1973 had dispersed in May, not even finishing our first year of school, and went in multiple directions for our required summer experiences. We had no opportunity to say our goodbyes, and with the exception of the twelve of us who went to the Indian Health Service, no one knew where the others had gone for the summer. We slowly filtered back to New Haven in early September. I ran into a couple of friends in front of the Harkness dormitory.

"What did you do over the summer?" I was asked.

"Well, I went to the Indian Health Service for a while, my father died…. and I got married. How about you?" My summer seemed to have had more to it than the others.

My second year of medical school involved a number of adjustments. I was now married, but Pat and I still had to learn how to live together, a challenge for two strong personalities. My mother informed me that she could not afford to send all three of us to school at once. Since I had already been through college, I was on my own. I went to the Dean of Students, Howard Levitin, MD and asked what my options might be. He asked what my family income was. "Zero." There was no pension for a solitary practitioner, life insurance was hard to come by for cancer survivors, and pediatrics had provided a good, but not lavish, livelihood. Without hesitation, he offered me a full scholarship for the year. Just like that. I got a loan from Yale for my third year, and finally, a Public Health Service scholarship for my fourth year, in exchange for a promise to return to the Indian Health Service for two years. Pat was working, which paid for rent and food. So with a little help, we made it over our first major hurdle, and it seemed likely that I would be able to continue studying medicine on schedule.

Pat had a punishing commute back and forth between New Haven and Mamaroneck, and after a few months, she found it difficult to add an hour and a half each morning and each evening to her work day. She was almost too tired to eat some nights when she got home. At that time, the federal government was opening neighborhood health clinics in places where there were few or no physicians, and one opened a few blocks from our apartment. We were in a racially mixed neighborhood, but there was a reasonably good sense of community, and Pat was offered a job in a project that provided health care to the poor people of the "Hill" neighborhood at the Hill Health Center. This was a particularly good fit for Pat and her unbending idealism. After about a year, they decided they needed mid-level "physician extenders", and sent Pat and another nurse to the University of Connecticut to become pediatric nurse practitioners, a new type of job in which the nurses had an unprecedented amount of autonomy. They became experts at normal child development, well child care and the common childhood diseases. This kept Pat challenged and happy.

Confronting the medical mystery

When I went to the library to study, I would occasionally doodle on paper to take a break—sometimes by making up math problems. One day, I found myself solving a simple statistical problem. If there were a risk of fifty percent for a binary outcome occurring among four people, what would be the likelihood that none would get one outcome, that one would, or two, three, or all four? Even without consciously thinking about it, I was calculating the genetic risks hanging over me and my siblings if we had a dominant cancer-predisposing disease. What was this disease? Was there a genetic explanation? The data I had collected suggested a dominant genetic disease, in which half of the offspring would be affected. But, in the 1970s, we had no clue of how to solve a question like this.

Yale Medical School has a prominent School of Public Health, so I took the family history I was gathering to one of the faculty. There was just one familial form of colorectal cancer known, and that was familial adenomatous polyposis—a disease that is easily recognized because, starting in the teenage years, the colon begins to fill up with hundreds of small adenomatous polyps, one or more of which will inevitably grow into a cancer. The records I had collected showed this was not the case in my father or anyone in his family. I sat down with an epidemiologist, and we discussed how likely it was that this represented a single gene-determined disease that hadn't made it into our textbooks. The discussion didn't last that long.

"Just a case of bad luck…" I was told, "…common tumors will eventually accumulate in a family just by chance." "There is no known disease that acts like this." So, the Bolands were victims of bad luck, for three successive generations.

"Bad luck?" I countered. "Why would colon cancer that typically strikes people in their sixties and seventies cluster in young people in one family, as early as age twenty-five? And what about the endometrial cancers?"

I got no convincing answers, and left feeling somewhat frustrated. I also had my introduction to the hubris of the established experts. I was just a second year medical student, but I was learning an important lesson about medical education. The job of the professors was not to know everything, and not to pull facile explanations out of thin air. Their job was to keep us grounded in what we actually knew, understand the principles of data-gathering, and to show us how to solve problems. I have no objection with that concept to this day. They didn't know what was going on, and neither did I. If I had a different idea, fine. Go prove it. It's in your court, dude.

Yale Medical School had a thesis requirement, and most of us started working on this in our third year. After a year of considering the pros and cons, I decided to take on the challenge of familial colorectal cancer as my research project. I decided that the place to start was by carefully gathering and annotating the full family history, and then find out how to solve a problem such as this using scientific principles. The first step was to carefully document as much of the family history as possible. One thing that helped was that our family was so large. Geneticists love big families. I decided that my medical school thesis project would be to figure out what was going on in the family. Unfortunately, I had no idea of how to attack the problem. Very few diseases that appeared to be genetic had a known molecular or biochemical basis. In fact, most of the diseases in my Pathology and Internal Medicine textbooks were "idiopathic". That is, we didn't know what caused them.

The first three semesters at Yale Medical School covered the preclinical material that most schools covered in four semesters. This included anatomy, biochemistry, cell biology, microbiology, pathology, pharmacology, physiology, and a few others. The summer between years one and two was used to get the first-year students out of New Haven, introduce us to clinical medicine, and help us think about what the preclinical sciences meant for clinical medicine. After the preclinical work, we had to pass Part I of the national board exams, which permitted us to move on to twelve months of clerkships in which we did a series of rotations in various aspects of medicine. So, after three semesters, we donned short white coats (the medical student uniform) and began hands-on interactions with patients (see the Class of 1973 photo as we headed to "the wards", *Figure 20*). The clerkships were broken into six week blocks. We had two blocks of internal medicine (which is central to all of the medical and surgical disciplines), two blocks of surgery (one in general surgery, and a second that included two-week rotations in three different surgical specialties), and blocks in pediatrics, ob-gyn, and psychiatry. We had to pass Part II of the national boards at some time before graduation. There were no other tests. We also had to write our thesis. So, by the middle of our third year, we had completed the basics of traditional medical school, and could take electives and work on our theses. Research was an important part of the curriculum, since medical information was huge, but unreliable and ever-changing. We had to know how medical and scientific information was generated, how to evaluate it, and ideally, how to add to it and improve it. Finally, students took a sub-internship in the fourth year for six weeks, and this time, it would be in the specialty that you intended to pursue after graduation. Gradually more responsibility was given to the student, which provided more familiarity with the field, and a final evaluation of your talents in the general field you had chosen.

Figure 20: Yale Medical School Class of 1973, about 1971, in front of Sterling Hall of Medicine, New Haven, Connecticut, in obligatory 1970s dress, in short white coats.

The MD thesis

I started my medical school thesis in the second half of my third year, in early 1972. I wasn't sure where to start. I knew I was dealing with a colon cancer problem, but there were also some uterine cancers involved too. I went to see Howard Spiro, MD, who was Chief of the Division of gastroenterology (GI), which seemed to be a good place to start. He was also a charismatic person, had an earthy sense of humor that was appreciated by the students, and he related well with us. He listened to my story, but he had never heard of a disease like this.

The first thing I had to do was make certain that the family history was accurate. So, I drove to Reading, Pennsylvania, and started visiting the hospitals where my aunts and uncles received their medical and surgical care. I got information from the Reading Hospital and St. Joseph's Hospital, and confirmed everything I had been told. The family reports were completely accurate. In 1972, I was able to walk into almost any hospital's medical records department, introduce myself, would be presented with all the charts I requested, and could take whatever notes I wanted. This permitted me to confirm the dates of the surgeries, I was able to review the pathological reports, and look up lab data. I found a few surprises, including that one of my uncles had a large polyp removed from his colon that I didn't know about. This particular uncle was the only one who held information back, and later refused to have his blood drawn for my research. (There's always one.)

I brought my notes back to New Haven, began to organize the data, and drew up a disease pedigree of the family. It was impressive and scary. I began to search the medical literature, and with some effort (prowling through the underground stacks at the Sterling Medical Library) I located the source of the single report of a family with multiple cancers of the colon and uterus from a pathologist named Aldred Scott Warthin, MD, PhD at the University of Michigan, published in the *Archives of Internal Medicine* in 1913. He referred to this family as a "cancerous fraternity", which must have sounded more attractive to him in 1913 than to me in 1972. I later found out that Warthin was—as was typical at the time—a believer in eugenics, so I wondered what his idea of a "fraternity party" might be.

I used an archaic medical reference tool called *Index Medicus* to find articles that had been previously published. This came out monthly as a periodical (in paper, of course), and was collated annually into massive tomes that listed the published literature by category. They formed a forbidding wall of volumes that dared you to open them up and try to get what you wanted. This was how the information was managed at the time. These books eventually morphed into the current versions of computerized searchable databases that we so casually use today; but it was all paper back then. One could search *Index Medicus* citations by topic, but there was very little indexed under the hereditary colon cancer topic heading. Therefore, I had to look up multiple terms, write individual citations on index cards, plow into the stacks at the library, pull the bound journal volumes one by one, and see what the article had to say. Of course, more often than not, the article provided no insight into the problem. Also, the journals were used intensively, and then replaced by hand; frequently the issue you wanted was missing. Better luck tomorrow. What is worse, each month, a new issue of *Index Medicus* would come out, and this had to be searched. Those who have only used computerized searches have no idea how tedious and time consuming this type of literature search was. Once you found a relevant article, you could look at the references cited in that article, but you depended upon the assumption that the authors had also searched assiduously. It's a wonder that anything got done.

Henry T. Lynch, MD

Eventually, I accumulated a small series of published reports of families with a cluster of cancers that sounded similar to what my family had. Furthermore, I found that a preventive medicine expert from Creighton University named Henry T. Lynch, MD had found other such families, recognized what they represented, published them, and called these familial clusters of colon and uterine cancer "Cancer Family Syndrome". I cringed at the term "cancer family" when I first saw it. The naming of this disease was making me quite uncomfortable. Henry noted that there was also an excessive number of cancers of the stomach and a few other organs in these families, but there were fewer breast and lung cancers than expected. I was very excited to find these reports, but didn't like the name Cancer Family Syndrome, since it sounded so pervasive, and did not acknowledge the selectivity of the risk for cancer to certain organs.

I contacted Henry by mail, and received an enthusiastic response from him, accompanied by a series of very large black and white glossy prints of the pedigrees from some of the families he had studied. Also, I later discovered that his work had been totally ignored by the cancer research community, and I was one of the first people to show an interest in the problem. So, we became kindred spirits from the beginning. He offered encouragement and told me about his work that was yet to be published. We started a life-long professional collaboration. At least there were two of us to share this medical delusion. In some ways, Henry took the place of the father I had just lost.

Into the laboratory at Yale

No one had any idea of what the genetic basis of Cancer Family Syndrome might be. It was less than twenty years since the discovery of the structure of DNA (!), and we knew the genetic basis of no specific disease at that time. We knew about the biochemical basis of a small number of diseases. A course on this subject was taught by Professors Coleman and Rosenberg at Yale. I was mesmerized by their lectures, and this facilitated the learning of the biochemical pathways involved in the production of the major intracellular molecules. This was, for me, the best course in medical school. Unfortunately, the only diseases we understood were disturbances of metabolism, and we only knew the biochemistry, not the genetics.

We knew next to nothing about cancer. The state of the art was that some carcinogens—such as those in chimney soot and cigarettes—caused cancer by damaging DNA, and that a virus was known to cause cancers in chickens. There was just a handful of rare familial diseases that caused a cluster of cancers, but the only accepted examples involved rare cancers or a characteristic "syndrome", which is how they were recognized.

A strain of mice was found that was particularly susceptible to virally-induced cancers, which had become a very hot topic at the time. One mouse strain with specific histocompatibility antigens (the ones you match up for an organ transplant) was more susceptible to the cancers than others. That provided me with my first hypothesis to study. Maybe there was a complex interaction between something in the environment—like a virus—and the "HLA type" (the human equivalent of the mouse histocompatibility antigens), and those who got tumors had a different "tissue type" than those who did not get tumors. This would be something I could test in the laboratory. I mentioned this to Howard Spiro, and he referred me to Marion Zatz, PhD, who was the director of the Yale Tissue Typing Laboratory. This lab was established for clinical purposes to identify matched donors for kidney transplants. I was permitted to use her lab and equipment, and she taught me how to do microcytotoxicity assays for the human tissue antigens. I could not use her antibody reagents (which the lab had purchased to determine the tissue types), so I had to write to various research labs around the US to get my own collection of antibodies, and create a platform for these assays. These labs all sent me the antibodies I requested, and she provided me with all of the supplies and reagents I needed. I just needed to stay out of everyone's way, and helped with a few of their procedures, such as drawing blood from her collection of rabbits.

Staying out of the way was not a problem, since I did my assays late at night. I would drive to Pennsylvania, and early the next day draw blood from my aunts and uncles (and later, my mother and siblings), put the blood on ice, drive back to New Haven, and set up the assay, which took about six hours to complete. The assays had to be done on living cells, so, I had to read the cells shortly after completing the assay. Since I wasn't getting back to the lab until pretty late in the evening, the assays were finally read, under a microscope, at two or three AM. The final read-out of the assay involved looking through a microscope into a ninety-six well plate in which each well contained a few hundred lymphocytes. The cells would either be red, meaning they had been killed by virtue of harboring the antigen I was testing, or clear, meaning they were living and the cells didn't carry that antigen. Because I couldn't use the commercially available antibodies, I had to use multiple different experimental antibodies for each antigen to gain a consensus on the tissue types. Consequently, I had to read about sixty microscopic wells for each subject I was testing. If I brought back ten blood samples, I had to set up the assay (taking perhaps two hours), let the antibodies incubate with the cells for another two hours, and then read all the plates. One of the first things you learn about research is that it takes a lot of time, and in the end, your eyes want to pop out of your head. If there had been any glamor, it was hard to appreciate at three AM.

My first set of assays came out completely negative. That is, it looked like no one had any tissue antigens—an impossible result. I reviewed my technique with Dr. Zatz, and it turned out that I used slightly too much heparin when I drew the blood. The blood had to be anti-coagulated in a way that didn't kill the cells, and heparin was the only answer. However, too much heparin interfered with the assay, and the amount I used was too high. So, back on the road for more blood samples. Eventually, I was able to determine the "tissue types" on my family members, but as luck would have it, my mother had a common tissue type (shared by all of her children), and my father's family had a wide range of tissue antigens. Moreover, I didn't have enough blood samples from living people who I knew had the disease, so it would take years to interpret the data. Failed experiment, and nothing to publish.

At that time, Spiro recruited an assistant professor to the GI Division, Frank Troncale, MD, who had just finished his research and clinical training at the Memorial Sloan-Kettering Cancer Center in New York City. He had learned about measuring a tumor-related glycoprotein called carcinoembryonic antigen (CEA, the latest new thing), and knew about how to measure cellular proliferation in colonic tissues. We measured CEA levels on family members to test the hypothesis that 'at-risk' family members might have elevated levels when they were healthy. We measured, and they didn't. Finally, one of Frank's mentors was looking for elevated rates of proliferation in the rectal biopsies of people at increased risk for colorectal cancer. However, we had no affected family members available to test, and this assay required a fresh biopsy from the rectum. Frank smiled sheepishly and suggested that he could get a rectal biopsy from me. I agreed to take one for the team. So, he put me on the sigmoidoscopy table, stuck in the sigmoidoscope, and took a chunk of tissue from my rectum. Actually, other than the uniqueness of having a ten inch metal pipe up my anus, I didn't feel a thing. Frank took the tissue to the lab for some incubations, and I went across the street to the library. After about thirty minutes, I went to the bathroom, and passed a plum-sized clot of blood into the toilet. I felt fine, but thought I should tell Frank about this. I went back to the lab, he shrugged his shoulders, and we both carried on. Nothing more happened. Also, my rectal proliferation was uninterpretable. I learned a lot about failure early in my research career, and became vaccinated against discouragement. My initial impression was that, research involved long road trips to get blood, eyes popping out of your head, being sodomized in the name of science, and nothing interpretable came of it. Just so you know.

In the end, what my MD thesis accomplished was to fully characterize what was at that time the second largest family with "Cancer Family Syndrome". My search of the medical literature uncovered six families characterized by Henry Lynch, and ten other case reports from Germany, England and Finland. My thesis reported that I was unable to learn anything more about the disease from the laboratory, in spite of my best, if naïve, efforts. The thesis was entitled "A Familial Cancer Syndrome", and a hard-bound copy sits in the Blake Medical Library at Yale.

As I got near the end of my fourth year, I asked Troncale who would write up the paper for publication. He told me that unless I did, he would write it and publish it without me. Welcome to the world of dog-eating. I went home and started writing, and eventually published it myself. Better to eat dog than be eaten. Later, I wrote up a second family we had found at Yale, and I included Troncale as a co-author, even though it was eleven years later. It was in 1984 that the term "Lynch Syndrome" was coined. I finally got away from those awful-sounding monikers for the disease. The term Lynch Syndrome is now is attached to the disease when it is confirmed genetically.

Fourth year of medical school (1972-73)

The fourth year at Yale Medical School involved focusing your professional career, taking the appropriate electives, finishing your thesis, and applying for internship. One of the first things I did during year three was to apply for a Public Health Service scholarship. The Vietnam War was clearly winding down, and everyone knew that the draft was going to end—which it did, in January, 1973. The draft had "inspired" many medical graduates to join the National Institutes of Health (NIH) or parts of the Public Health Service (PHS)—including the Indian Health Service (IHS)—which were alternatives to a trip to Vietnam. With the draft ending, there was a concern that interest in the IHS would wane, and it would not be possible to recruit young physicians to the Indian reservations. So, a scholarship program was created. If you signed on for a two year stint in the IHS, the government would pay for your last year of medical school; this was the "Senior Program". I applied, and specifically asked to return to the Navajo reservation in New Mexico, for unfinished business, and I was selected into the program. Also, at this time, I didn't see myself pursuing a career in laboratory-based research, and wanted to have more intensive clinical exposure in a place where the care was desperately needed. This meant that I committed to dropping out of my post-graduate training program after one year (internship), do two years in the IHS, and then return to the training program for two more years of residency. This was fine with me, but unfortunately, this would be considered disruptive to the training program director. Since post-graduate programs had been losing their trainees for decades to the draft, I didn't think this would be a problem. Furthermore, it meant I wouldn't have to borrow for another year of schooling, and it also permitted Pat and me to do what we thought was important work for our country, and for our indigenous population, which was seriously underserved medically.

In my third year of medical school, I briefly considered that I might only take one year of training after medical school—a general internship—and then go to a small town as a general practitioner. In part, this was a response to a sense of doom. I thought it was likely that I would die young, so why bother with a lot of training that would never be put to good use? However, by the time I reached my fourth year, I was beginning to think about the longer term (that I might live to age thirty or longer), decided that I would pursue training in internal medicine (which meant an internship and two years of residency), and was beginning to think that I might even specialize in gastroenterology. The anxiety and maladaptive response to learning about the presumed family disease was settling down, and I was starting to think more like a normal twenty-four year old medical student. For now, it was internship, IHS, and perhaps specialty training. Too early to tell.

Where to do one's internship was the major topic of discussion among my fourth year classmates. I wondered where my training might take me, and what I would end up doing. It was an exhilarating time, since it was all unknown to us. I thought about training in the Northeast or the Southeast, but the "Promised Land" at that time was San Francisco. That was probably the most popular destination, and not many would make it. Pat and I began to take road trips and look at various medical schools and training programs. We were all sure that we would be desired candidates. It didn't occur to me that, without any test scores (except Part I of the national boards), the program directors wouldn't have much information on fourth year Yale students. Our self-confidence may have been somewhat greater than how we were perceived by others.

I made an appointment with the Dean of Students (still Howard Levitin), for advice. I told him about the places that interested me. He pulled out my academic file, and reported that one of the residents, named David Berry, had put a negative report in my file after my first internal medicine rotation. I had no idea, but recalled that we had an interaction that obviously was more important to him than to me. We had a patient admitted with some form of encephalitis, and no one knew what was causing it. I was assigned the patient, and put my "work-up" into the chart. I went home for dinner, and the newest copy of the *New England Journal of Medicine* had been delivered that day. There was a review article by an infectious disease expert from Harvard on *Herpes simplex* infections that discussed encephalitis caused by this virus, and also mentioned that affected patients may have had a history of "cold sores", which are caused by this virus. So, I came back, spoke with the patient's wife, found out that our patient had such a history, and wrote an additional note in the chart to that effect. The next morning, Barry sarcastically said:

"Boland, do you think you are an attending physician around here?"

I said that I had just read a review article that was fresh off the press, from an expert from Harvard. (That didn't always go over well in New Haven.) Unbeknownst to me, Barry had done his Yale MD thesis on *Herpes simplex* virus, and he considered himself as the expert on this subject. He asked who the author was—somewhat dismissively. I told him and he stormed off to find the article; the author had been his father-in-law. I didn't think much of it at the time, although two of my classmates had to stifle smirks. It seemed as though Berry had the final word on this. I will never know for sure, but there was a great gulf between the Yale medical students and some of the interns and residents just a few years older than us. We were radicalized anti-war types, wore our hair longer, looked different and had an attitude about authority. This probably annoyed some of them, and perhaps they were looking for ways to punish those who didn't follow their rules. Who knows?

None the less, the rest of the academic file was fine, and I had no idea of how this one spot would affect my application. Fortunately, there would be a cover letter from the Chairman of the Department of Internal Medicine, who would provide the most important document for my application. During my four years at Yale Medical School, we had three chairmen of medicine. When I arrived, it had been a man named P.K. Bondy, MD. We never got to know him; during our second year, he went on sabbatical in England. A popular nephrologist named Franklin Epstein, MD stepped in as interim Chairman of Internal Medicine in Bondy's absence. At that time, the medical school decided to seek a new Chairman, which Epstein wanted. However, the search committee recruited a new Chairman from the University of North Carolina, Louis G. Welt, MD. Being passed over, Epstein left Yale, and within a couple of years, was a professor at Harvard, and Chairman at one of the top hospitals in the country. When Welt arrived, he clashed with some of the old guard in his department, which was not unusual, but one of those he was trying to oust was my thesis mentor, Howard Spiro. I was in Howard's office one day, and overheard a nasty quarrel between them. Welt was going to take charge, and leave his mark on the Department and on the medical school.

Fateful meeting with the Chairman

At the beginning of our fourth year, it was announced that everyone who would be applying for an internship in internal medicine should make an appointment with the new Chairman, so that he would know us better for his letters of recommendation, which he was going to write personally. In the fall of 1972, I did so. He had a letter from Barry in front of him, but also, some other evaluations. I had only one test in the file (the national board score), and had scored very high on that. I felt comfortable that I would be in good shape for a competitive letter.

Then he asked me about my thesis.

"I identified a family with hereditary colon cancer, tried to study it in the lab, didn't get far, but I think this is a disease that we should know more about."

"What can be done about it?" he asked.

"I don't know."

"Do you think these people should be sterilized?"

I was stunned at the question, but assumed he was testing my moral convictions. None the less, the comment triggered anger within me that I dared not show. I shifted around in my chair, and leaned forward.

"I think that people in these families ought to be told about their possible risks, maybe preventive measures can be developed, and moreover, some people in these families might be productive in spite of their cancer risks." I paused. "Also, this is my family."

He said no more and dismissed me. I assume that I have passed the interview, but wondered about the subtle suggestion of eugenics. Ugh—not eugenics again.

So, I continue my internship applications, and generally applied to competitive programs. After all, I had applied to just four colleges, and two medical schools. This was presumably going to be easier than that. I ended up applying to four top programs (including UC San Francisco, everyone's dream), and listed Kentucky as a "safe" fifth application, just in case. A month or so later, I did my subinternship in internal medicine, the key rotation for my fourth year. The resident was Bill McGuire, MD, who was a notable rebel, but who got along very well with the medical students just a little younger than he was, since we shared similar political views. I enjoyed that experience more than anything I had done before, and was sure that internal medicine was for me.

One night on my subinternship rotation, I admitted a thirty-nine year old man who had a pulmonary embolus (blood clot lodged in the pulmonary artery). We administered anticoagulants for this, and found that he had blood in his stool. A sigmoidoscopy revealed that he had colon cancer. He was one of twelve siblings, and he was the sixth to get colon cancer, but no one had the other types of cancers that Henry Lynch and I had found. His family was similar to mine. Eleven years later, Frank Troncale and I wrote the paper in which the terms "Lynch Syndrome I" (only colon cancer, as occurred in this patient's family) and "Lynch Syndrome II" (all the other types of cancer, too, like mine) were used. It would be another thirty years before we understood how this happened.

Near the end of the subinternship, McGuire came to me and said "terrific job, you are getting an A+ for your rotation. Also, I am going to Welt's office today and make sure this gets into your letter before they send them out".

The next day, he reported that he had spoken to Welt, told him to be sure to include this, and that Welt responded, "I've written the letter already, it's too late to rewrite it, and your evaluation won't make any difference anyway." Bill and I took this as good news. I must have already had a great letter if an A+ in the subinternship wouldn't change things.

The disastrous "Match Day"

Sometime in early 1973 all fourth year medical students submitted our choices for internship to a computerized system that coordinates the students' choices with training programs' choices, called "The Match". I made my choices and submitted them. My next task was to finish writing my thesis, type it, and have it bound. The thesis took up a lot of my time, so I had no chance to study for Part II of the national boards. I wasn't worried. Standardized tests were my specialty. I dropped off my thesis at the Dean's office literally on my way to the national board exam, which was in February or March, 1973. To the best of my recollection, I did not study a single day for the test. I wasn't sure if one could actually study for this, since it tested broadly all areas of clinical medicine. I figured either you knew the material, or it was too late to start.

About six weeks after this, the all-important internship Match Day was looming, and our scores on Part II of the national boards were also about to come back. On the night before Match Day, I was in the library with a classmate, David Pickar. We were both applying for internships in internal medicine, and we had a discussion about where we might end up as interns. I knew that I had a potential problem because I had disclosed that I would be leaving the training program after one year to go to the IHS. David was planning to become a psychiatrist, and he would be leaving after a year as well. We knew that there were no tests or class ranks, so that Yale Medical School grads might be considered wild cards. We found out that we had both listed Kentucky at the bottom of our match lists, "just in case". We sang a line together from the song "My Old Kentucky Home", and laughed. We wished each other well, and planned to see each other the next morning to celebrate the beginning of the next stage of our lives—for the first time not as a tuition-paying student.

The next morning came early. Pat and I were living in a beach house in East Haven, a short drive from the medical school, with four other medical students. About seven AM the phone rang, and it was Howard Levitin, the Dean of Students.

"Is Boland there?" I went to the phone, and found out that I did not match with any program for internship.

"What?"

"Come to my office at eight AM so we can find a place for you." This was inconceivable to me. Then, he proceeded to ask to talk with one of my roommates, Tom. Same story. Tom then had to find Jim, a third roommate, for the same news. What was going on? Three classmates from one class—not matched? Inconceivable.

At eight AM, a total of six of us sat in the Dean of Students' office. All six had applied for internships in internal medicine, and failed to match. This was unprecedented. No applicant for any other specialty failed to match. Usually every student matched. This year six did not—all in the same specialty. The only thing we all shared was a letter from Louis Welt. Levitin seemed annoyed with us, but said nothing about the irony that we all failed to match in one specialty. So, one by one, we picked places we had never seen before from a list of programs that hadn't filled all their internship positions. I had previously heard lectures from a Yale professor named Steven Sulavik, MD, who had recently moved to St. Francis Hospital in Hartford as Chairman of Internal Medicine, and I knew that he was an excellent physician and teacher. Levitin gave a private call from his office (as the humiliated six waited outside), and he told me that, although they had filled all their positions, Sulavik would add one for me. I had to go to Hartford and meet with him. This was the most humbling moment of my professional career. I couldn't go to the student center where my classmates were all celebrating their good fortunes, and as I ran into them over the final two months of school, I had to painfully admit my failure to them. When I ran into David Pickar, he hung his head and told me he had matched at Kentucky. No longer a joke. As luck would have it, he later met his wife there, and he has told me he enjoyed the year. The winner of the San Francisco sweepstakes was our classmate Lee Goldman, who matched at the University of California, San Francisco (UCSF). He was to have an extraordinary academic career, came back some years later as the Chairman of Internal Medicine at UCSF, and eventually become the Dean of the medical school at Columbia University.

I was despondent and discouraged about where my career might go. If one had any academic ambitions (and at that time, I did not), it was necessary to do house staff training at a prestigious university hospital. I had never experienced this type of failure. I ran into Bill McGuire on the wards, and he asked where I would be going? I told him I didn't match, and would be going to a community hospital in Hartford. He was flabbergasted. What about Tom (the roommate, whom he also knew)? Same story; there were six of us. "What?" he exploded. "I am going to see Welt about this". So, he marched down to the Chairman's office and asked how our class could have done so poorly in our applications for internships in internal medicine. Bill asked to see my letter. Welt showed it to him. When I saw Bill next, he told me that I could not have gotten into any program with the letter Welt wrote, and that Welt wanted to meet with me again. (What for? Humiliate me further, or suggest my sterilization?) Bill suggested that Welt had some misgivings.

So, I made an appointment, and sat in the same chair where we had the discussion about hereditary disease some months earlier.

"Well, Mr. Boland, perhaps you were a late bloomer, or perhaps we made a mistake. When you finish up your tour in the Indian Health

Service, give me a call and I will have something for you." I have no idea what he had in mind, and had nothing in writing. Unfortunately for everyone involved, Welt died at his desk at Yale on a Sunday night, about eight months later.

I spoke with Howard Spiro, who expressed surprise at the no-match story, and when I told him that I was interested in a fellowship in GI, he too told me to give him a call when I was ready for that and he would have a fellowship for me. I finished up my final clinical electives, and Pat and I decided to go on vacation rather than show up at graduation. I couldn't go through with it. They mailed me my diploma.

The internship year (1973-74)

I went to St. Francis Hospital humbled, but with a positive attitude. I had so much to learn, and thought there might be some benefit to a less competitive atmosphere. A few of the attending physicians had come from Yale, and they made a particular effort to make me feel comfortable and to teach me. I was the only one of the interns who would regularly read about a dozen medical journals, and cut out the pertinent articles for my files. I was put in the intensive care units for the first three months of my internship, and by the end of that period, I was quite comfortable with people who were very sick, and learned how to manage all sorts of disasters. This was fortunate, because Yale students were encouraged to be scholars, but did not have as much hands-on experience. The old saying was that we made lousy interns, but excellent residents. So, I got what I needed. We were on-call every third night for the entire year. This meant that we came in on Monday morning, worked a thirty-six hour shift and went home by seven or eight PM on Tuesday (if everyone was stable), come back for a regular twelve hour day on Wednesday, and then start the cycle again on Thursday. The cycles went through the weekend the same way, so, you had either one Saturday or a Sunday off every other week. I estimated that we worked about 120 hours a week, and our weekly take home paycheck was for $117. The Middle East oil embargo occurred during the 1973-74 academic year, which limited travel, but that was not a problem for us. We were given an apartment across the street from the hospital, so, I barely drove at all. Pat worked nearby at another neighborhood Health Center. When we had a Saturday afternoon or Sunday off, we would plan a short outing in Connecticut, but it had to be done on less than a tank of gas. I scarcely recall any political events of the year. It was simply a time to learn how to keep people alive until the appropriate specialists arrived, and St. Francis did an excellent job of that. By the time I headed out to New Mexico, I was capable of fending off medical disasters. It was, ironically, a very good year for me.

During my internship, I was given one month for an elective, and mine came at the end of the year, in June, 1974. A liver specialist that I had known well at Yale named Bob Scheig, MD had moved to the University of Connecticut in nearby Farmington, and took over as head of the GI Division. I did an elective month with him, and for a brief while, thought about becoming a hepatologist. At the end of the month, Bob told me to call him when I finished the Indian Health Service and my internal medicine training, and he would have a GI fellowship position for me at the University of Connecticut. There I was collecting offers for GI fellowships, and still had two years to go on my internal medicine training.

Back to the Indian Health Service (1974-76)

In July, 1974, Pat and I drove from Hartford to Gallup, New Mexico, where I started my two year stint as a General Medical Officer (GMO) at the Gallup Indian Medical Center. The hours were demanding and we were paid just under $14,000/year. There were fifty doctors for a 200 bed hospital, and we were the primary care physicians for about 50,000 Navajos. Of the fifty physicians, about thirty were fully trained specialists, and twenty were GMOs—the foot soldiers who took the primary call at night. There were four medical services where the GMOs ran the patient care first hand—Internal Medicine, Surgery, Ob-Gyn and Pediatrics. There were some other specialists who worked alone. Some GMOs asked to spend their entire time on just one service, but four of us requested a broader experience, and were assigned three months on each of the four services. Pat and I arrived after a three day cross-country trip, and with the help of the Gallup staff, got an apartment in town, near the hospital. The evening we arrived, one of the staff Ob-Gyn's, James Smith, MD, came by to greet us.

"See you in the morning", he said.

"Where?" I asked.

"Ob-Gyn, of course," was his answer.

I didn't know that I was to start on that service, and had a brief moment of panic. Although I wanted a broad experience, I had a minimum of obstetrics experience. So, I found my obstetrical text book, and showed up in the morning on the Labor and Delivery ward. We introduced ourselves, and I found there were three GMOs assigned to Ob-Gyn. I was the only one who had never delivered a baby on my own. "No problem; we will show you how." My learning curves were quite steep on each of the rotations, and as I went through the Ob-Gyn, Pediatrics and Surgery, I listened and learned. The challenge was to do as much as you could by yourself, and then know when to ask for help. Within a day or so, I was up to speed on the deliveries, since we had backup from the permanent Ob staff, and could call them in if anything started to look complicated. I ended up doing 125 deliveries, including twenty-five cesarean sections, and had no complications. The only place where I did not feel a comforting degree of competence was in Pediatrics. It was harder for me to know when a child was sick than it was with an adult, and that responsibility was hard for me to handle. After two months on Pediatrics, I asked to be put on the internal medicine rotation, which got me back in my comfort zone. Ultimately, IHS was an enjoyable challenge, and it gave me a unique experience and perspective that served me well as I progressed through my career pathway, becoming more and more narrowly specialized each year.

For some reason, there was quite a medical toll on the GMOs that first year in Gallup. In October, 1974, I developed viral meningitis, and had to spend my first night in the hospital as a patient. A patient across the hall went through alcohol withdrawal and howled loudly all night. The next day, I asked to go home to get some rest. It was valuable to know what it felt like to be in the hospital bed rather than peering over the bed railing from the outside. A second GMO developed a case of bubonic plague the same weekend that I got meningitis, but it was quickly recognized, and he didn't require admission to the hospital. A third of the GMOs drowned in a nearby lake, forcing a change in the service coverage.

The second year in Gallup was spent on Internal Medicine. We were again on call every third night, but if things were quiet, we could go home. The time in the hospital was not as intensive as it had been during internship, but the patients were sicker, in general. In addition, we all had to take periodic call in the Emergency Room and serve as the "house physician". For the GMOs, that involved spending most of a weekend in the hospital. This occurred once every couple of months. The IHS got a lot out of us, but the patients were grateful, and they got genuine attention and care from most of us. The exposure to challenging cases was enormous, and I saw cases of infectious diseases that I would never see again in any university hospital. That period helped me recognize the value of dedicated general physicians.

Pat and I also had a chance to observe the Navajo culture closely. We attended several cultural-religious ceremonies, including a Zuni Shalako ceremony, and a Hopi snake dance, which is a spectacular initiation ceremony for adolescent boys on the Second Mesa of the Hopi Reservation. During the ceremony, they handled live rattlesnakes with the help of an adult male, in front of their friends and families. Anglos—as we were known—usually weren't permitted to observe this, but for that one year, we were allowed, and it was very impressive.

Starting a family (1975)

During my internship in Hartford, Pat and I made a major decision, which was to start a family. We thought that the period in the IHS would be the right time to have a child. Interestingly, we had no hesitations about having a family in spite of the "family illness" hanging over our heads. We made the simple decision that our lives were worth living regardless of the health outcome, and that our children would see it the same way. It was probably a naïve and overly optimistic decision in light of how little we knew about the disease, but we were young, and just went ahead with it. I have never questioned the decision. What if my father had made a decision not to have a family?

We had no idea how long it might take for Pat to get pregnant, but we got our answer immediately. Pat was already pregnant when we arrived in New Mexico. In spite of that, the need for help in pediatrics was high, and she was put to work as a Pediatric Nurse Practitioner in the Pediatric Clinic. When I was on the Pediatrics service, Pat and I worked side-by-side in the clinic; she was much better than I was with outpatient care. I knew about disease, but she knew about health, well child care, and child-rearing. Pat read extensively about normal child development and family-raising strategies. It served us very well over the years.

Pat went into labor with our first child on Saturday night January 25, 1975. I was in the hospital as the house physician, and had been up all of Friday night dealing with an influenza epidemic. I got to go home and sleep at eight AM on Saturday after an all-nighter, but had to return at six PM to resume my role again. When I arrived at the hospital that evening, the parking lot was as full as if it were Monday morning, the waiting room was packed, and there was a stack of forty charts waiting to be seen. Multiple episodes of trauma came into the Emergency Room, we had twenty-five hospital admissions throughout the twenty-four hour period, and I had to take a woman into a rewarming tank in the hospital basement after she had been pulled out of a freezing river. That day, 256 charts were pulled for outpatient evaluations (the most ever for one day at the time), and there was just the weekend staff available. In the midst of this, at ten PM, Pat called and told me she was in labor. I dashed home (one mile) and brought her back while someone covered the hospital. I took her to my on-call room. Word got to the nursing supervisor ("Dr. Boland, we understand you have a woman in labor in your on-call room"), so she was sent to Labor and Delivery. I would visit her a few minutes as she labored, and then be called back to the Emergency Room or clinic. As Saturday night wore on, there were more and more trauma patients, and I was running up and down the steps between the clinic and Labor and Delivery. A car wreck came in with multiple injured patients. Pat's labor progressed slowly. Finally, at five AM, one of the surgical GMOs, Rick Fein, MD, offered to pick up the last few hours of my shift, and I got to join Pat.

At noon on January 26, our first daughter, Tara, was born. I had only a few hours to spend with Pat, call family, and suddenly it was six PM again, and I had my third consecutive all night shift. When I returned to the clinic, there was another stack of forty charts waiting, and all of them were pretty sick. No one was going to wait four hours for a minor symptom. I called in the on-call pediatrician (Jurgen Upplegger, MD) who lived in an apartment on the hospital grounds, and was very efficient. I was rarely so happy to have a colleague join me in the trenches. We took care of almost everyone by about ten PM, and I had a little more time with

Pat. Interestingly, my father was an intern when his first child was born; history repeated itself.

Pat had been adamant about having a "natural" delivery using the Lamaze method, which utilized breathing exercises instead of analgesic medications during the contractions. In fact, she took no form of anesthesia for any of her three deliveries. We had no family nearby—like most of the staff in the HIS—and everyone learned how to cope and provide mutual support.

Our children became the center of our lives. We didn't plan on having another child right away, and Pat had an intra-uterine device placed, while she nursed Tara. A few months later on a Friday night, she told me "I feel that way again". I didn't believe it, but the next morning I had to cover the internal medicine service, which required me to run the simple lab tests on the inpatients. So I did the pregnancy test—five times. When this pregnancy test was positive, there is no "result" on the slide. So, I figured I had done something wrong, and kept repeating it. She was pregnant again, and was ultimately pregnant for fifteen of our twenty-four months in New Mexico. Maureen was born just a month after we left Gallup, in August, 1976.

From Indian Health back to internal medicine residency: another lucky break

My two years in Gallup were challenging and fulfilling, as we were young and energetic, but I realized that I couldn't continue as a generalist. Actually, it was too hard. Because of my prior training, I wanted to know more about the complexities of disease, and didn't like having to send the most challenging and sickest patients somewhere else. So, when I was in my second year in the IHS, I knew it was time to find a residency in internal medicine and complete my clinical training. There was a problem that I had not anticipated, although I should have. Large numbers of physicians had been drafted out of their training, or had volunteered to do so as I did, and were returning to the training programs they left; there wasn't room for everyone. About half of the GMOs in Gallup were interested in internal medicine training. We all called around, and there were very few training positions available. I called my Yale classmate Lee Goldman, who was now a third year resident at UCSF, he did some looking around, but called back and said nothing was available in their system.

We had a family wedding in New Jersey—brother Jim—and while we were in the East, I took a side trip to Hartford and asked about the availability of returning to St. Francis Hospital. Steve Sulavik was still the Chairman, was very generous, but he had no open positions. Nonetheless, he said he would try to make one available for me. I told him that I was grateful, but needed a little more time before I could accept, as I was looking into the West Coast. When we returned to New Mexico a week later, a letter was waiting for me from Sulavik. He told me that he was unable to procure the extra position, but that one was available at the University of Connecticut, which was very close by, in Farmington. I didn't understand this immediately, but shortly thereafter, found that he was about to resign as Department Chairman at St. Francis, and took a position as Chief of the Pulmonary Division at the University of Connecticut. I think he couldn't tell me about that when I spoke with him, but was looking out for me.

We were preparing to make a decision about returning to Connecticut when a bit of luck came our way. I do not underestimate the value of talent as a determinant of our life's trajectory, but luck has intervened many times to help me out. As Bob Dylan crooned in one of his songs, "I can't help it if I'm lucky." There was a Public Health Service (PHS) Hospital in San Francisco, sitting in a prime location on the Presidio. This was part of the Federal Bureau of Hospitals that was established in 1798 to take care of merchant marines. Merchant marines are sailors working on commercial ships. They are essential for ordinary commerce, but are also very important in times of war. Because of their international travel, they can (and do) bring infectious diseases back into the US when they return to port. As world travelers, they typically did not have a personal physician, certainly not in the eighteenth, nineteenth and early twentieth centuries. So, a national system of medical care was set up for them to protect the public health. There were hospitals in critical port cities such as San Francisco, Boston, New York, New Orleans, and Chicago, and there was a leprosy hospital in Carville, Louisiana. These hospitals and the IHS were all part of the "Uniformed Health Service", under the umbrella of the PHS and the Department of Health and Human Services.

The San Francisco PHS Hospital was a choice assignment, highly sought after, and had an affiliation with UCSF, the medical school in town. The San Francisco PHS Hospital had an internal medicine training program that took four interns each year, and these four would become the second and third year residents thereafter. For some reason, there had been a long-standing rule that the staff at the PHS hospitals must wear uniforms, but by tradition, no one did, and the rule was never enforced. An edict came from Washington mandating that all of the commissioned officers in the Uniformed Health Service must wear uniforms. For some other reason (the spirit of the times explains this), the four internal medicine interns drew a line in the sand and refused to wear them. This was a bad decision, as there was a long line of GMOs in the PHS who were looking for residency positions. All four interns were fired.

In Gallup, I heard that four positions had become available at the San Francisco PHS, and immediately called them. They were interested, and I got on the next flight to San Francisco. I met with the Chairman of Medicine, Donald Mason, MD, who was a locally well-known clinician and educator, and he offered me a residency position on the spot. He asked if I cared about wearing a uniform, and I immediately responded "no sir", followed by, "incidentally, what is the uniform?" It turned out to be a khaki open-collared shirt and khaki pants. Nothing fancy, pretty comfortable, no tie, no coat. Actually, this saved me the trouble of deciding what to wear in the morning. So, lady luck smiled again, as she had during my fateful drive from South Bend to Indianapolis in 1968, and now we were headed to the Promised Land, San Francisco. It would get even better.

San Francisco PHS Hospital (1976)

When I first arrived in New Mexico and was sent to work on the four services, I was initially unprepared clinically because of the way we were educated at Yale. There had been no emphasis on hands-on clinical activity, and my internship had been in internal medicine. Yale was training scholars, and we were expected to be clever enough to figure out the rest. Eventually we did, but these things take time. Contrariwise, when I got to the San Francisco PHS Hospital as a second year resident in internal medicine, I had more clinical training and experience than any of the third year residents in medicine, and I had gotten out of the habit of asking for help. In the IHS, we were expected to take care of business. We learned quickly, and the culture demanded that you not bother the specialists unless it was necessary. I heard occasional mutterings that "so and so cannot take care of a simple problem." The expectations were different in an academic training program, so that took some adjustment. I had an unexpected sense of comfort with clinical medicine that I hadn't previously experienced. It was good to be moving up the food chain, since at this point, I had two extra years of clinical experience compared to my peers.

Just six weeks after arriving in San Francisco, Pat gave birth to Maureen, so, I was suddenly a resident in internal medicine with a family of four. The residency was a good one, had fewer emergencies than I was accustomed to at St. Francis, and fewer infections and trauma cases than in Gallup. The best part was that eight of my twenty-four months were electives, and I took as many as I could at UCSF.

Many of the staff at the San Francisco PHS Hospital had academic interests, research projects, and academic appointments at UCSF. The clinical activity at the hospital was essentially run by the residents under the supervision of the specialists. All of the upper level residents were given an office where we could review charts, examine the patients (who often slept on open wards with twenty or more other people), or meet with the students and interns. By coincidence, my office was next door to the Chief of GI, Mark Rosenberg, MD who had just finished his GI fellowship at UCSF. In fact, there was a connecting door between our offices. He was just a few years older than I, we became good friends, and by this time, I was certain I wanted to do a GI fellowship.

It was during my first year of residency in San Francisco that I wrote the article describing the medical history of my family. It was my first publication, entitled "Cancer Family Syndrome", and it was done essentially without mentorship. I ended up getting hundreds of written requests for reprints of the article. I kept making more copies of the article, and mailed them out myself. It felt good to know that someone might be reading the article.

Shortly after my arrival in San Francisco, it was already time to apply for GI fellowship, even though they wouldn't start for almost two years. Mark Rosenberg encouraged me to apply to UCSF (which was one of the most competitive GI fellowships in the country), and said I would be as good as any they had. He wrote a letter of support for me. I interviewed (along with lots of others) for the six positions they had each year. I also called Bob Scheig, who was still the Chief of GI in Connecticut. He had two fellowship slots each year. He offered me one over the phone, and talked about grooming me to do a year of research training and eventually join his faculty. I told him that sounded excellent, but I wanted to check other options as well. He said he would call me when he had to make his final selection. Unfortunately, there was no uniformity of deadlines for fellowship selection; everyone had their own schedule.

I called Howard Spiro at Yale to ask about that offer three years earlier, and he informed me that he was stepping down as the GI Division Chief, and that the new Chief was to be Jim Boyer, MD. I knew Jim from my first year of medical school when he mentored my first clinical training experience with three other first year students. Unfortunately, he was in the process of moving to Yale from Chicago, and no one knew where he was or who was managing the fellow selection. There was no email, no cell phones, and often times, letters were written, and it was never clear whether anyone read them or if they were lost in a stack somewhere. The fellowship program at Yale seemed temporarily chaotic, and I never finished applying there.

In January 1977, almost a year and a half before I would finish Internal Medicine and move into GI, and Bob Scheig called and said that he would give me forty-eight hours to either take the fellowship at the University of Connecticut, or he would offer it to someone else. I called UCSF, and spoke to the Division Chief, Rudi Schmid, MD, PhD. I told him of my situation, but he said that they weren't going to make their selections for several months. He told me that they had trimmed their list to nineteen candidates, I was on the list, but that they were only going to take five fellows for July 1978 because of a financial shortfall. He suggested that I should take what Scheig had offered. I thanked him and told him I would do that. I called Bob Scheig back and accepted his offer. He told me that he was planning on having me work with a new faculty member who would be coming and was working in copper metabolism. That didn't thrill me much, but I wasn't really sure of what I would do in the long run, and that sounded as good as any place to start a research career. Bob called a month or two later, and said that the copper guy wasn't coming, but that we would find another research project for me. I was getting a little worried about that situation.

Meanwhile, Mark Rosenberg and I had some discussions about familial colon cancer, and we were trying to figure out how to take care of me and my family members. One day he mentioned that UCSF had one of the nation's top colon cancer researchers at the San Francisco VA Hospital—Young S Kim, MD. I knew nothing about this. I recalled the challenges of research when I was a medical student, and thought about the possibility of doing research in colon cancer. The problem was that I was a clinician, had modest formal training in laboratory-based research, and had no idea what the state-of-the-art might be at this time. It was mid-1977, and I was about to make a fateful decision about where my life and career would be headed.

Chapter 9

From Running to Fighting (1977-1979)

"*The Hour I First Believed*", *Amazing Grace,* John Newton.

During the earliest years of my training, I would occasionally wonder—what would I do, where would I go along the way, and what path would I take? As I moved along, the issues became more concrete, and choices had to be made. Pat had been an important steadying influence on me. I had two daughters, and had to make responsible decisions. I was getting over the "I won't live to be thirty" fantasy, which was of no benefit to me. I began to recognize it as a maladaptive, adolescent attitude. Time to get over it.

The evening of October 18, 1977 was the night before my thirtieth birthday. Just before midnight, I was sitting in a chair in our living room in San Francisco, reading the latest copy of the *New England Journal of Medicine*—my idea of late night entertainment. I glanced at my watch, and watched the second hand sweep past midnight. I had made it to thirty after all! As I reflected about what this meant, I realized that it was time to make some longer-term decisions about life. I was now one of those people over thirty. I had a moment of exceptional clarity—perhaps similar to the "vision" my father had when he was ill. I wasn't ill at all, but I had been behaving as if some illness was going to reach out and strike me at any moment. I was running from something I couldn't see, and didn't understand. I realized that this was foolish and doing me no good. I knew I had been given some native talents, and should make an effort to maximize those and do something important with my life. My heart must have been very excited about this, because just as I had this thought, I had a brief cardiac arrhythmia—something called paroxysmal atrial tachycardia. It gives you a disturbing sense of palpitation in the chest and slight shortness of breath. Although I had cared for patients with this, I had never experienced this myself. (Rarely since, either.) It stopped spontaneously after about ten seconds. That was the second part of the "vision". Don't be too smug or sure about anything in life. Take it when you can. Life can be robust or fragile. You don't really know what might be coming. This convinced me that it might not be wise to wait too long before making some specific decisions about my life.

As I look back, I wonder why it took so long to wake up to this realization. The fact that I had reached age thirty in the context of my family history was a symbolic event for me. That was the moment I realized that some of my thinking and decision-making were based on the false premise of a shortened life expectancy; it was a rational, if maladaptive, response to fear. The most critical insight I gained that night was that I was waiting for someone else to come along and solve the familial colon cancer problem—for me. Why would anyone else do that? It was *my* problem. I even felt angry at times, but had no idea who I was angry with. I realized at that very moment that I had to stop running away from some abstract existential threat, turn, and fight. I had no idea how I might do that, but the critical point was to resolve that I would enter the fray. How I would go about it would become a tactical detail. That was it. I would become a medical researcher, learn everything I could about the conduct of scientific research, and hope the opportunity would come along that would permit me to direct my energy against the vexing problem of familial colon cancer. On that night, I overcame a rational fear about dying young, and made a different rational decision to change my attitude.

Lucky a third time

Good luck was about to enter my professional life a third time, and this was perhaps the luckiest turn of all. It would be convenient to say that I had some skill that led to this next opportunity—but it was mostly luck. I was becoming concerned that the GI fellowship at the University of Connecticut wouldn't get me where I wanted. Pat and I had grown very fond of San Francisco, but our plan was to go back across the country to Connecticut.

On Friday night, December 30, 1977—New Year's Eve—I got a phone call from Mark Rosenberg. UCSF had taken only five GI fellows earlier in the year for the July 1978 program, but they optimally needed six to cover the work load. There were three hospitals in the system, and they needed two at each one. Earlier that day, the Chairman of Medicine at UCSF, a canny academic giant named Holly Smith, MD, had given Rudi Schmid and the GI Division a sixth GI fellowship position, and they called Mark to ask if I was still available. I told Mark that I was having some misgivings about the University of Connecticut program, and would consider it. He went on to say that although GI fellowships were two years in length, UCSF might only have funds for one year. Not perfect. But, if I was interested, I should contact Schmid and discuss this. Also, someone was flying in from New Mexico right after the New Year to apply for the slot. The problem was that most of the competitive applicants for the 1978 year had already been recruited into a program. There was no formal mechanism to get word out, no one knew what talent might be available. I discussed the issue with Pat, and she was happy to stay in San Francisco.

The fact that the UCSF position became available was just part of the luck involved here. Monday January 2, 1978 was a national holiday, and everyone started the year on Tuesday January 3. I had previously selected (probably eight months earlier) to do an endocrinology elective at UCSF in January, 1978. By chance, the Division of Endocrinology office was immediately next door to the GI Division office on the UCSF campus. I lived near the UCSF campus, and showed up at the door of the Endocrinology Division at eight AM sharp.

However, none of the endocrinology faculty or fellows had arrived yet. So, I walked around the corner, saw that the door to the GI Division was open, and two secretaries were at their desks. I entered, introduced myself, and asked if Dr. Schmid was in. "Not yet," they told me, and I was instructed to come back later. I turned to walk out when Rudi's associate director, Bob Ockner, MD arrived. I told him about my phone call with Mark Rosenberg, so he asked me to sit down with him for an interview. He remembered me from my initial interview over a year ago, but I told him that my research interests were more focused on colon cancer now. He seemed interested in this, but said that no decision could be made without Dr. Schmid's input; so perhaps I could come back later. I agreed, but as I turned to leave, Dr. Schmid arrived. We sat down in his tiny office and had a ten minute discussion (we hadn't met previously), after which, he asked me to wait for a moment. He and Ockner had a brief discussion outside his office. He returned with a big smile, shook my hand and congratulated me and announced that I was about to become a fellow at UCSF.

I was flummoxed, and told him that I had to deal with Bob Scheig and the University of Connecticut fellowship. Rudi waved his hand in the air. "Don't worry about it. It's your career. He will understand and fill that slot immediately." I accepted the offer on the spot, and left their offices. It was just 8:30 AM on January 3, and my life had just taken an abrupt change in direction once more. This future was wide open, and it no longer mattered what anyone thought about not matching for my internship, or why I chose to go to the Indian Health Service.

Now I had a difficult phone call to make, as I respected Bob Scheig, and we had a warm relationship that went back to my first year at Yale. He was not very happy, and said he wanted my decision in writing. I did so, but even before he received my letter, I got a letter from him indicating that the Chief Medical Resident at the University of Connecticut had made a late decision to seek training in GI, and the position I gave up had been immediately filled. I was relieved at that outcome, but was ecstatic about the possibilities that were now ahead for me.

As I returned to the endocrinology offices, I ran into one of the GI Fellows who had been a student one year ahead of me at Yale, and he was accompanied by one of the GI faculty. I told him that I was just offered a GI fellowship for next year. The faculty member muttered:

"That is impossible. I am on the Fellowship Selection Committee and we haven't made that decision yet".

I stayed away from that discussion, recognizing the political delicateness of my situation. The strangest part of all was that the next day, a person I had known briefly from my days in Gallup and the IHS had flown from Albuquerque to San Francisco to seek the fellowship slot that had just been offered to me. I only discovered who it was many years later, when I mentioned my "accidental" fellowship to a couple of friends (which included this fellow, Bob Lane). He had become a gastroenterologist in spite of this disappointment, but he glared at me and told me about his unfortunate trip to San Francisco. Actually, neither of us knew about the other in this episode. We sometimes muddle about in a small and unpredictable world.

Young S. Kim, MD

Everything changed. I made an appointment to meet with Young Kim, whose laboratory was at the San Francisco VA Hospital. Dr. Kim had immigrated to the US from Seoul, Korea as a college student at Stanford. He came from an extremely accomplished and wealthy family in Korea. He had a brother who was a Professor, a brother who was a touring solo violinist, and a brother who was a highly successful lawyer in Seoul. He grew up in a home that was contiguous with the Royal Palace in Seoul, and there had been some connection of the family to royalty in the past. Young's wife also came from a prominent Korean family, and was herself an attorney. Her father had been a notable Korean novelist. Young went from Stanford to Cornell Medical College in New York, became a Gastroenterologist, and ultimately a Professor at UCSF. He had been recruited to the San Francisco VA by Marvin Sleisenger, MD, who had been brought to the San Francisco VA from Cornell Medical College by Holly Smith, the Department Chairman at UCSF.

Marv had turned the San Francisco VA into an academic powerhouse. There was a slight bit of academic rivalry between Marvin Sleisenger at the VA and Rudi Schmid at the University Hospital, even though the VA was part of UCSF. Rudy once said to me that Marvin actually wanted his job as Division Chief at UCSF. Marvin scoffed at that, had already been a Division Chief at Cornell, and moreover, he had turned Rudi's job down a year before he was took the job as Medicine Service Chief at the VA. Marv was Associate Chairman of Medicine at UCSF—second in command to Holly Smith. These political shenanigans were the normal state of affairs at UCSF, and it never really slowed anyone down. Just a side show. In any event, Young Kim became a nationally and internationally known biochemist for his work on glycoproteins in the stomach and intestine. He had a big lab, and plenty of grant funds. In the late 1970s, the National Cancer Institute (NCI) began to set up individual cancer research programs that were focused on the most common types of cancer: colorectal, lung, breast, prostate, etc. Young saw an opportunity, and began to direct his research from the study of the glycoproteins in the normal gut to the biochemical abnormalities in colorectal cancer. By 1978, he had one of the largest grants in the nation from the National Large Bowel Cancer Project. I realized this was where I had to be.

I read as much as I could about colorectal cancer over the next several weeks, and met with Dr. Kim in the February or March of 1978. He was a humble, unassuming man, and had an office in the basement of the inauspicious Building-12, the oldest laboratory building at the VA. His office was essentially doubly land-locked. It was below ground, and you had to go into one office and through a door into his tiny office without windows. First lesson confirmed: research is not glamorous. He was very kind, and listened to me as I asked him if I could join his lab and learn everything I could. I did not mention the familial colorectal cancer issue. That topic was to be sealed and buried for many years. I had become a true Boland. I was afraid that my interest in science in general and cancer of the colon in particular would be discounted if it appeared that I was doing this for personal reasons.

Young asked me what ideas I had. I told him that, from my reading, I thought that cancers take many years to develop, and that it might be possible to find some abnormality in the normal-appearing colon that would tell us that a cancer would eventually appear in that location. He smiled gently, and said that some other people had the same idea. He offered me a spot in his laboratory starting after my clinical year of GI fellowship. He gave me a tour of the laboratory, showed me what cultured tumor cells looked like, mentioned that this was the optimal way to study cancer at that time, and showed me the basic pieces of equipment they used. I was now able to make long-term decisions, and was feeling very positive about what was to come. Moreover, it was exciting to enter the lab, see the equipment, and think of what I might be able to do with it.

I still had three months of medicine residency in the PHS before going to UCSF. I arranged to do two GI electives over my final three months. From April until mid-May, I did a GI elective at UCSF, gave a case presentation at GI grand rounds, and gained familiarity with the other fellows and faculty. From mid-May until the end of June, I did a GI elective at the PHS Hospital with Mark Rosenberg. He taught me how to do endoscopy—even before I started my fellowship—and it came easily to me. I had previously told Mark about my family history. On the last day of my residency, Mark performed a colonoscopy on me—the first of many I was to have over the years. It was negative. He didn't use too much sedation. So after he finished, I put my uniform back on and assisted Mark with several more procedures on other people. (That was a unique situation, and never happened again.)

GI fellowship at UCSF (1978-79)

In July 1978, I started my fellowship at UCSF. The first year involved purely clinical training at the three hospitals: the University Hospital (called "Moffitt"), the San Francisco VA Hospital, and San Francisco General Hospital (called "the General"). My first two months were at the General, and there was a new Division Chief, John Cello, MD, who was just out of his fellowship at UCSF. I was paired with a fellow named John Haughom, MD, who had just finished as Chief Medical Resident at UCSF, a prestigious position. He was well known to everyone. I was the new guy from the PHS Hospital. John Cello was a highly dedicated clinician, but as a new Division Chief, he was very determined that there would be no mistakes at his hospital. He set a high bar for quality, and he was always looking over our shoulders. Moreover, he was not above stepping into the clinical arena (unlike his laboratory-based peers), nor was he too fastidious not to help us perform endoscopy in a sea of blood. I sensed that John was worried initially that I—the new guy from across town—might make mistakes that would reflect badly on him. However, once he saw that I could handle the consults and endoscopes, we became good friends, and near the end of my third year, he asked if I would come to the General with him when I joined the faculty. So, I passed my initial test at UCSF, and that was that. Cello was always the favorite GI faculty member to the fellows.

My clinical year of GI training went well. I arrived with additional clinical experience due to the Indian Health Service. I had a head start in doing endoscopy because of Mark Rosenberg. The discipline came easily to me. Also, I carried a small notebook in my pocket with hundreds of references from the literature—which I continuously updated—and would annotate my consultation notes with references, like a research paper. The year passed quickly. It was fun, and I knew I was in the right place.

My first research grant application

In November, 1978, the faculty had to decide what to do with the six first year GI fellows. There was a crunch looming for the second year (which hadn't been specifically promised to me anyway), as too many of us wanted to become laboratory-based researchers in our second year. In an orderly predictable world, three of the six first year fellows would stay on as second year clinical fellows, one for each hospital (to teach the new first years), and the other three would go into labs. This was accomplished through the Division's "training grant" from the National Institutes of Health (NIH), which had six positions. This permitted three individuals to be trained for two years each after their clinical year. Unfortunately, not only did four of the six first year fellows want to pursue research training, Rudi had previously promised two slots to the current group of second year fellows. They had struck the following bargain: if you serve a second clinical year, we will put you on the training grant for your third and fourth years of fellowship. This was a big problem, since we now had six people seeking three training slots.

They discovered that one of the second year fellows was Canadian, and would not be permitted on the NIH-funded training grant. So, they helped him find a training slot elsewhere. They then picked two of the remaining five, myself and Peter Ells, MD, and asked us to write our own grant applications for our salaries. If you get it, you can stay; if you don't get it, you are gone. The funding rates for these applications were about 25%, so the prospects would be dicey. I was asked to write my own because I was the last one on board, and I had a more definite idea of what I wanted to do. Mainly, I was expendable. My biggest problem was that I had never even seen a grant application before, let alone written one. Also, I had just under two months to do this—at the same time that I was tending to the clinical service. Fortunately, I was at the VA for November and December, and had access to Young Kim for guidance and his secretary for typing. I took a look at one of his grant applications—sixty pages long, single spaced. Furthermore, these grant applications were all written by hand

and transcribed by the secretary. Word processors were still a few years away. I wasn't sure I could get this done, but there was no time to dither.

So, Young and I found some articles about the familial form of colon cancer called familial adenomatous polyposis (FAP), in which a researcher at Memorial Sloan Kettering (named Levi Kopelovich, PhD) had found some abnormal behaviors in the skin fibroblasts of FAP patients. So, we decided that I could get some of these fibroblasts and perform glycoprotein biochemistry experiments on them. The rationale was reasonable. I wrote the background sections explaining why this might work, and we then cut, scotch-taped, and photocopied a variety of experimental approaches, and ended up with the requisite fifteen page fellowship application. It was a bit stressful, and I had no clue whether what I was writing would be compelling to the reviewers. The last thing I wrote was a required "personal statement" about what I wanted to do, and what my commitment might be to a career in research. This was placed at the beginning of the application, and was considered to be as important as the scientific portion. I tried to make it personal, but would never mention that I was seeking an answer to my own family's problem. I assumed that might be a show-stopper.

Rudi had an antagonistic attitude towards Young Kim, Marvin Sleisenger, and the VA in general. He insisted on seeing my grant application before it was sent out. I nervously took it to him, about a week before it had to be submitted. He read it that night and called me into his office the next day. He said it was terrible. He was totally focused on the personal statement for some reason, and said that I wrote "like a high school student", and it might be an embarrassment to UCSF to send this out. ("This is not Oklahoma, you know", he said.) This was particularly insulting, as Rudi was Swiss, and spoke English with a thick and sometimes incomprehensible accent. But, he was the boss, and an experienced grant-writer.

I picked up the copy of the grant application (which was bleeding with his red ink), and went to my assigned clinic that afternoon. The attending physician that day was a supportive person, in private practice, but he had briefly trained in Rudi's lab.

"What's the matter, Rick, you don't seem yourself today."

"Had a meeting with Rudi today who didn't like my first-ever grant application."

"What did he say?"

"That I wrote like a high school student."

"Really? That's actually pretty good! He always told me that I wrote like a kindergarten student. You're almost there."

His humor picked me up enough that I went home, rewrote my personal statement, had it retyped, and reassembled the application. I took it back to him. I used his suggestions as best I could, and he acknowledged that it was better—if still not excellent. He agreed that we may as well send it off anyway. So, it was submitted to the NIH for an individual training award. A few months went by, and we got the reviews back. My application and Peter's were approved and funded. Rudi crowed at a meeting of the GI Division. "Only twelve of these were funded in the entire United States, and we got two of them. We knew that Rick and Peter would deliver for us." Oh well. Back on top again. I came to learn that a certain degree of abuse was required for learning in certain circumstances.

By June, 1979, the first year of my GI fellowship was over. I had essentially finished my clinical training, I was completely comfortable with my expertise in internal medicine and GI, I had my own research grant, and I was about to walk into a setting where I would suddenly be the dumbest guy in the room.

Chapter 10

Learning to do Research (1979-84)

Making a decision to become a biomedical researcher was one issue, but making it happen was another challenge. On Monday July 2, 1979, I entered Young Kim's GI Cancer Research Lab at the San Francisco VA Hospital. He had a vast number of rooms and amount of space—allegedly more than any other single research laboratory at UCSF at the time, as Marvin Sleisenger had ceded his space to Young as well. The lab was well-equipped, and there were about twenty-five lab workers ranging from senior scientists, to post-doctoral fellows, technicians, and a secretary. Since my meeting with him in the winter of 1978, Young had been given a larger office in a different building, near Sleisenger. I was given a desk in a large room with a group of other post-docs on the first floor of the old research building. The animal care facility was close to our lab, which ensured a steady supply of cockroaches. When I came into the lab late at night and turned on the lights, several roaches would jump off the walls. One of the first things I learned was that cockroaches can actually fly a short distance when they jump off walls. I was hoping to learn even more.

Most of the members of the lab had PhD degrees in biochemistry. Everyone knew something about doing research, and I was the newcomer. Some of the members of the lab were very helpful, most were friendly but otherwise neutral, a couple hated the idea of an MD in a basic research lab, were resentful of my presence, and were capable of sabotage. One colleague with whom I later shared a small office later admonished me "watch your back" after there were some odd occurrences in the lab. I hadn't anticipated that aspect of a research lab. There were mostly normal regular people in the lab; there were also a few strange characters.

I had entered the lab with some specific goals. First, I planned to learn more about colorectal cancer than anyone on the planet. Anyone, anywhere. Really. This was an ambitious goal (which I shared with no one but Pat), and fortunately there was no testable outcome, so I could declare myself successful any time that suited me. Second, I wanted to learn enough about glycoprotein biochemistry to be able to conduct reasonable experiments that might provide insight into how colon cancers either started, grew or spread. There were reasons to believe that understanding glycoprotein structure was a reasonable place to gain insight into how cancers functioned. The ultimate point was to learn enough about the conduct of cancer research that, when the appropriate time came, I could turn my attention to hereditary colon cancer. Actually, from the very beginning, I was most interested in how tumors began. What was the ultimate origin of a tumor? How did something like a cancer arise from normal-appearing tissue? This focus has been a constant in my career, although my work has gone in tangential directions, it is always traceable back to that central interest.

I also wanted to learn about the academic process. Some of my peers were far more familiar with the process than I was. I was quite naïve and just beginning to learn about tenure, promotions, getting grants, how to publish, and the things that were essential for academic survival. Unless I survived in the academic world, I would accomplish nothing. For some who went into the lab, their research was a means toward academic advancement. For me, it was the other way around. Research intensive medical schools like UCSF have a small core of individuals whose salary is paid by the state or the VA, but the overwhelming majority are self-funded through their grants. Since I had gotten my first award, I was now a fledgling member of the club. The challenge was to continue, survive, and thrive.

My first lesson in glycoprotein biochemistry

On my first day in the lab, Jim Whitehead, PhD, who was the most senior scientist in the lab, approached me with a sincere smile and said:

"Rick, you look a little confused. Do you know any glycoprotein biochemistry?"

"Almost none," I responded, honestly.

"Well, let me show you a few things." Without further ado, he gave me a thirty minute tutorial on the basics of how sugars were bonded together and attached to proteins, and he reviewed what we were doing in the lab. He was generous, patient and gracious. This gave me a positive feeling about coming into the lab—and defused my initial anxiety about perhaps being in the wrong place. I then went to the library for more resources, and to the bookstore to snap up more books on the subject. Glycoproteins are one of the more complicated aspects of biochemistry, most scientists avoid it, and I knew I had a long haul in front of me. Also, most of the techniques in the lab were totally unknown to me—a variety of types of chromatography and electrophoresis, tissue culture, and so on. If I had been thinking in terms of a short-term victory, I would have been well-advised to turn around and leave. But I wasn't thinking that way.

During the last few months of my clinical fellowship (in the spring of 1979), I went to the Kim lab when I could to get a head start on some of the technique they were using. There was a GI fellow from Canada, Hugh Freeman, MD, who had completed his clinical training in Toronto, and was doing a two year research fellowship at UCSF with Young Kim. He was using a novel class of biochemical tools called lectins that could be used on sliced sections of intestinal tissues, and one could determine which carbohydrate structures were being made in each location of that tissue. Lectins are naturally-occurring proteins that are extracted from plant seeds, invertebrates, and other sources that have the curious ability to selectively stick to very specific complex carbohydrate (sugar) structures. They are called "agglutinins", since when mixed with red blood cells, they selectively agglutinate the cells based upon what carbohydrates are on their surface membranes—which includes our blood types. The lectins I was using were tagged with a fluorescent marker, and one could use a fluorescent microscope to look at the tissues and record what sugar groups were present in various parts of the tissue. So, I met with Hugh on a couple of evenings and Saturdays prior to my entry into the lab (as he had accepted a job in British Columbia, and was scheduled to leave just as I would arrive), and he showed me how to do these experiments. They weren't complicated. I just had to learn a bit more about the pathology of colonic tissues, and a little more glycoprotein biochemistry to interpret what I saw. The day after Hugh left, I arrived and took his desk.

When I arrived in the laboratory in July, I knew it would takes me a while to get fibroblasts from patients with familial adenomatous polyposis for the research proposal we had written. So, Young asked me to get a panel of fluorescent lectins and study human colon cancer tissues from the Pathology Department—which routinely received and processed all of the surgically resected specimens. Pathology kept portions of the cancers in their archives for decades. Colon cancer tissues and colonic polyps were particularly abundant in the VA system. For a variety of reasons, middle aged and older male veterans have a lot of polyps and cancer. Young said: "I don't know what you'll find, but I'll bet there is a story there". So, I sought out the pathologist with the most expertise in the gastrointestinal system, Carolyn Montgomery, MD. She taught me how to interpret the slides and we formed a collaboration to get the tissues I needed. She was a natural teacher, and we got along well.

I have attributed several turns of fortune to "good luck" thus far, and there was at least a little luck involved in my first months in the lab. But I was determined to find something, and developed the skill of recognizing the organizing principles from raw data. First I found an interpretable pattern of differential glycoprotein expression that corresponded to the maturational state of the cells in normal colonic tissues. The normal tissues were prepared for microscopic evaluation in such way that you could tell where the new cells were first "born", and follow their paths as they matured and finally were expelled into the intestinal contents. I discussed the findings with Jim Whitehead, and we made sense of what was happening during normal tissue development. To explore the carbohydrate structures in greater depth, Jim would regularly give me additional fluorescent lectins (ones that I had never heard of) and suggested that I try them out. These lectins would progressively tell us about how the sugar molecules were hooked up one to another, and tell us more about the complexity of glycoprotein structure in the colon. Some days, Jim would walk by my desk, smile, and toss a handful of tiny plastic tubes containing new lectins on my desk, and suggest that I "give these a try." Before long, I found a unique glycoprotein structure present only in the cancers and tissues immediately adjacent to the cancer, but virtually never in the normal colon. In fact, I had almost given up on this lectin, because it didn't stick anywhere in the normal tissues I initially studied. I quickly realized that this might be important. I was able to get progressively more detailed structure by using a broader panel of lectins, all of which came from a company called Vector Laboratories, which was conveniently located nearby in the San Francisco Bay peninsula.

One day, I asked Jim how he got these lectins, and he said that he knew people from Vector. The lectins kept coming, and eventually I asked Jim:

"Who is Vector, anyway?"

He responded "I am". After he left the lab each night, he drove to his second job, where he was the founder and president of Vector Laboratories. About nine months after I joined the lab, Jim left the Kim lab to take over running the company full time. Before he left, he taught me what I need to know to get started. His company has been very successful over the decades, and is still the leader in that field.

First abstract submission

Within six months of entering the lab, my data were accumulating, and I was starting to see the "story" that Young Kim had predicted. In January, 1980, abstract time came. Once a year, the GI fellows would write up their newest findings in a short, half-page summary called an "abstract" and submit them for possible presentation at the annual meeting of the American Gastroenterological Association (AGA), which occurred each May. This was the most prestigious scientific meeting of the year in gastroenterology, and we all wanted to stand up at the podium and discuss our findings in front of our colleagues and friends. It was an honor, and also, it was a way of getting recognized, perhaps for a future job offer.

There were probably a dozen of us in the lab writing up our work and handing the drafts over to Jim Whitehead and Young Kim for their advice and approval on the deadline day. The comments on my first attempt at doing this was that it was too dry and had too many biochemical details.

"Think about what you are really trying to say; tell us a story" was the suggestion. So, I went back for a rewrite, and brought it back to our circle of reviewers. Jim looked at the abstract for a longer time than usual, looked up at me with a sly smile and said: "Are you trying to write an abstract or a press release?" I finally found the "just right" tone in-between, and submitted the abstract.

One of the other new guys in the lab was Jim St. Hilaire, MD, who had joined the lab directly from his Internal Medicine residency, and was hoping to do clinical GI training later. He was given a new hormone to work with called "EGF". No one was sure if it was important in cancer, but there were reasons to believe that it might be involved in regulating growth. (It is.) Jim had a year of training in an endocrinology lab, and knew how to work with hormones. He went about his experiments putting EGF on cultured cancer cells, but I didn't know exactly what he was doing. He submitted an abstract along with the rest of us, but he kept muttering that his work was unimportant and that no one would be interested. He submitted an abstract anyway. Later in March, we got the results of our abstract submissions by mail; the letters all arrived simultaneously. We reassembled our circle, and opened the envelopes together, like Christmas presents. The first fellow, Akira Morita, MD (from Japan) proudly announced that his paper had been accepted for presentation, as a poster, and he was pleased. I opened next, and found that my paper had been accepted for an oral presentation—an invitation that occurred in about ten percent of the abstracts. I was delighted—better visibility. Jim St. Hilaire was the last to open his envelope. He paused for a moment and then said "What's the Plenary Session?" We all had a big laugh. He was just invited to present his paper in front of about 3,000 people. It is the highest honor an abstract can get. When we told him this, he froze with fright and shook so hard that the letter dropped to the floor. Over the next two months, we practiced our presentations over and over, first to the lab, then to Young and Marv, and later to Rudi and the GI faculty and all the other UCSF fellows. Jim overcame his stage fright, and we all had our first experiences in front of a national and international audience.

By the end of the first year in the lab, I was getting a lot of data as a result of my initial lectin studies, which resulted in the publication of two papers in prestigious journals. I was extending the work into colonic polyps, ulcerative colitis, fetal tissues, and also colonic tissues from mice and monkeys that developed either inflammation or cancer. I had gotten momentum considerably faster than I had anticipated. As we entered the second year in the laboratory (which was the third year of my fellowship), decisions had to be made about whether to invite us to join the faculty at UCSF, help us find a job elsewhere, or send us packing.

Three of the members of my initial group of GI fellows had done sufficiently well to be considered for faculty appointments. One was Dick Weisiger, who had a PhD in biochemistry in addition to a MD from Duke, and two years of additional post-doctoral research experience at the National Institutes of Health (NIH). He was the prize pony. He was working with Bob Ockner at Moffitt Hospital, and had published an article in *Science*, which is one of the most prestigious journals. He also had won a Hartford Foundation grant, and was certainly one that they wanted to keep on the faculty at Moffitt. Most importantly, he was a liver researcher, as were Rudi and Bob, and they wanted to keep the best hepatologists in their labs. The second fellow in the group was Jim Grendell, MD, who was working with a physiologist on pancreatic function. He was the only GI fellow in that field. He was also a very competent clinician, and they targeted Jim to join the faculty at the General Hospital, with John Cello. I had just published a paper in the *Proceedings of the National Academy of Sciences* (with Rudi's blessings and progressively less harassment), and another one in *Gastroenterology*, so I was chosen to join the faculty at the VA hospital, with Young Kim. They planned to add one new faculty member to each of the three hospitals. The only catch was that we all had to come up with money to pay our own salaries, and UCSF was expected to pay none of it. Since this was the University of California, they had to advertise the positions nationally, and we had to apply for each respective position. The advertised positions were very narrowly defined, which would make it unlikely that some other person would fit the description. However, one morning, John Cello (who chaired all three Search Committees) told me that someone else was applying for "my" position. She was a productive researcher from one of the Harvard hospitals, and was very interested in UCSF. Her interest immediately diminished when she found it was associated with no salary support. So, we are all "selected", but still had to win some grants if we actually wanted to take the jobs.

First academic appointment

In the fall of 1980, Pat became pregnant with our third daughter, Brigid, who was born in San Francisco in May, 1981. I had written three grant applications based upon my lectin findings, but had to wait until April or May of 1981 to find out if the grants would be approved. The odds of success with these grants were thought to be about ten percent for applications to the NIH, but better for grants to the VA and some other foundations—maybe up to thirty percent. Now, my commitment to the lab was being pitted against the responsibilities I had to my family. I had a meeting with Rudi Schmid and asked him what would happen if I failed to win a grant. He suggested that I could borrow from my family. I told him that would not be possible. He then told me that he would keep me on for one more year of fellowship—which was paying $17,500 per year. I thought that was challenging for a family of five in San Francisco, but kept that opinion to myself, as complaining about money was the worst thing you could do at UCSF. You were expected to suffer quietly. Furthermore, MDs were better off than PhDs, and since we all stood shoulder to shoulder in the lab, there was no sympathy for such complaints from basic scientists. If you don't like it, go into private practice.

After the grant applications were sent out, I had to wait and see what would develop. To hedge my bets, I sent out a series of letters to the Chiefs of GI Divisions at six other universities. I explained that I wanted to pursue research, wanted to do it at UCSF, but if I couldn't do it there, I was open to relocating. Looking out for myself and applying for positions was something I had done each time that it was appropriate (for college, medical school, house staff, fellowship), so it seemed appropriate that I should take care of myself this time, too. As soon as each of these Division Chiefs got my letter, they immediately called Rudi Schmid to ask if I was any good. Totally unbeknownst to me, this was the wrong thing to do, and as soon as Rudi heard about this, he hit the roof. To this day, I do not understand the dynamic behind his furious response. I thought I was doing the right thing, and furthermore, I was candid and said that if I was successful in getting a grant, I preferred to stay at UCSF. I was called on the carpet and told I had been a "bad dog" by Rudi, Marv and Young. Live and learn. The whippings were only words.

Still concerned about the future, I quietly inquired about other backup situations, in the clinical world. I was a very competent clinician who just happened to be fixated on solving a cancer problem and wanted to do research. I was offered a job at the Kaiser-Permanente Hospital in South

San Francisco, and was sitting on that possibility, thinking about the fact that I was just getting started in the lab, and hated the thought of leaving that behind. Suddenly, in April 1981, the dominos fell my way, all at once. I was returning to the lab from lunch. Young Kim met me on the sidewalk and told me that my VA grant application was approved, meaning that the VA would provide my salary for the next three years. I was on top of the world. About a week later, I found out that my NIH grant application was also funded, which would permit me to hire a technician and contribute supply money for lab supplies. A few days after that, the National Foundation for Colitis and Ileitis (now called the Crohn's & Colitis Foundation of America) called and asked if I wanted their grant. That application overlapped with the NIH application, so I had to turn it down. In just a few weeks the uncertainty turned into a fantastic opportunity. Rags to riches. I was to be fully funded for three years, appointed as an assistant professor, and everything was looking very positive for me. I was thirty-three years old, had a loving wife and three daughters, I wasn't concerned about an early death from cancer any more, had my first job, and my plans seemed somehow within my reach.

Meeting another Department Chairman

Shortly after receiving the appointment as Assistant Professor of Internal Medicine at UCSF, I was asked to set up a meeting with the Department Chairman, Holly Smith, MD. He was a soft-spoken gentleman from the small town of Easley, South Carolina, who possessed such depth of charm that he was able to herd a very large and talented department of superstars, egotists and sociopaths into one of the strongest academic departments in the world. No one was ever sure how he did it, but he was as responsible as anyone for the phenomenal growth of UCSF from a minor, middling medical school before his arrival from the venerable Massachusetts General Hospital in 1964. Under his deft leadership (aided by the fact that Stanford Medical School moved from Pacific Heights in San Francisco to Palo Alto in 1959, leaving the whole city to UCSF), UCSF became the perennial top grant winner from the NIH. He brought the San Francisco General and San Francisco VA hospitals into the fold, and oversaw their growth in stature along with the University Hospital. He also helped launch the careers of three Nobel Laureates.

I went to his office, not sure of what to expect, and he was welcoming, kind, and encouraging. His office was on the north aspect of Moffitt Hospital, and his desk had its back to a window that looked over a spectacular view of the Golden Gate Bridge. I sat and chatted with him, dividing my attention between his advice and the view of the bridge and Marin headlands. He spoke about traditions, and mentioned that his medical school class (Harvard, 1947) contained a number of luminary academic physicians—including Marvin Sleisenger, whom he had recruited to lead the VA Hospital Medicine Service. He looked at me and said "isn't that a wonderful picture?" I immediately agreed, looking over his shoulder on that clear July morning. Fortunately, I quickly realized that he was referring to the Harvard Medical School Class of 1947 class picture that was on the wall to my right. I looked over, and the graduates were shown alphabetically, and there in a cluster were Marv Sleisenger, Holly Smith and Howard Spiro. Quite the club. I agreed that it was indeed a great picture. He wished me well, and whenever I see him—years later at national meetings—he shakes my hand and says "how are you doing Rick, and how is that colon cancer research coming?" He possessed rare charm, and I don't think I have ever known anyone quite like him.

The Assistant Professor

I spent three years as an Assistant Professor at UCSF, as a member of Young Kim's lab at the VA hospital. I hired a technician, and met with her daily to plan the experiments. In addition, I picked up a lot of clinical and teaching responsibilities—probably more than I should have, since it wasn't actually part of my job description. There were five Gastroenterologists who were full professors at the VA. Marv Sleisenger was Chief of the Medicine Service, there were three full GI positions at the VA filled by senior people like Young Kim, only one of whom actually practiced clinical medicine to any degree, and there was a cell biologist who was initially in the GI section, and then became the Chief of the Research Service at the VA. There were two junior people—a hepatologist named Tom Boyer, MD, and me. Tom and I were expected to monitor all of the clinical activity in the GI Section, train the fellows, oversee the clinics, and take care of the patients. The irony was that Tom and I were supported with awards that were specifically designed to guarantee time to pursue our research, and the full time positions were ostensibly to ensure patient care. In actuality, we had reversed our activities. I spent a lot of time seeing the patients and being involved in the conferences, but the clinical issues often came up urgently, and tended to crowd out the less urgent issues of working in the laboratory. I was the only VA staff member in the GI section who was comfortable with all aspects of patient care. This involved doing the endoscopic procedures, taking out the colonic polyps, or managing the patients who came in with gastrointestinal hemorrhage. Before long, I had also been asked to learn how to do the biliary procedures, which involved putting an endoscope in the duodenum and threading a catheter into the bile ducts—and even performing the procedure to remove gall stones that got stuck and blocked the bile flow. I was very flattered to be doing the teaching and patient care at UCSF, and proudly agreed to do that work. However, I gradually recognized that the clinical work would eventually overwhelm my laboratory efforts. Everyone was happy that Tom and I were willing to carry the ball for them, as that protected their time for research.

I initially performed a number of experiments with the lectins on a variety of different types of premalignant or inflamed tissues, since I was comfortable with this technique, had a good partner in Carolyn Montgomery, MD, and my early papers were being accepted with minimal revisions. However, I knew that this technique would not get to the heart of the colon cancer problem, and began to collect specimens of colon cancers and other tissues for extraction of the glycoproteins for more detailed biochemical analysis. Unlike the fluorescent microscopy experiments, the biochemical analyses were technically much more challenging, very time consuming, and a month's work could easily go down the drain with one bad day at the laboratory bench. I did my best to keep the papers coming with the microscope work as I learned the new analytical techniques.

Some of the people in the lab were very helpful. I shared a tiny office, now in the basement where Young's office was previously, with an experienced biochemist named Roger Erickson, PhD, who was helpful. Young Kim would make general suggestions about the directions I should take, but to execute the experiments, I needed to consult with the ground troops in the lab. Nothing was in a book. You took experimental procedures from the manuscripts that other people had published, and hoped that they told you everything they did, just exactly as they had done it. If you were lucky, someone in the lab had some prior experience with that technique. Often times the procedures that were published wouldn't work when repeated. I do not believe that other researchers intentionally misled their peers. Rather, these procedures would evolve over weeks to months, and when the papers were written up, I think they forgot what changes they had made in the protocols. So, there was a lot of trial and error as you tried out new approaches.

Unlike the lucky two years of fellowship, the early years of assistant professorship were a more uncertain time. Furthermore, we anticipated that one needed about twenty-five papers, of which ten to fifteen were "substantial" contributions, to be considered for the next academic step, which was promotion to associate professor, and the consideration of academic tenure. Tenure was mainly important at the UCSF level, since the VA had its own way of supporting the permanent staff. However, the procedure at the University of California was that after no more than six years as an assistant professor, you were evaluated and "up or out". My salary was supported by a research grant, so I was actually a temporary employee. What's worse, there were about twenty-five of us at the VA on the same type of temporary grants called "career development awards". We had all successfully competed for these awards nationally through the VA, and these grants were in part developed to encourage young researchers to join the VA, and to stay on as permanent staff. That worked better in the heartlands of the US than in San Francisco. We all wanted to stay on, but there would never be room for all of us.

I met weekly with Young Kim, and he encouraged me to be optimistic, and to hope that a permanent slot would open up. I had not been in the academic world very long, and to me it looked like a closed system as no new positions were created. The GI section at the VA had the senior full professors and the young assistant professors, but there were no mid-level faculty (associate professors). The same was the case throughout the Division. One time, a representative of the Internal Medicine faculty at UCSF came to the VA to speak with the hopeful assistant professors who were on our temporary awards. He noted that the real point of the career development awards at the San Francisco VA was to develop faculty to go to other VAs. He said: "there are plenty of other VAs out there who would love to have you". That was surely true, but not what we wanted to hear. I asked what strategy I should adopt. One day Young told me that perhaps someone would have a heart attack, and I could move up. I thought that was a slightly morbid thing to hope for.

During the next three years at UCSF, I published everything I could, and made sure that I presented preliminary work as abstracts at the national meetings. I began to get letters of inquiry—unsolicited this time—from other medical schools who were interested in recruiting me. One day I got a letter from a gastroenterologist at Stanford University named Peter Gregory, MD. They were looking to recruit a junior faculty member at the Palo Alto VA. I was reading his letter, and Young Kim just happened to walk into the lab, looked over my shoulder, and asked me what I was reading. I showed him, and he said "it's a form letter, throw it out". So, I put it aside. A couple of weeks later, the secretary told me that Peter Gregory had called and was trying to contact me. None of us had our own phones, so all communications went through the secretary. I went to the phone (in a different room) and Peter asked me why I hadn't answered his letter. I told him I had been advised that this was a mass-mailing. He said it wasn't and he wanted to interest me in a job at the Palo Alto VA Hospital and an appointment at Stanford. He asked a few questions about my research and clinical skills, and then asked me what he thought was a critical question: "Do you own a house?" I told him I did, and he was delighted. It was very difficult to recruit young faculty to San Francisco or Palo Alto because the housing was too expensive for those moving from the East or Midwest. I asked what kind of position he had to offer. He said that they had a part time VA appointment (i.e., part of a full VA position like Young Kim and the others had at the San Francisco VA). The plan was to offer seven-eighths of a VA position, which would pay about $45,000 or so a year. I asked why they carved off the last one-eight of the position. "That would make the salary too high compared to the Stanford University salaries, so we had to adjust it down." (That was interesting.) The GI Division Chief at Stanford was another glycoprotein expert, and he thought I would be a good complement to their group. I eventually was invited for a lecture, but other opportunities came along before any offer was made. I was about to discover that I was entering into the academic marketplace, and a young person with two grants and clinical skills was a valuable commodity.

UCSF was a competitive institution, and standards were high. You were expected to become the top person in your field in the nation to be considered fully successful. I spent most of my time at the VA, and although there were occasional dangerous interpersonal dynamics between the VA and the University Hospital, Young Kim and Marv Sleisenger were protective of my interests.

During my second year on the UCSF faculty in 1983, Rudi Schmid was chosen to become the Dean of the UCSF School of Medicine. He had been on the faculty for twenty years, had been elected to the prestigious National Academy of Sciences, and the only surprise was that he had been a Division Chief, but never a Department Chairman. There were no rules on the subject, but he essentially jumped over one level in the administrative structure, presumably because of his academic stature. By all accounts, he was an excellent dean. He made the choice to appoint his protégé, Bob Ockner, as his successor as Division Chief. Bob was a successful academic researcher, a full professor, seemed to have all the tools. But within a few years as Division Chief, he was overwhelmed. He simultaneously served as Division Chief, director of a large and prestigious NIH-supported Digestive Disease Center, and he also accepted the position as Editor-in-Chief of the journal *Gastroenterology*. It was a work load that few mortals could have mastered. I had been in Rudi Schmid's office when he was contacted by Jim Boyer, MD, the hepatologist from Yale, who was urging him to become the Editor-in-Chief of a new liver disease journal. Rudi refused on the phone saying:

"I cannot possibly continue as Division Chief, director of the Center, and become editor of the new journal."

Unfortunately, Bob tried, and the Division began a long, slow decline from its position at the top of American gastroenterology. During my three years on the faculty, we never had a single meeting of all of the GI faculty. One by one, everyone was succeeding, but the Division was fraying as an integrated group. A process that I likened to "reverse natural selection" began to take over. UCSF could recruit the best fellows, put them into the best labs, bring the best of those onto the faculty, but then, the most promising young faculty members would be recruited away, one by one. My turn would come.

I began to recognize what was happening. There were a lot of outstanding faculty at the top, junior faculty were brought in at the entry level and they were doing most of the teaching and clinical work. It was difficult to move up in the system. My initial sense of pride in being asked to teach such outstanding students was beginning to conflict with my underlying interest in solving the familial colorectal cancer problem. I had three daughters and the public school system in San Francisco had gone into a steep decline, which forced us into an expensive private school system. Also, I had to win grants to pay my salary, and these were term awards with a three year expiration date coming up in June, 1984. In my third year on the faculty, I prepared more grant applications, but I wouldn't get the outcomes until April or May of 1984, which would give little time for developing an alternative strategy for July should the application fail.

An invitation to Michigan

In the winter of 1983-84, I was getting inquiries about possible recruitment to other institutions when I would present my work at scientific meetings. At a national meeting in Chicago in November, 1983, several people approached me, and one was Tadataka (Tachi) Yamada, MD. He was a fast-rising star in the GI world, was one of the first "molecular biologists" in our field (i.e., he was using the newly developed genetic techniques that had transformed medical research—but seemed out of reach to ordinary biochemists or physiologists), and he had just moved from UCLA to the University of Michigan (UM) to become Division Chief in Ann Arbor. When he moved at age thirty-eight the prior year, he was one of the youngest Division Chiefs in the country. He needed a Section Chief at the VA Hospital in Ann Arbor, which was right across the Huron River from the UM medical school. I had met him at the national meetings, and we had jogged together with a group of young gastroenterologists. Also, a good friend, Jon Kaunitz, MD had spent a year with me in Young Kim's lab, and then moved to UCLA to work with a well-known physiologist. Young researchers were drawn to Tachi, and he spent a lot of time cultivating those relationships and encouraging those around him. Before Tachi left for Ann Arbor, Jon said that there was a hidden secret at UCSF in Young Kim's lab who could be recruited away. Jon referred to me as "Cinderella" with a sly wink.

Tachi and I ran into one another during a social gathering at the Chicago meeting, He approached:

"Hey Rick, how long do you think you will stay at UCSF?" he asked.

"I don't know."

"Do you have kids?"

"Three daughters."

"So, do you think you will raise them there?"

"Probably not"

"Well, I have a job for you in Ann Arbor."

"Thanks, but for now, I have one in San Francisco".

We spoke for a few minutes, and he ended with, "Send me your CV (curriculum vitae)."

I had a couple of other Division Chiefs approach me at that same meeting, as junior faculty from a top institution were thought to be ideal recruitment candidates. They would be well-trained, and the parent institutions would surely be taking advantage of them, so they were probably hungry and moveable for a modest recruitment package. However, Tachi and one other called me about a week after the meeting to follow up.

"Rick, you didn't send me your CV."

"Yeah, I figured that if I sent you my CV, I would be obligated to take a recruitment visit to Michigan, and I am too busy right now. I didn't want to mislead you." (At that time, I thought that traveling once every two months was too much travel.)

"Well, I want you to come and take a look. It's a great opportunity".

"I don't want to spend more time away from my wife."

"That's what I am saying. I want you to bring your wife, too."

"I don't have family in San Francisco, and cannot afford babysitters"

"I'll pay for them."

"OK." (Short pause.) "By the way, what airport do we use to get to Ann Arbor?"

"Detroit." I must have seemed very naïve at that point. I was.

So, in the first week of December, 1983, Pat and I flew to Ann Arbor, leaving on a sunny San Francisco morning, and getting in on a chilly afternoon in Michigan. As we went to dinner that evening at a fancy French restaurant called L'Escoffier, it was seven degrees. Fortunately, we still had some east coast winter jackets, although Pat's suitcase didn't arrive at the airport and she had to borrow clothes from Tachi's wife Leslie—and boots from her daughter Sanae.

We stayed at the Yamada's house that first evening, had a three hour time zone change, and I was very excited by Tachi's attention and his vision for the GI Division at the UM. As a result, I don't think I slept the entire night. I tried reading, but just couldn't get to sleep. I usually went to bed at midnight or one AM, and when everyone else retired, it was about eight PM San Francisco time. The next day, I was up early, had to give two lectures—one at noon and one at 4:30 PM, had a series of interviews one after another, and then another sumptuous dinner. I hadn't been so tired at the end of that day since I was in intern. Tachi offered me the position as Section Chief at the Ann Arbor VA and an academic appointment at the UM. I would become his first lieutenant and right hand man, providing leadership at the "other" hospital in the academic system. All this just three years after finishing my fellowship. More importantly, for the first time in my life, I might actually have a permanent job with a salary. Moving from San Francisco would allow us to have a bigger house, and we would be in a family-oriented community. It was all starting to make sense. Suddenly, it didn't seem so important to stay in San Francisco. We loved the city, but we realized that eventually we would leave.

Meeting with yet another Department Chairman

During my visit, I met with the Chairman of the Department of Internal Medicine, William Kelley, MD. He was another of the daunting, confident, successful giants of academic medicine. He was at the top of his field, was assembling a new textbook of internal medicine, and well-connected to all of the sources of academic power in the US. We sat down in his office across a coffee table from each other, and he looked at my CV. He asked me how it happened that I had gone from Yale Medical School to St. Francis Hospital for my internship. I told him that I had made some mistakes, but learned my lessons, and earned my way back to the top. He nodded as if to say "OK", and that was it. I believe that was the last time anyone inquired about my unusual academic progression, and I was happy not to revisit that uncomfortable issue again.

Kelley had come to Michigan in 1975 as a very young professor and Department Chairman. He aggressively "cleaned house", much as Holly Smith had at UCSF a decade earlier, and began bringing in young rising stars like Yamada. Initially there was push-back as some of the traditional clinician-teacher professors were replaced by young, laboratory-based researchers. By 1983, the old resentments were mostly gone, and everyone was energized by the growth in the stature of the institution. When I visited, the UM Hospital—called "Old Main"—was the oldest university hospital in the country, built in 1925. There were open wards with ten or more beds, and it looked all of its sixty years. However, they were in the process of building a new university hospital, which was to be huge, and completely re-outfitted. The UM was poised for sharp upward movement. I initially thought that anything but UCSF would not be suitable, but UM looked like a medical school on the rise.

A look at Johns Hopkins

After getting back to San Francisco, Tachi called and wanted me to come for a second visit to Ann Arbor. Although I was getting inquiries about recruitment, I had no comparisons for the UM. I then got a call from Ted Bayless, MD, from Johns Hopkins School of Medicine, who asked if I would take a look at a faculty position there. That would be a good way to compare. So, in early February, 1984, I flew to Baltimore. Ted was well-known in academic circles, and graciously tried to interest me in joining their Division. I flew in one evening, had dinner with Ted, and the next morning, we had a meeting with the Chairman of the Department of Medicine, a towering figure in the field of genetics named Victor McKusick, MD. He was imposing and took himself extremely seriously, which was a major distinction compared with my interactions with Tachi, who was just two years older than I, which created an easy social connection. For some reason, Ted stayed in McKusick's office with me during the interview. I sat in a great leather sofa across from McKusick's desk, and immediately behind me was a larger-than-life oil portrait of William Osler, MD, one of the inaugural pioneers of US medicine, who had been a prior Chairman at Hopkins. I was surrounded. Dr. McKusick pointed out some of the historically important sights visible from his window. Johns Hopkins was one of the top medical schools in the country, and it had an august—and intimidating reputation. McKusick played it to the hilt. I may as well have been in the Oval Office.

He cleared his throat and looked at me for a moment. He had my CV in front of him, and was scanning it. I might have misinterpreted, but I concluded that he hadn't looked at it prior to this moment. After a quiet moment, he looked up and asked "Do you have family?" My brain almost froze. What was this question? Is it a polite opener? I'm coming from San Francisco. Is he asking if I'm gay? He's a geneticist. Has he been informed about my interest in familial colon cancer and is he asking about my cancer risks? (No, it can't be eugenics—not that!) I gathered my composure and calmly answered that I had a wife and three daughters. He nodded approvingly; that seemed to do the trick. After a brief chat that included reminding me again of the role of Hopkins in American medicine, he pulled out a book he had written in which he reproduced some of the chapters from Osler's original textbook of medicine, proudly signed it, and gave it to me.

I then went through the ritual of meeting with various faculty members, including the Division Chief, Tom Hendrix, MD, who reminded me some of Holly Smith—charming, an easy smile, and very friendly. I gave a noon conference on my work on glycoproteins in colorectal cancer. Immediately after the lecture, I was greeted by an enthusiastic person from the audience I had never met previously, Andy Feinberg, MD, MPH, who was a new Assistant Professor at Hopkins. He dashed up to the podium, introduced himself, and effusively said that it would be great for me to join the research group that he was in. I thanked him for this, but we weren't scheduled for a meeting, which I never understood. Moreover, I didn't know that his research partner was a young rising star named Bert Vogelstein, MD. Both Andy and Bert were to become major figures in my research life over the next nine years. I just didn't know it yet.

I visited some of the other labs, and met a young researcher named Gordon Luk, MD, PhD, who had made some important discoveries in the tissues of people with familial adenomatous polyposis (FAP, the disease that my fellowship grant proposed to study). For some reason, his lab was separated from the GI people—and Feinberg and Vogelstein were somewhere else as well. If they had been adjacent to one another, I might have made the connection to what they were doing. So, for better or worse,

I did not envision that Hopkins was the place to go at that time. It's a waste of effort to wonder "what if", but in the end, things worked out very well in Ann Arbor.

In 1981, Young Kim took me to a meeting of the National Large Bowel Cancer Workshop, held in Houston in July (which is, incidentally, not a good idea). Young was on the Steering Committee of the group, and one of its major grant-holders. I was a junior researcher, considered to be an extension of Young Kim, and these meetings were tremendous learning experiences for me. I saw the leaders in the field discussing what colon cancer was all about. Of course, none of us knew much about carcinogenesis at that time. Moreover, there was no agreement that there was a familial form of colon cancer other than FAP, so, I kept my mouth shut about my hypothesis. Each of the investigators brought his or her latest findings on a poster—typically on a piece of rolled up paper measuring four by eight feet, and set it up for display. There were sessions for viewing the posters and interaction among the investigators.

I carefully looked at each poster one by one during the meeting. I came across a poster in which the investigator had counted and catalogued all of the abnormal chromosomes found in individual colorectal cancers. The results were a heterogeneous mess. Every tumor had a different group of abnormal chromosomes, and I couldn't imagine making sense of it. I thought to myself—this is no way to solve the mysteries of colon cancer. The author of the poster took Young Kim aside, as Young represented the power elite of the group, and complained that he was having a hard time getting his work appreciated or winning a grant from the NIH on this topic. I didn't run into this fellow at that time, but his name was Bert Vogelstein, MD, and before long, this problem would permanently disappear.

Making the decision to move

Early in 1984, I took a second trip to Ann Arbor. Upon arrival, Tachi gave me a formal, written offer to be the Section Chief in gastroenterology at the Ann Arbor VA Hospital, and join the faculty as an assistant professor. I took the offer letter back to San Francisco, decided that I should not move unless I was offered an academic promotion to associate professor—and called Tachi to tell him that. He told me that my CV wouldn't make it through the committee on appointments and promotions at the higher level, and asked me to reconsider. He even offered a little more salary, but that wasn't the issue. I called a good friend, Peter Lance, MD, who had been a fellow with me in Kim's lab, and asked his opinion. He challenged me with:

"Are you concerned about the security of tenure, or the title you have on your letterhead?"

I told him I thought tenure was meaningless, and it was definitely the latter issue.

He replied "Just so you understand what you are doing." Peter usually said what he thought.

I told Tachi that I probably needed another year or two at UCSF to publish a few more papers so that I could qualify as an associate professor, and that I didn't care a bit about tenure. I even told him I wouldn't go anywhere else until I was ready to come to UM at the next level. Tachi then offered to go with Bill Kelley to meet with the committee and see if they would grant an appointment at the associate professor level, without tenure. I said OK. He did, they approved, and I accepted the offer.

In February, I told Young Kim and Marv Sleisenger about the offer from the UM. They encouraged me to stay, but we all knew that the only way I could stay would be if I got the next step in the VA Career Development Award system, which depended upon the outcome of a competitive grant application. The grant application had been submitted, but we wouldn't know the outcome until April or May. Young and Marv appealed to Bob Ockner and Rudi Schmid (I was unaware of this, and only heard about it from Marv years later), but the Division had nothing to offer. Everyone was on "soft money", that is, they were living on their grants. So, I took the UM offer. It was an unusual experience. I had spent the last eleven years wanting to get to San Francisco, and now I was about to walk away from my faculty position at UCSF. I discussed it with Tom Boyer, MD, who was now the Section Chief in GI at the San Francisco VA and a good friend. He quietly encouraged me to get out while there was a good offer on the table. In a few years, he would be recruited to Emory as the GI Division Chief. In fact, many of the best people were sequentially recruited away over the next few years as natural selection worked in reverse for UCSF's GI Division.

Once I decided to leave San Francisco, I was approached by a couple of faculty members from other Departments and Divisions to withdraw my application for the VA career development award, which would reduce the competition among others at the San Francisco VA who had their applications under review. I did. By May, I found out that my grant through the NIH was renewed for five years, and that would travel with me to Ann Arbor. I had the first permanent job ever at age thirty-six, which permitted me to make my first contribution ever to my retirement fund. The housing market in San Francisco was seriously overheated. We put our house on the market, had a four-hour open house, and four offers were made on the house that evening. We took another trip to Ann Arbor to look at houses, and decided to build a new house on a lot that was next door to Tachi Yamada and his family. It was the beginning of a beautiful friendship.

Lynch Syndrome gets a proper name

I accomplished one final task before leaving UCSF, which was to become an important legacy over time. I wrote up and published an article describing the differences between the cancer occurrences in my own family—which included cancers of the uterus, stomach, and a few other organs—and compared this with the family of the patient I had admitted to the hospital at Yale during my subinternship in 1972. That family had six colon cancers among twelve siblings and in one of the parents, but there were no other non-colorectal cancers. I thought there might be something important in this observation. I decided to call these two entities "Lynch Syndrome I" for those with colon cancers only, and "Lynch Syndrome II" for the families like my own that had the other tumors. I hated the term that Henry Lynch had initially coined, "Cancer Family Syndrome", since it implied susceptibilities to cancers everywhere, but there were no apparent increases in the common cancers such as lung, breast and prostate that we could see at that time. The term actually bothered me. I called Henry Lynch and told him of my idea. He enthusiastically approved. I then called Frank Troncale—as the Lynch Syndrome I family was under his care in New Haven, got the additional follow-up data on the family, and the Boland-Troncale paper was published in the *Annals of Internal Medicine* in May, 1984. This was a minor issue at that time, since many clinicians and researchers were still reluctant to believe that this was an actual clinical entity. However, time would be kind to us. Curiously, Henry Lynch then coined the term "Hereditary Non-Polyposis Colorectal Cancer", or HNPCC, for the same entity in 1985! This was a mouthful of unnecessary letters, and eventually several of us in the field felt that the term should be dumped. I once attended a lecture in which the "expert" on colon cancer had misspelled HNPCC on his lecture slide, and butchered it verbally; I resolved to get rid of that name once we figured out what the disease actually was.

Chapter 11

MICHIGAN, MOLECULAR BIOLOGY AND CANCER GENETICS (1984-1990)

Our years in Ann Arbor, Michigan were among the best both professionally and for the family. During my eleven years at the UM, the field of cancer research also underwent a revolutionary change that made solving the genetics of cancer possible. Pat was happy, and the girls grew up in a safe and supportive community.

I was the first recruitment to the GI faculty since Yamada had arrived in 1983. The transition from UCSF was like Dorothy moving from black and white to color in *The Wizard of Oz*. Tachi had touted my arrival as a great recruitment, and everyone was on board. I became the tenth faculty member in the GI Division that July. Within six years, the Division would have more than thirty members, and have a nationally prominent research program. It was a time of growth and excitement.

Tachi is one of those extraordinary people you meet only a few times in your life. He was born in Tokyo, Japan in June, 1945, as the city was being pummeled and scorched by the US near the end of the war. His father was a prominent industrialist who was top executive of Nippon Steel, the largest steel company in Japan, and his mother, although fully Japanese, had been born to a prominent physician in New York City, but found herself back in Japan at the outbreak of the War. Tachi was (and is) a terrific athlete, and competed with the Japanese national ski team. He was sent to Philips Academy Prep School in Andover, Massachusetts at age sixteen, where he excelled academically and in his athletic endeavors. He went to Stanford as a history major. He was initially bound for business, but decided against it after spending a summer with his brother in the financial district of New York. He decided to go into Medicine—against his father's preferences, who had a dim view of medicine. Tachi went to New York University Medical School, and after his Residency in Virginia, was drafted into the Army. He volunteered to do research at Fort Detrick, Maryland, where he had an introduction to protein biochemistry. He learned the discipline quickly, and after three years in the Army, went to UCLA for a GI Fellowship. His talents were immediately recognized by the senior people there, and his closest mentor, Mort Grossman, MD, selected him to go to a lab in Chicago to learn the field of molecular biology, and specifically, the cloning of genes. He was among the first in the field of gastroenterology to tackle this new technology. Even before he had cloned anything, it was perceived that he was one of the top scientists in our specialty.

In the early 1980s, he was on everyone's recruitment list. I first heard him speak when he was brought to UCSF by Rudi Schmid but Tachi refused his invitation to move. He looked at a job at one of the top Harvard hospitals, and almost took that position. However, moments after accepting their offer over the phone, he had buyer's remorse, and called Bill Kelley, who was also trying to recruit him at the same time. Bill was not to be outbid.

"Did you sign a contract?" Bill asked.

"No."

"Then you have no deal."

Bill flew Tachi back to Michigan for a whirlwind recruitment and his best offer. Tachi took it, not because of what it was, but for what he saw it could become. He then had to find others to join in his vision. It was hard for anyone older than Tachi to go to the VA as his associate, so he had to look at younger candidates, and that was not a problem for me. When I arrived, it was like the return of the conquering war hero. Just before arriving, my NIH grant was renewed for five years, and I immediately started getting additional grants through the VA research system. My office was across the hall from the VA Endoscopy suite, so I was easily available to help out when needed. Whenever I walked into the room to assist, the procedure seemed to go more smoothly. The power of suggestion and perception were beginning to work on my behalf now. Tachi would brag about his division wherever he went, and just like Tachi, my reputation began to grow even faster than the reality. One thing led to another, and after a few years I had three grants, which allowed my lab to expand.

About the same time, many of my colleagues at UCSF were beginning to struggle, the lab space was inadequate for growth, and grants were hard to obtain. The contrast was striking—and unfortunate—as I had left good friends behind. There were at least six other young faculty from UCSF who moved to Michigan the same time that I did, including one cardiologist with whom I shared a GI rotation at UCSF; he lived two doors down the street.

Life in Ann Arbor

Tachi and I began meeting in our driveways at 5:50 AM and jogged together for seventy minutes through Ann Arbor's back-country roads. It involved running through some fields and crossing the Huron River twice. Tachi was sure the route was ten miles, but by my measurements, it was under nine miles, which made for interesting debates. During those runs, I was tutored in the ways of the academic world. Tachi was very well connected with the GI research community, and was on one of the panels that reviewed grants for the NIH, called a Study Section. This permitted him to see grant applications from everyone in the field, and he likened it to a grocery store for new talent. Every time he reviewed a brilliant application from a promising young researcher, that person would be invited for a recruitment visit.

Over the first five to ten years, the long morning jogs were required to keep from getting too fat, as we had so many dinners with the recruitment candidates. I became an enthusiastic supporter and cheerleader for the VA during this time. When I arrived, there were just two of us in GI at the VA—myself and Jorge Gumucio, MD, a hepatology researcher. Five years later, we had ten in the GI Section, using all of our permanent positions, adding to this with grants and the VA career development award system. Tachi and I had come from the inside that system, and we knew exactly how to take advantage of it.

Coming to Michigan brought some unexpected insights. With Rudi's encouragement, we were convinced that we had the world's best GI Division at UCSF, and the grants and manuscripts coming from the division could support that contention. However, after arriving in Ann Arbor, I realized that we hadn't been as good at clinical gastroenterology in San Francisco, and that the Ann Arbor group was more broadly skilled in clinical medicine. I developed a close relationship with Tim Nostrant, MD, who was the clinical "kingpin" of our group. Interestingly, we were both born within twelve hours of each other on October 19 and 20, 1947, about 200 miles apart in upstate New York. Once we entered GI fellowship, we went in different academic directions, I to the research lab and Tim to the endoscopy lab. Tim had seen much more than I had—not to mention that for the prior five years, I had been practicing at a VA Hospital, and although I tried to know everything possible about colon cancer, there was a lot more to know. Repeatedly, I would encounter something new clinically, and not recognize what it was. I would call Tim, describe it, and he would say:

"Oh yeah—that's the x disease or a y complication."

He didn't swagger too much with his expertise in front of me, which made it easy. I respected what he brought to the table, and visa-versa. It was a very good arrangement, and it kept my learning curve steep, and enjoyment high. We became good friends, and as my birthday was the day before his, I could always get a rise out of him by saying:

"Wait until you get as old as I am." I was about twelve hours older, and got the same groan and eye-roll every time.

The GI Division under Yamada experienced an unprecedented period of success. Everyone got along like a family (a functional one, at that), and there was a very high sense of pride about being at that place at that time. Yamada was almost worshipped by the fellows and junior faculty. He convinced a substantial proportion to get involved in research and join the faculty. At one point, in about 1988, he was approached by three different medical schools for recruitment as a Department Chairman. He seriously considered one of these—Penn State in Hershey, Pennsylvania—and even challenged Bill Kelley by convincing ten of the GI faculty to leave Ann Arbor for Hershey with him. Fortunately, Kelley sweetened the GI resources enough that Tachi called the recruitment off. However, the fact that he had so many on board to move *en masse* was something that no one could have imagined. He was a phenomenon. We had monthly GI Division meetings in which we discussed what was happening in the division, chose our fellows, discussed possible recruitments, and generally supported one another. Even though Tachi made all the decisions, there was a democratic feel to the discussions. We also had annual photos of the GI Division, with Tachi proudly in the center, surrounded by his "family" of faculty members, fellows and technicians (*Figure 21*). I realized that we had never had one faculty meeting at UCSF, and never a single faculty or fellows' photo. Michigan was a happening place and churned out top recruitments to other medical schools.

Figure 21: GI Division Photo, University of Michigan. Fourth, fifth and sixth from the left, front row, Drs. Tim Nostrant, Tachi Yamada and Chung Owyang. (late 1980s)

The birth of a new era of research

At the UM, I dove deeper into the biochemistry of the altered glycoproteins I had identified in the first few years of my research using a microscope. I used fresh tissues and other animal models to extract the glycoproteins, and then went about the process of purifying various fractions from the mixture. The discipline was difficult, and there were few automated methods to analyze the molecules I was interested in. Everything was done painstakingly, as these large complex molecules had to be disassembled piece by piece and purified for individual analyses. I was publishing papers, but was not making the progress I really wanted, and we were nowhere near any kind of breakthrough in cancer. I knew it might turn out this way, but I was impatient for more. The search for a cause of familial colon cancer seemed as far away as it did when I was a medical student in 1973. There seemed to be no way to start looking for the genetic basis of the disease, and we still couldn't identify people at risk until an affected person developed a tumor. Moreover, their cancers looked like tumors that anyone else might get. We were stuck, and I was particularly on edge, since I wanted to solve one particular problem.

Starting in the late 1970s, the world of biomedical research was undergoing a gradual transformation from old-style analyses to a new type of biology. Very complex techniques were gradually coming within the grasp of investigators who were willing to take the time to add new analytical approaches to their toolboxes. I saw this happening, but it wasn't initially apparent how I could apply the new technologies to the problem I had selected. There was a new, parallel universe of science, complete with its own language and thought processes, and it took some time to recognize what it meant. So much had happened in science during my lifetime.

For example, in April, 1953, I was in first grade, and the structure of DNA was deduced by Watson and Crick. By 1966, I was already a sophomore in college, and relationship between the triplet genetic code and how the code was translated into amino acids and proteins was determined by Nirenberg, Khorana and others. By 1972, I was in my third year of medical school, and the first cloning experiments were reported by Herb Boyer and Stanley Cohen from UCSF and Stanford. I was growing up side-by-side with the evolving technologies, and none of it had been taught in any of my academic coursework. It was too new, too fresh, changing too fast. One had to keep reading and listening. The value of the Yale Medical School approach to education, which was not to teach what was known but rather the process of learning, had paid off. Along the way, automated methods for sequencing DNA were falling into the grasp of the ordinary scientist, and we all were trying to figure out how we could become familiar with and master these techniques, and apply them to the problems we had individually chosen to pursue.

In the late 1960s, J. Michael Bishop, MD had been studying poliovirus, but he abandoned this after the development of effective vaccines, and yielded to the allure of San Francisco. He joined the faculty of UCSF before it was a powerhouse, and began to work on retroviruses, since they seemed to cause cancer in certain animals. He was joined in 1970 by

Harold Varmus, MD, and they became a formidable team in the world of cancer research. By the mid-1970s, they realized that these viruses caused tumors by ferrying mutated copies of genes from one cell to another. The unexpected part of their work was that the cancer-causing genes had been picked up by the viruses from a host cell (chickens, in their particular case), and the virus served as a transmission vector and amplifying machine.

This led to the discovery that one could chop up DNA and deliver it into fibroblasts in culture plates. When a critical fragment of DNA was transferred, the fibroblasts looked a little bit like mini-tumors on the culture plate, and it was possible to then isolate the DNA fragment responsible for this transformation. They called these tumor-causing genes "oncogenes" triggering a revolution in our thinking about cancer, and won the Nobel Prize in Medicine or Physiology in 1989. I was at UCSF when they were reporting these discoveries, and couldn't help but take note. But the experiments they were doing involved unusual tumors in animals, it was not immediately clear how this was relevant to human cancer. Perhaps more importantly, the techniques seemed impossibly difficult for ordinary scientists. Moreover, it was in no way clear how this would lead us to an understanding of familial cancer syndromes. But, our time would come.

From 1979, when I started in Young Kim's lab, until the mid-1980s, I learned the biochemical techniques that were being used in his lab, and had to watch these new, exciting disciplines develop from the sidelines. As additional concepts developed one month after another, it gradually became clear that all cancers were caused by aberrations at the genetic level—not just the familial forms. I realized that I needed to be studying DNA, not glycoproteins.

Meanwhile, back at Johns Hopkins, Andy Feinberg and Bert Vogelstein (on the road not taken to Baltimore) were publishing work in basic science journals about how DNA was altered in cancer cells. As if we were in a Dickens novel, Feinberg was recruited to the Howard Hughes Medical Institute (HHMI) at the UM, and in 1986, we were at the same institution. He was interested in a process in which DNA was modified by the addition of methyl groups to cytosine (called DNA methylation). Positions in the HHMI were not only prestigious, they came with a funded salary and recurring laboratory funds, so the investigators didn't necessarily have to worry about having grants (even though they all did worry about it). The

HHMI investigators had the advantage that they didn't have to disclose what they were doing in a grant application until they were sure they were correct. They could perform high risk experiments with fewer concerns than the rest of us, who had to show continuous progress in writing, which disclosed our progress sooner than we wanted, and left us vulnerable to having our ideas poached.

One of the first tasks Andy and I undertook at the UM was to write a grant application on familial colon cancer—which we submitted even before he arrived. We had an additional co-investigator on the grant named Francis Collins, MD, PhD, who would later direct the Human Genome Project and eventually become Director of the NIH. We wrote the application in response to a "Request for Applications" from the NIH, which came with a specific topic and a short deadline for writing and submission. The grant was not funded, but it had a favorable review and provided an opportunity for Andy and me to get to know one another.

K-ras and colorectal cancer

In May 1987, a watershed finding was reported in the field of colorectal cancer. Two independent laboratories, one led by Bert Vogelstein, MD from Johns Hopkins and another led by Manuel Perucho, PhD, who was at Stony Brook, New York at that time, found that one of the Bishop-Varmus oncogenes (called *K-ras*) was frequently mutated in colorectal cancers. The papers appeared side-by-side in *Nature*. Finally, one of these oncogenes was linked to a common human cancer. Based upon what we knew about *K-ras*, it was also likely that this mutant oncogene was functionally important in the genesis of the cancer.

There was an interesting back story to these two publications, which appeared simultaneously without specific collaboration. Vogelstein's group finished their work and submitted a manuscript first. Then there was a scientific meeting, and the post-doctoral fellow involved in this work encountered the post-doctoral fellow from Perucho's group who was working on the same subject. Allegedly, Perucho's fellow was a sufficiently attractive woman that Vogelstein's fellow tried to impress her by boasting that their paper was under review in *Nature*. She immediately told Perucho about this, as their work was nearly finished, and they quickly submitted their own manuscript. Both were finally accepted and published in the same issue. Perucho was and is a passionate researcher, not to mention, competitive and interested in leaving his mark on science. It was however only the first time that Perucho was to feel the heat of competition with Vogelstein's group.

Tumor suppressor genes

Over the prior several years, it was recognized that there was a class of genes that were inactivated in the process of tumor formation. These genes normally functioned to ensure a mature form of cell development, restrain additional cell growth, and prevent cancers from evolving from normal tissues. They were consequently called "tumor suppressor genes". Whereas oncogenes could be identified on the basis of a sequence alteration (mutation) or amplification (multiple copies of the gene), tumor suppressor genes were inactivated or even disappeared from the tumor cells, and these alterations were somewhat harder to find. Vogelstein developed a clever way to identify the losses of these genes—or alleles, as each copy of the gene would be called—and published a pair of landmark papers in September 1988 in the *New England Journal of Medicine* and April 1989, in *Science*. He analyzed fifty-six colorectal cancers and compared the pattern of gene loss—which he called "allelic loss"—in the tumors compared to the normal tissues. Pieces of DNA were missing all over the genome, but tended to cluster in certain chromosomal locations in different tumors. Vogelstein presciently predicted that these clustered spots of allelic losses were places where tumor suppressor genes reside in our genome. This was essentially correct. Then, he analyzed a series of benign colon tumors called adenomatous polyps compared those results with what he found in cancer, and determined the progression of genetic alterations as tumors grew from the smallest adenomatous polyps, to larger ones, and eventually to a malignancy. He discovered that there was a sequential ordering of the genetic alterations, some of which were simple mutations, and others of which were losses of pieces of chromosomes. We now know that the story is much more complicated, but this was the first rational explanation for how colon cancers grew in a progressive way, and has been the framework for the characterization of many other tumors.

The "Vogelgram"

This was it. Tumors were caused by genetic alterations. There were lots of them, and they came in many varieties. Some were simple "point mutations" (change in the code), others were genetic losses. They occurred gradually and sequentially. Vogelstein and his colleague Eric Fearon, MD, PhD published their conceptual formulation with an iconic figure that came to be known as "The Vogelgram" (*Figure 22*). The boat was in the harbor, and it was essential for me to climb aboard before it set sail. I was following this amazing scientific revolution, but I didn't understand it sufficiently. I had to concentrate on each technique, and could not yet think quickly and creatively as a scientist must to determine how to pursue problems in the lab. I had to learn. There was only one way. I had to become a post-doctoral fellow again. I had to go back to the bench and learn a new set of skills.

Multistep Carcinogenesis (1990)

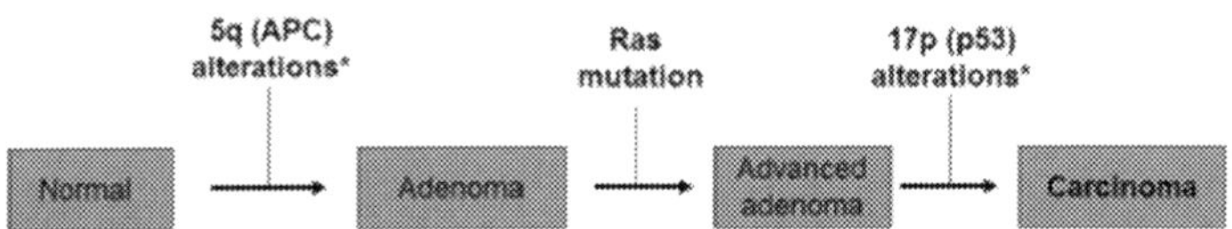

Figure 22: The Vogelgram**.** This is a scheme of the genetic events involved in the development of colorectal cancer. The concept, revolutionary at the time but seemingly obvious now, is that cancer develops through a sequential series of genetic alterations, and that explains why—at least in the colon—we had been able to identify the progressive pathological stages ranging from normal tissue to the benign stages (adenoma) to cancer, and why cancer didn't suddenly emerge as a fully developed malignant tumor. Vogelstein's group put the altered genes in sequence and attached them to the pathological stages of colorectal neoplasia in this iconic scheme, affectionately called the "Vogelgram".

Chapter 12

The Sabbatical (1990)

Recruitment Overtures

My decision to do a sabbatical in molecular biology has a deep back story, but in the end everything fell into perfect alignment, against any reasonable expectation. Our first six years in Ann Arbor were excellent; the family was happy and the lab had gotten into a number of new glycoprotein-related projects. Tachi would sing the praises of the UM GI faculty, and I got frequent overtures about recruitments to other institutions. It was nice to get the attention from other institutions, but life was good and I didn't bother pursuing any of them for the first five years. Then, in September of 1989, I got a call from Rex Jamison, MD, who was Chairman of Medicine at the University of Rochester, who asked me to look at the job as Chief of their Gastroenterology Division. This was somewhat interesting to me because of my roots in upstate New York, but also, my sister Alice lived there, and a college roommate, Jim Schubmehl, MD is a psychiatrist in Rochester. Also, when I was a student, the Department of Internal Medicine at the University of Rochester had a reputation as one of the best in the country. The irony was that I was passed over as an internship candidate in 1973, and sixteen years later, they wanted to recruit me into a position of leadership. Fate surely has a sense of humor.

An unexpected illness

At the end of October 1989, my mother had been living in south Florida and developed a mysterious illness. Her doctors in Fort Lauderdale could not come up with a diagnosis. I asked her to fly to the UM for an evaluation. When I picked her up at the airport on Thursday October 26, her face looked a little puffy, and she told me her story, which included an unexplained low potassium level, new hypertension, and blotchy skin lesions that had been attributed to the sun (but were also occurring in non-sun exposed areas). When we arrived at our home in Ann Arbor, she was unable to get herself out of the car without my help. Before we got into the house, I suspected she had Cushing's syndrome.

I got her an appointment to see the specialist in that condition at the UM, and he evaluated her the next morning. He agreed with my suspicion, and decided she needed a five day evaluation in the Clinical Research Unit at the UM Hospital to discover why she had this. We scheduled admission for Monday, Oct 30. Unfortunately, I had a previously scheduled trip to Kobe, Japan, for the international hereditary colorectal cancer meeting (called the International Collaborating Group on Hereditary Non-Polyposis Colorectal Cancer, or ICG-HNPCC). I dropped Mom off at the UM Hospital, got her admitted, and then went to the airport for the long flight across the Pacific Ocean. When I got to Kobe, Henry Lynch was there, and he was pleased to see me as we were among the few who recognized this problem nearly two decades earlier. On the first evening of the meeting, he wanted to introduce me to Burt Vogelstein, whom I had never met, and was by now a risen star in the field. Bert didn't attend the reception. Unbeknownst to me, luck was turning bad in Ann Arbor, and I would not run into Bert face-to-face for another five years.

I went to bed, got up early in the morning to jog, and when I got back to the hotel, Tachi was on the phone. Mom had gotten a CT scan, they found a large tumor on her adrenal gland that seemed to extend into her liver, and also found that she had suffered a clinically silent perforation of her colon, which required emergency surgery. They had taken her to the operating room, did what they could, but she had a catastrophic reaction to the colonic perforation and Cushing's syndrome and was desperately ill in the ICU, on a ventilator. I told the meeting organizers of my problem. I gave the first talk in the meeting, and then quickly left for my return home, not twelve hours after landing in Kobe. When I got to Ann Arbor, she was ill, and beginning a two year illness during which she was in the hospital for nearly eighteen months. She finally died of an adrenocortical carcinoma which invaded and destroyed her liver in November, 1991. By the time she died, we all knew that she had suffered too much and when she fell into a coma as a consequence of the tumor, we all felt relieved. We were all at her bedside at the time of her death, at sister Sue's home.

One minor consequence of Mom's illness was that I had totally lost track of the Rochester overture. In February, 1990, I got a call from Professor Dean Lockwood, MD from the University of Rochester, and he said, "I guess you are probably wondering why you haven't heard from Rex Jamison for the past few months." (In fact, our conversation had totally slipped my mind, under the circumstances.) He told me that sometime around New Year's Day of 1990, Rex had been sacked in some type of political upheaval at Rochester, and no one had picked up the gastroenterology recruitment until it fell to Lockwood. So, we resumed the discussion where it had dropped off several months ago. A month later, I flew out to take a look, and saw some value in a promotion and the proximity to family. I thought it over. Pat and I took a second visit. Meanwhile, Jamison landed on his feet in a position of leadership at Stanford. I never ran into him again.

Academic politics are constantly roiling. At this exact same time, Bill Kelley (Chairman of the Department of Internal Medicine at the UM) left Ann Arbor to become Dean at the University of Pennsylvania School of Medicine. A national search ensued for his replacement at the UM, and in the end, Tachi was appointed Chairman in mid-1990. This led to a search for Tachi's replacement as GI division chief at the UM. Tachi knew I would be interested in the position, but also, half a dozen of the others in our division also wanted the position, and it would be considered a choice job on a national level. This led to another Search Committee, and attendant intrigue.

Tachi and I went jogging one morning, and out of the blue, he said:

"Rick, I know you want this job, but you are not ready for it."

"Why not?"

"You need to push your science into molecular biology and genetics."

"I've been thinking about that too."

"You should learn molecular biology and retool your lab. Also, don't go to Rochester. You'll just get stuck in the glycoprotein business. You will be an expert in that, but it won't get you where you need to go in cancer research. You need to change." I agreed; he was correct.

He then suggested I should do a sabbatical, and that when I finished, he would give me the lab space at the University Hospital that he had gotten as part of his recruitment package. He would give me enough money to buy the equipment needed to convert my lab into this new area. I immediately agreed—while we were running—and it was to change my life. My good friend Chung Owyang, MD, who had been a member of the division since before I arrived, was chosen to serve as Tachi's successor. He has continued to serve as a highly respected Division Chief ever since then—over twenty-five years. In fact, under Chung's leadership, it was next to impossible to recruit the GI faculty away from Ann Arbor. Everyone loved Chung and his leadership style.

Sabbatical with Andy

My daughters ranged in age from fifteen to nine and were well-adjusted to their schools, so leaving Ann Arbor was not a good option for a sabbatical. I decided to look into spending time with Andy Feinberg's group, who was now at the University of Michigan Howard Hughes Medical Institute. I went to see him one afternoon in March of 1990, and told him that I needed to learn genetics and a new set of laboratory skills. He opened one of his lab refrigerators and showed me a group of Eppendorf tubes (small sealable plastic tubes for storing laboratory samples in a refrigerator or freezer) lined up in a rack. Andy boasted: "I purified these DNA samples at Hopkins several years ago, and they are still stable and good to use. Show me a protein or a glycoprotein like that". He simultaneously convinced me of the practical side of DNA biochemistry, while reminding me why that molecule has been entrusted by evolution to carry our genetic code from generation to generation. He was happy to have me join his group. After all, I was already an established scientist, and would work for him for free.

I decided to start in July, 1990. I had to figure out how to keep my lab running while doing this. I was chair of a major committee at the medical school, and I was getting into a totally new discipline. It wasn't going to be a time for rest. I applied for a six month sabbatical through the Department of Medicine, and it was granted to me. I was puzzled that only three people in a department of about 350 had applied for and were granted sabbatical time. Off I went.

Back in the saddle again

On July 2, 1990, I walked into Andy's lab, revisiting the sensation of being the "dumbest guy in the room" all over again. His lab was large, and I was given my own laboratory bench—one that had just been vacated, but my chair backed up against the radioactive waste container (a large rubber garbage can with a lid that was sometimes on and sometimes off). Every morning I scanned my chair and the surrounding floor and bench areas with a Geiger counter looking for evidence of radioactive contamination. Surprisingly, there never was a trace to be found. I got a copy of the standard lab manual for molecular biology, and began reading that at night. Everything was new and exciting. I loved every day of it.

I decided to launch straight into real experiments even before I had read very much, and saw value in continuously making *new* mistakes. Andy and I got together a week or so before the sabbatical officially began, and he asked me what I could do. I told him that I was a reasonably competent pathologist with colon cancer tissues, that I had collected some fresh samples of colon cancer, and frozen them in an airtight preservative for future use. He had a cryostat, which is an instrument that permits you to slice frozen tissues into very thin sections (like meat or cheese at the deli counter, only these slices were *really* thin), and place them onto glass slides. No one else was using it, but I figured out how to make it work. In short order, I was able to look at cancer specimens under the microscope, and using tissue stains on the frozen sections, could individually isolate and extract the normal tissue and cancer from the slides, as well as the intermediate stage between normal and cancer (which is the adenoma stage).

We decided to test the hypothesis advanced by Vogelstein's group about the sequence of genetic events that mediated the emergence of a full-blown cancer in the colon. On the first day in the lab in July, I cut "frozen sections" from the tumor samples, put the slides under a dissecting microscope, and using a scalpel blade, picked up tiny pieces of tissue under direct visual control, and placed each into separate Eppendorf tubes. Each piece potentially represented one of the visually recognized stages of cancer evolution, and our hypothesis was that each step was driven by a novel genetic alteration. We had normal and neoplastic tissues to study with minimal contamination. Now, the trick was to find a way to analyze the

DNA in each of these pieces of tissue, which were very small. I took care of the tissue dissection, and Andy was going to help me figure out how to analyze the DNA.

I met with Andy on a regular basis—every couple of days. He was astonishingly brilliant. It wasn't that he has a greater fund of information than everyone else (although that part was very good and complemented what I knew), it was the speed with which his mind worked that was so impressive. We were discussing a topic that involved an issue called "genetic linkage", which required determining a LOD score (and it doesn't matter what this is other than to note that it requires solving a moderately complicated mathematical equation) and he did it in his head—as we were talking. That said, he had strangely underdeveloped interpersonal skills. He would occasionally chew out a student or technician in my presence, and act surprised when I mentioned that the object of his derision might have had his or her feelings hurt. He acknowledged my assessment, but didn't really care, and the behavior never changed. So, you take your choice in life. I could tolerate the social oddities in exchange for the research training. I got what I wanted. I didn't join his lab to judge or change his approach to others. He gave it to me too, sometimes, and I learned from his blunt comments. It just wasn't my style.

DNA, PCR, and VNTRs

The first experiments were to extract DNA from these tiny pieces of tissue I had removed from the slides and determine what was happening in the DNA of each sample. Most of the other work done on the molecular genetics of cancer involved taking a large chunk of a tumor mass—which could include the cancer, normal tissue, adenoma and other elements mixed together—extracting the DNA, doing some type of analysis on the DNA, and comparing the cancer with normal tissue. That approach was the state-of-the-art in 1990. However, it took a lot of DNA to do most of those analyses, and this limited the precision with which we could focus on the discrete steps involved. Did these genetic changes occur all at once, or did they slowly evolve, step by step, as proposed? We had to microdissect the tissues to find out and look at small, well-defined samples.

What changed everything in the mid-1980s was the advent of the polymerase chain reaction—or PCR—which permitted us to amplify a specific DNA target a million times over. The amount of DNA one could extract from the very small pieces of tissue I was obtaining was too small to analyze using classical techniques. PCR provided a powerful tool to permit the next wave of experimentation. How did the ability to amplify DNA help?

Initially, Andy suggested that I use PCR to amplify "variable number tandem repeats" or VNTRs from the DNA extracted from these tiny samples to find chromosomal deletions. We have three billion nucleotides arrayed in a string in our DNA. Only 1.5% of this encodes for genes that produce proteins. These sequences are very similar between different people, which is why most humans are identifiable as members of a single species. But, the other 98.5% of our DNA is non-coding, and much of it tandemly repeated DNA sequences, the function of which is currently obscure. We began using VNTRs called "minisatellites", in which the repeated sequence is from 10-60 nucleotides long. The minisatelllite sequence is repeated like a series of beads on a string (*Figure 23*). DNA sequences are written using an "alphabet" of just four nucleotides: A, C, G, and T. These letters refer: adenine, cytosine, guanine and thymine. The beads of the VNTR are the repeated DNA sequences. Sometimes the repeated sequence consists of a one or two nucleotides; in other instances, the repeated sequence can be hundreds of nucleotides long.

VNTRs were valuable sequences for analysis because they are variable in the number of repeats from person to person. Everyone inherits a complete set of genes from each parent, so we have two copies of everything. Let's say you have one hundred of these necklaces, each with a different number of beads on a string. You could easily lay them out on a table and sort them in order according to the number of beads on each necklace, from the longest to the shortest. A few could be the same length, but there would be a lot of variation.

Now let's then say that each person owns exactly two necklaces, and necklaces in the population vary in their lengths. Depending upon how many different length necklaces there were in the population, from a statistical perspective, you might be able to identify people by the lengths of their two necklaces. VNTRs work the same way, as illustrated in *Figure 23.*

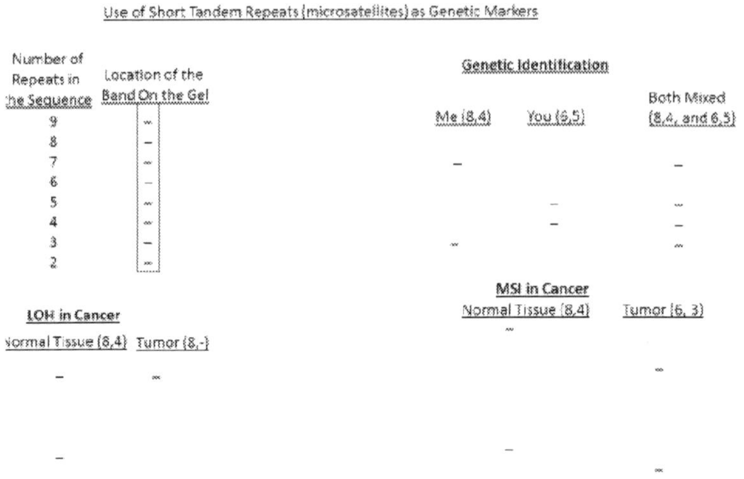

Use of Short Tandem Repeats (microsatellites) as Genetic Markers

Number of Repeats in the Sequence	Location of the Band On the Gel
9	–
8	–
7	–
6	–
5	–
4	–
3	–
2	–

Genetic Identification

Me (8,4) You (6,5) Both Mixed (8,4, and 6,5)

LOH in Cancer

Normal Tissue (8,4) Tumor (8,-)

MSI in Cancer

Normal Tissue (8,4) Tumor (6, 3)

Figure 23: Schematic explanation of the use of short tandem repeats (VNTRs or microsatellites). There is variability in the number of repeated elements at variable number tandem repeat (VNTR) or microsatellite sequences, but this has no strong effect on gene expression. This diversity in sequence appears to be random. In the upper left of the figure, we see that some in the population have 9, 8, 7, 6, 5, 4, 3, or 2 repeats at this location in their DNA, and we can identify each one by its location when separated by length on the analytical "gel". In the upper right, we can tell if we are looking at my DNA (as one allele has 8 repeats and the other 4), versus yours, which has one allele with 6 repeats and one with 5. Moreover, we can detect a mixture of our DNA when we find 8, 6, 5 and 4 in the same batch of DNA. In tumors, microsatellite analysis was initially used to detect loss of heterozygosity (LOH) in a cancer, as shown in the lower left in which my tumor has lost the chromosomal fragment containing the microsatellite with 4 repeats. The phenomenon of microsatellite instability (MSI) was discovered by Perucho and others, when they found that there were deletion or insertion mutations within the microsatellites, changing the length of the repeat and their subsequent positions on the gel. In the tumor shown above, the 8 allele lost two repeats, becoming a 6, and the 4 allele lost one, becoming a 3, and the mutant alleles move to a different position on the gel.

If you were working with necklaces, you could hold the necklace by the string at each end, and count the number of beads in-between. PCR permitted us to count the VNTR. These sequences were specifically chosen because they are highly variable in the population. When we did the PCR reaction on the normal tissue, some proportion of the population gave us a result containing two different sequences, because the mother and father contributed a different number of tandem repeats in that VNTR. We didn't care which parent contributed which piece; we just wanted to find two different "alleles" in the patient's normal DNA. The object of the experiment was to find two "PCR products" in the normal tissue, and one that was lost in the tumor. This phenomenon has had many names in cancer research, but the term "allelic imbalance" is the most accurate term for this. Vogelstein called this "loss of heterozygosity", or LOH.

We knew the chromosomal location of each VNTR from published reports. The concept was that the location of the LOH would suggest the chromosomal location of a possible tumor suppressor gene. When the chromosomes in cancer cells begin to go haywire, large chunks tend to be deleted, duplicated or rearranged. We now know that each tumor has a unique collection of genetic alterations, and that deletions are common in colon cancers. Some are common to many tumors, whereas others are more specific to one type of tumor. We were interested in the colorectal cancer-specific genes, and to test which were involved in the progressive steps between normal and cancer.

How do you find missing genes?

Other groups had already identified many of the major genetic targets of the progressive cancer-producing process. We were interested in discovering the tempo and sequence of these events during the evolution of a tumor. Most colon cancers have undergone multiple chaotic cellular divisions, and it was hard to understand how these heterogeneous events could be so variable in different tumors, yet still be involved in tumor cells growth. Presumably there would be some decipherable pattern to these genetic alterations.

Cells have evolved a brilliant strategy to prevent such mitotic catastrophes from surviving. When a cell does not divide perfectly, the two daughter cells each get imperfect copies of the genetic plan, and this should frequently have lethal consequences. Bad plans lead to failure. However, there are genes that direct a cell to stop growing, the ones we call "tumor suppressor genes". When these genes are lost, a cell might gain the capacity to overgrow its neighborhood, like an invasive weed.

For a bacterium, bad mitoses are not necessarily a problem. Mistakes are made during the replication of DNA, and if the cell still works, it survives. If it's a catastrophe, the bacterial cell dies which makes room for the neighboring cells that got it right. Multicellular organisms work differently, since the cells must have a high degree of cooperativity. To prevent mitotic aberrations, the nucleus in all higher organisms (beginning with yeast) have "cell cycle checkpoint genes" that monitor how accurately the replication of DNA is going. If it doesn't go just right, the cell hits the "abort" switch, and the cell dies. The concept of monitoring cellular mitosis has been extensively studied, and resulted in a Nobel Prize in 2001 to Paul Nurse, PhD, Leland Hartwell, PhD and Timothy Hunt, PhD.

The cell cycle checkpoints are diverse, complicated, and wonderfully efficient in preventing abnormal cellular mitoses from being perpetuated in daughter cells. However, in most cancers, some of the checkpoint controls have been disabled. When this occurs, the tumors have wild abnormalities in the number and structure of their chromosomes, called "aneuploidy". Once the cell cycle checkpoints are disabled, unbalanced mitoses take place, and some of the daughter cells may "delete" critical tumor suppressor genes. One could inactivate a tumor suppressor gene by a mutation—which is a frequent way for inactivation to happen. But, the results of mutations are unpredictable, and may disable a gene or have no effect. A highly efficient way to disable tumor suppressor genes is to delete them from the genome through an unbalanced mitosis, where one daughter cell gets both copies of a gene, and the other cell gets neither. The cell that deleted the tumor suppressor gene might then have a growth or survival advantage over its sister cell.

One of the hardest things to detect in a tumor is a piece of DNA or gene that isn't there. The problem is that a tumor consists of a mixture of pure cancer cells together with all of the supporting cells—the blood vessel cells, the connective tissues between the tumor cells, and even cells from the immune system that are sniffing around for trouble. In fact, in many tumors, the majority of cells in the mass are not cancer cells at all; these genetically normal collaborators are referred to as "stroma", and they constitute the tumor microenvironment. Vogelstein had shown, using whole chunks of colon cancers, that tumors frequently have an imbalance of the DNA in certain chromosomal regions. For example, he had found that part of the short arm of chromosome 17 (called "17p") and the long arm of chromosome 18 (called "18q") were unbalanced in three quarters of colon cancers compared to that person's normal DNA. In two landmark papers from 1988 and 1989, Vogelstein's group showed that these DNA deletions, or allelic imbalances, were preferentially occurring at specific chromosomal locations. The process presumably began randomly (we still aren't certain why), but the chromosomal losses that provided an advantage in growth or survival would be "clonally amplified" in the tumor. He concluded that there must be tumor suppressor genes on 17p and 18q. This was correct, and his landmark observation stands as a milestone in the history of cancer research. He reached this conclusion using the tools available in the 1980s. We were trying to refine this because of the availability of PCR, which we hoped would get us closer to the putative tumor suppressor genes.

Doing PCR on very tiny pieces of tissue

On the first day of my sabbatical, I turned on the cryostat and sliced thin sections from my frozen chunks of tumor, picked up tiny tissue pieces under the microscope, extracted the DNA from each piece, and performed PCR reactions. To my delight, I found that I could perform PCRs on the DNA from these tiny pieces, and identify the PCR products (defined amplified pieces of DNA) using a gelatinous film and an electric current (called polyacrylamide gel electrophoresis, or PAGE), which separated the amplified DNA fragments in a neat column, according to their size. When I did this, I felt like I had discovered something unique. I now know that other labs were thinking and doing the same thing, and working feverishly to exploit this new technique. I looked at my first successful experiment, taped the resultant photo of the "gel" in my notebook, marveled that I could amplify DNA from such a tiny fragment of tissue, and wondered if anyone in the world had seen this before. They had, but it was quite thrilling to me at the time. Furthermore, I realized that I had taught myself a new technique. No one in Andy's lab had done any of this previously. It was the power of collaboration at work. The sabbatical was becoming great fun, and I had been at it for only five weeks. This helped soften the blow when I learned that I was going to lose about fifteen percent of my salary while on sabbatical—something I didn't learn until I was about a month into it. I figured this was why only three people took sabbatical leave that year.

Andy had made the suggestion that we could use PCR to amplify VNTRs and then analyze the PCR products on polyacrylamide gels. When the technique worked, we got two "bands" on the gels: one would be the mother's allele and the other would be the father's. We could then compare the DNA from the tumor tissue with that from normal tissue. If there had been a deletion of a piece of DNA in the tumor, then one of the two "bands" would be missing in the tumor (*Figure 23*). If I could microdissect a whole tumor into a grid under the microscope, I could find out which chromosomal arms were deleted in each piece, reassemble the tumor like a jigsaw puzzle, and determine what was deleted at each step of tumor development. Given enough time, we might eventually find VNTRs that were very closely located to a large number of tumor suppressor genes. We knew that the chromosomal deletions were typically quite large, and the hypothesis was that the VNTR (which was functionally inert) would be lost along with the nearby tumor suppressor gene.

So, I looked up the published details on many VNTRs, and selected those that were close to the chromosomal positions of possible tumor suppressor genes involved with colon cancer. I started with my collection of frozen colon cancer specimens. This worked, but to get even more samples, I had to obtain tissues that had been archived in the Pathology Department after surgical resections of colon cancers. These samples had been fixed in formaldehyde and embedded in paraffin (the standard approach), which gave me access to a much larger group of samples that were well-characterized. I began getting help and important technical advice from two particular members of the Feinberg lab who were at adjacent benches: David Law, PhD, and Minoru Koi, PhD. Both were patient teachers and excellent colleagues. I began to find frequent deletion events in the tumors, and was greatly encouraged that we now had a powerful technique to analyze multistep carcinogenesis.

A mid-course correction to "CA repeats"

Once I started using the colon cancer samples from pathology, I found frequent chromosomal deletions in the tumor samples. Early success is a great motivator. As I looked at the results, however, I noticed that the deletions were substantially more common in the longer VNTR alleles. The deletions should have been random, occurring equally in the shorter allele or the longer one, but the genetic losses were occurring preferentially on the longest alleles. We calculated the sizes of the larger and smaller alleles, and realized that my results were an artifact of the way the tissues were "fixed". The formaldehyde, we realized, was breaking the DNA into small pieces, probably in the range of 500-1000 nucleotides, or even smaller pieces. The VNTR targets ranged in size from a few hundred nucleotides to several thousands. They would be broken to pieces in the fixation process, and the longer alleles would be more likely to have been broken. We would then not be able to amplify the longer, broken alleles, whereas the shorter ones were more likely to have been preserved. So, that approach was not going to work.

Andy and I discussed the problem. He then said:

"You are going to have to use 'CA repeats'".

I responded: "What are they?"

His reply: "Get out of my office and read some more." That was it. Get out and read.

What are CA repeats?

So, I started to read more about repeated DNA sequences. Human DNA contains over a million copies of a repetitive sequence from the "Alu family", which are considered "short interspersed nuclear elements (or SINEs—we love abbreviations in science). These sequences are imperfectly repeated elements of about 300 nucleotides, and this family alone makes up about 10.7% of our genome! However, I found that another common VNTR in the human genome is made up of repetitive elements that are just two nucleotides long, C-A, and these are called "CA repeats".

Tandem repeats in which the repetitive element is very short (one to six bases long) are called "microsatellites". These are very common in the genome, and again, the number of repeated elements at each of these locations ("loci") is variable throughout the population, so panels of these microsatellite sequences have been developed to "fingerprint" DNA, and essentially, it is possible to find a unique microsatellite fingerprint for every person on the planet. The value of CA repeat microsatellites was that they were small (the entire repeat cassette is usually under 200 nucleotides long), and within the range of PCR using the formalin-fixed, paraffin-embedded tissues. In addition, a scientist at the Marshfield Clinic in Wisconsin named James Weber, PhD, had developed a technique for rapidly characterizing these, and was publishing the details of each one, including how likely was each person to have two alleles that were not the same lengths. I called him up, and he sent me a print-out that was several inches high of all the CA repeats he had characterized, their chromosomal location, and the conditions for doing the PCR. I had access to a large number of colorectal cancer specimens from pathology, and a seemingly limitless number of microsatellite sequences that were PCR-friendly from which I could map out the sequence of events during the evolution of a colorectal cancer. Luck was coming our way. I had no idea how much was just around the corner.

The lab migrates from glycoproteins to microsatellites

By Thanksgiving of 1990, I realized that I was able to perform the techniques that I needed to convert the focus of my own lab from glycoprotein biochemistry to tumor genetics. In December, I started to move the performance of the experiments from Andy's lab at the HHMI on the main campus to my lab at the VA hospital, about half a mile away. You could see the University Hospital from the VA, and shuttles ran back and forth regularly. Tachi Yamada made good on his promise to provide the funds to retool the lab. We bought thermocyclers ("PCR machines") and apparatuses to separate the PCR products on polyacrylamide gels.

A post-doctoral fellow from Japan, Juichi Sato, MD, PhD, joined my lab and mastered the art of microsatellite analysis. I hired a technician to cut the colon cancer specimens and place them on glass slides for us to microdissect. Now we had to analyze enough samples to make sense of the progressive genetic changes in cancer, assuming that not every tumor would be the same. We obtained every variety of colon cancer we could find. We collected samples of adenomatous polyps, the precursors of colon cancer. We collaborated with a gastroenterologist who had worked with me as a fellow when I was at UCSF, Bob Bresalier, MD. He collected thirty-two specimens each of which contained normal tissue, the adenomatous polyp precursor, and cancer—all in the same specimen, an invaluable contribution that he shared.

We worked on this project from the beginning of 1992 until 1994, and eventually published what would be an important paper in *Nature Medicine* in 1995. We confirmed the role of the *APC* gene (which was on chromosomal arm 5q) in mediating the emergence of the first neoplastic lesion in the colon—the benign adenomatous polyp. We found that there was a chaotic series of chromosomal losses (on chromosomal arm 18q) in the progressively more "dysplastic" (cancer-like) portions of the benign adenomatous polyp. We had Bob's thirty-two slides that contained normal, premalignant and malignant tissues read by an expert GI pathologist, Henry Appelman, MD, who was "blinded" to all of our genetic results. We had picked multiple small pieces of tissue off the slides, numbered the "holes" to identify where the tissue had been taken, and then determined exactly which cells had been removed for analysis. Henry read the slides, identified each group of cells removed, and gave us a definitive diagnosis for each piece. When we broke the code, we found a perfect correlation between loss of chromosomal arm 17p and the appearance of colorectal cancer from the antecedent adenomatous polyp. We felt an enormous sense of accomplishment, as Vogelstein's group had identified the *p53* gene on 17p as the tumor suppressor gene involved in this process, and our work confirmed that the loss of the gene occurred precisely at the moment of the "adenoma-to-carcinoma" conversion. It never happened earlier. That was a genuine cancer gene.

The Michigan HHMI

I recall my five months in the Howard Hughes Medical Institute (HHMI) as a time when my learning curve shot upwards in the way it did as a medical student. Other members of the HHMI at that time included Francis Collins, MD, PhD, who later became director of the National Institutes of Health; Andy Feinberg, MD, MPH, who later took the endowed chair in Genetics at Johns Hopkins; Gary Nabel, MD, PhD who headed the NIH Vaccine Research Center in 1999, and later became Chief Scientific Officer of a large pharmaceutical firm; Craig Thompson, MD, who first headed the cancer center at the University of Pennsylvania and then became President of the Memorial Sloan Kettering Cancer Center in New York City; Jeffrey Leiden, MD, PhD, who became CEO of a large pharmaceutical firm after his time in Michigan; and David

Ginsburg, MD, who is a leader in the field of blood clotting, and shared office space with Andy while I was there. I sometimes felt that you could get smarter just eating lunch and breathing the air in the place. There were some extraordinary minds at work, and they got a phenomenal amount of financial support from the HHMI. Those were the days, and it is hard to believe that so much occurred in those five months.

Chapter 13

SOLVING LYNCH SYNDROME (1990-1994)

While I was in the process of catching up with the rest of the world in tumor genetics, abundant progress was being made elsewhere. In fact, more had been accomplished in our understanding of colorectal cancer between 1987 and 1992 than in all the years of colon cancer research prior to 1987. However, what happened between May, 1993 and the end of 1996 was unprecedented in cancer research.

Finding the gene for familial adenomatous polyposis (FAP)

When I was a medical student, the only recognized form of familial colorectal cancer was the disease called FAP. This was a clear-cut autosomal dominantly inherited disease in which the affected individuals begin to develop colonic polyps in their teenage years. For many, when the disease reaches full bloom, the colon can be filled with thousands of polyps, and cancer of the colon is an inevitable consequence. The polyps are "ordinary" *per se*, and it is thought that only a small percentage (perhaps five percent or fewer) eventually become a cancer. But in FAP, the overwhelming number of polyps makes it likely that at least one is likely to become cancerous. Moreover, the median age to develop colon cancer is about forty years, three decades earlier than usual. No one had any idea what gene was involved, or even what kind of gene might do this. By the end of the 1980s, we knew the location and function of only a few disease genes. There was no facile approach for finding genes, and it required a major, focused effort by the best genetics researchers in the world to find each disease gene. Even if you were sequencing DNA right in the middle of the gene of interest, it was difficult to know you were actually *there*.

In 1986, a surgeon from Roswell Park Hospital (where my father had his surgery in 1970) named Lemuel Herrera, MD identified a patient who had FAP, as well as several other seemingly unrelated developmental abnormalities. Neither parent had any of these features. One explanation for such an occurrence is that the patient's nucleus had lost a chunk of a chromosome—a piece that contained multiple genes—during the formation of the sperm, egg, or in the early embryonic developmental period. Herrera asked Avery Sandberg, MD, DSc, a well-known expert in cytogenetics, for a chromosomal analysis of the patient. A large deletion was found on chromosome 5q (the long arm of chromosome five), and they correctly predicted that the gene for FAP would be found in this region.

This finding led many groups on a hunt for what genes in this region of chromosome five were deleted in this patient. In 1987, a British group led by Walter Bodmer, PhD confirmed that the FAP gene was in this region, and narrowed its chromosomal location to 5q21-q22. Then, in 1991, a group of collaborators that included Bert Vogelstein, his associates Kenneth Kinzler, PhD and Yusuke Nakamura, MD, PhD, a group led by Ray White, PhD from the University of Utah, and several others, collaboratively identified the gene that caused FAP, which was either mutated or deleted in affected families. In a remarkable display of cooperation, they published four articles simultaneously in the journals *Science* and *Cell* on August 9, 1991. They called it the *APC* gene, for *adenomatous polyposis coli*. Although this was an incredibly talented group of outstanding scientists, I imagine that many of them had never met a patient with FAP, and the name of the *APC* gene came from an arcane term once used for the disease. Cooperation was high at the time, but was to go out of style when the competition heated up for the Lynch Syndrome genes.

The gene responsible for FAP encodes a protein with a unique structure previously unseen, and its function is to regulate the intracellular concentrations of the protein β-catenin, which is the main driver of growth in colonic epithelial cells. Most of us are born with two copies of *APC*. If only one copy of the *APC* gene is defective, nothing abnormal happens. However, when both alleles of *APC* are inactivated or deleted in the colon, there is no ability to regulate the amounts of β-catenin in the cell, and the colonic epithelium produces many more cells than are lost each day. The cells pile up on one another, and this permits polyps (bumps in the mucosa) to emerge from normal colonic tissue. This mechanism took everyone by surprise, and reminded us that nature has her own way of doing things, and our job is to keep the level of science high, keep it honest, observe carefully, and learn.

FAP is a serious disease, and affects about one in 7,000-10,000 people around the world. It results in innumerable adenomatous polyps of the colon and eventually cancer in almost every affected person. It can usually be controlled by removing the colon surgically, although there are other clinical consequences of having a mutated copy of the *APC* gene in every cell of the body. Studies of *APC* also confirmed the concept of the tumor suppressor gene. The protein produced by the gene plays an essential role in controlling the growth of colonic (and some other) tissues, and its *loss* leads to excessive proliferation and the growth of a tumor. So, it is a "tumor suppressor". This is very different from an oncogene (from Bishop and Varmus fame), which plays a role in cancer by overactivity. Oncogenes act positively and tumor suppressors work negatively. Vogelstein's multistep model proposed that a combination of events at both kinds of genes (and other events in other instances) are required for a cancer to occur.

The tumor suppressor gene concept also helped us understand one way a familial predisposition to cancer could occur, and how a person can be born looking perfectly normal, but be at increased risk for a disease involving multiple colonic polyps or cancer. In FAP, the disease is inherited by the transmission of a single mutant *APC* gene to a child. This is a classic autosomal dominant mode of transmission, and on average, half the offspring will be affected. The presence of the single mutant gene (an inactivated form or a deletion of the gene) either produces no abnormality, or a very minor one. In the case of tumor suppressor genes, a "second hit" occurs in a colonic cell which inactivates the other copy of *APC*, that is, the one inherited from the uninvolved parent. This is referred to as a somatic mutation, since it is not passed on to the next generation through the germ cells. It is the loss of both copies of *APC* that permits unregulated growth—which leads to cancer as more genetic alterations accumulate in that cell. In this regard, the disease works like a recessive disease at the tissue level, requiring a defect in both copies of the gene. This concept was confirmed when multiple groups showed that there was loss or mutation of the other copy of the *APC* gene in the adenomatous polyps or cancer. FAP and *APC* were huge educators for colon cancer researchers.

Bert Vogelstein later stated that understanding the genetic events in FAP represented the "training wheels" for the next milestone. Although we didn't know it at the time, Lynch Syndrome is perhaps ten times more common than FAP; it was just harder to know who had it. It is possible to identify most cases of FAP because of the large number of polyps, but patients with Lynch Syndrome have no abnormalities to indicate their condition. As a consequence, there was no way to know who had the disease until a tumor occurred; even then, there was nothing distinctive about the tumors when they occurred. Not surprisingly, even into the early 1990s, many argued that there was no such distinct disease. Even Henry Lynch used the term "hereditary non-polyposis colorectal cancer" or HNPCC, illustrating how the more readily identifiable FAP dominated our thinking at the time. But, if it wasn't familial polyposis, why mention it in the name of the disease?

It is easier passing closed windows on the first floor

In early 1993, my lab had moved from the old laundry room in the basement of the Ann Arbor VA Hospital to one of the research buildings on the medical school campus, as Yamada had promised. We were collecting a lot of data from colon tumors using microsatellite analysis—essentially using microsatellites as landmarks to localize the allelic imbalances (gains and losses in DNA) in tumor specimens. Chromosomal gains might indicate the presence of oncogenes; losses might suggest tumor suppressor genes. My lab was supported by three federal grants at that time, all of which had been focused on abnormal glycoproteins in cancer. I knew I had to change this, and was trying to convert all three grants into those focused on tumor genetics during the renewal process, which typically comes up every five years. The problem was that I had no publication record in the field—and was not to have my first published paper using these techniques until 1994. I was so involved in redirecting the lab that my publication record slowed down, and I had nothing to show in tumor genetics. I was passed over for an honorary medical research society called the "Young Turks", when nominated just before my forty-fifth birthday—which is the oldest one can be elected into this group. This was disappointing to me, but reflected the reality of where the field was and what I had published by that time. My first attempt to redirect a grant application into tumor genetics was rejected. More disappointment.

At that time, the NIH gave an applicant three chances with an application—the initial submission and two subsequent revisions in response to the critiques. Three strikes, and you are out for that idea. By March 1993, I had written the second (and last permitted) revision of a renewal application for one NIH grant, refocusing it on the new approaches I had learned on my sabbatical. I had let a second NIH grant lapse because it was directed on a separate issue and was going to be a distraction for the new push. I had written a renewal application for my VA grant based on the microsatellite work, but had only preliminary data and no publications in the field.

I was pretty worried about the challenge, and wondered if I would survive this transition. One snowy March morning in Michigan in 1993 I looked out the window from my first floor office and chuckled to myself. If I jumped out, I wouldn't hurt myself since I would fall about three feet into snow. There is more than one way to "keep passing the open windows", and at this time it was to live on the first floor during the winter in Michigan and to keep the windows shut. I considered alternative academic career options, but decided to put all my chips on the table to solve the hereditary colon cancer mystery. I had come a long way to get this far, I knew that tumor genetics could finally get me closer to the Lynch Syndrome answer, and I felt that this was the way to do it. I had no idea how close we were.

"What's this?"

One day in the fall of 1992, Juichi Sato, MD, PhD, the research fellow working with me and doing most of the microsatellite analyses, showed me an inexplicable result on one of the polyacrylamide gels we used to characterize the microsatellites in DNA. In the middle of a row of PCR products from a tumor sample was a single result in which the amplified DNA fragment was smaller than expected, and I concluded it could not have come from that patient. The DNA fragment of interest was about 200 nucleotides long, and located outside of any gene that made a protein. We were using these microsatellite sequences as mapping markers, and assumed that they were of no functional significance. Therefore, these sequences could not drive tumor growth if mutated, and we didn't expect to find mutant versions in tumor DNA.

Neither Juichi nor I had ever seen this before. It made no sense that there might be a mutation in this random, non-functional segment of DNA. We discussed it, and I told him that it was unlikely that we had isolated a mutation in a randomly selected 200 nucleotide target from cancer tissue. There was no precedent for this, so he must have mixed up this person's DNA with that from another person. I asked him to go back to the original tumor tissue, and repeat the experiment. He did this, and a few days later he just came to me and showed me the exact same result. There was no mistaken identification, just an inexplicable mutation in an unimportant DNA sequence. We looked at each other and shrugged. I took it to Andy Feinberg, and he shrugged. No one thought this could be anything other than a lab error. I should have been more persistent, but the fact was, I didn't know enough about genetics at that time. In fact, until that time, no one did.

Unexpected good luck

Not having a grant to support your lab is a very big problem, as universities and research institutes usually don't provide much (if any) financial support for research labs; they just give you a hunting license. Just when I feared I might be out of luck, things began to change—first slowly, then faster. In 1992, a family from Minnesota with a foundation and a familial problem with colon cancer gave me $120,000, out of the blue with no strings attached, to study hereditary colon cancer. I have never met them, but the seed money they provided ultimately gave rise to a grant that is still funded over twenty years later. I had to fight Yamada a couple of times to keep him from taking a share of the money. I put the money into a university account, waiting for the right time to use it. I told him that this was for hereditary colon cancer and nothing else. I protected it like a mother cub, and put the funds into a university account waiting for the right time to strike.

Then, in April 1993, I got news that my VA grant was funded for another five years even though I had no papers published in the field. They trusted that I could do the work. Third, also in April, the NIH gave me a "Shannon Award", which was a bridging grant of $100,000 to get me through the year until my grant renewal application would have its third (and final) review. I was saved by a three-headed *deus ex machina*. So, my aspirations had a one year reprieve. But I had no idea what a year was about to blossom. Once again I realized that there is no substitute for good luck.

The saga of Manuel Perucho and microsatellite instability

In May, 1993, the field of hereditary colorectal cancer experienced an explosive transformation. Three laboratories, working independently, all discovered the secret to Lynch Syndrome at the same time. Each brought a unique piece to the table. The first among them was Manuel Perucho, PhD, the one from the mutated *RAS* gene story and the race with Vogelstein to publish their papers in *Nature* in 1987. Like the rest of us, he was looking for tumor suppressor genes using microsatellite analyses. He utilized a variation on the theme in which multiple PCR targets were chosen arbitrarily and the DNA amplified all at once, in a so-called multiplex reaction. Literally, the PCR primer sequences, which determine the targets of the DNA to be amplified by PCR, were selected by rolling dice; the technique was consequently called "arbitrarily primed PCR". By using just the right number of randomly selected primers to amplify DNA from normal colon and colon cancer, he would generate several thousand PCR products that were separated by size using gel electrophoresis, and each result would be specific for one person's DNA—a unique fingerprint. Perucho used this to hunt for differences between normal tissue and tumors. He separated the PCR products, placed the normal and tumor results side-by-side, and looked for difference between the tumor and that person's normal tissue. If he compared two gels taken from different normal tissues from the same person, they looked identical. He then compared the DNA from cancer tissue with the normal DNA from that patient, looking for deletions of one or more of the PCR products in the cancer—allelic imbalance. Naturally, he found multiple examples of allelic imbalance, as predicted by the Vogelstein paradigm. But, his careful eye also noticed that in a small proportion of the tumors, instead of allelic deletions there were changes in the sizes of the PCR products; some of the bands were smaller, and moved further down the gel. This is just what Juichi Sato had showed to me.

Perucho first recognized this in early 1992. More importantly, he discovered the reason some of the PCR products had shifted. Deletion mutations had occurred within the microsatellite sequence itself and changed its length—not what anyone was looking for or expecting. We had all been using the microsatellites as markers of a genetic loss adjacent to the microsatellite sequence, and never suspected these "marker" sequences would themselves be mutated. Microsatellites were a tool for finding the adjacent genes that were functionally important in cancer. Perucho showed that these non-coding sequences were mutated at a high frequency in about 12% of colon cancers. He estimated that in this group of tumors there were more than 100,000 such mutations!

Perucho extracted the mutated PCR products from the gels for DNA sequencing, and found that the mutated sequences were simple *mononucleotide repeats* (which are repetitive runs of the same nucleotide, such as AAAAAAAA…. or TTTTTTT…., etc.) and *dinucleotide repeats* (our old friends, the CA repeats). He also found that the colorectal cancers with these strange microsatellite mutations were slightly different clinically than other tumors, and were significantly less likely to harbor mutations in the *RAS* and *p53* genes compared to other colorectal cancers. One of the patients he studied had four separate tumors showing this pattern, raising the possibility that there could be some constitutional form of this. It is considered appropriate to name a new process when you discover it, so that others will know what to call it. Manuel came up with the unfortunate mouthful—"ubiquitous somatic mutations in simple repeated sequences," and suggested that it reflected a new mechanism or pathway for carcinogenesis. He was the only person ever to use that term, but it actually did represent a novel mechanism for tumor formation.

On April 9, 1992, there was a scientific meeting in Toledo, Spain near Madrid, and Perucho was involved in its organization. He was able to get Bert Vogelstein to participate, which added to the meeting's luster. Bert discussed his work on multistep carcinogenesis in the colon involving the genes *APC*, *RAS* and *p53*, and reported that one could find these mutant genes in feces and urine. Manuel sat next to Bert for much of the meeting, and discussed his findings on the mutated microsatellite sequences, and called this catastrophic process the "mutator phenotype" at the meeting. This was the first time he had discussed this in public. Being careful not to disclose too much before this group of experts in his own field, he did not mention that the mutations were occurring in microsatellite sequences during his lecture. He spoke too long (some scientists regularly do this), so there was no time for questions from the audience after his talk. Apparently after one of the other talks, the moderator, Robert Weinberg, PhD, a major contributor to the oncogene concept and our understanding of cancer, asked the audience if there might be "two different pathways" to colon cancer. Manuel thought there was, but he remained silent and no one pursued that conversation. After the session, Manuel and Bert picked up their slides from the speakers' room at the same time, and Bert asked Manuel what kind of sequences were involved in this process. Manuel wanted to impress Bert, so he told him that they were mononucleotide and dinucleotide repeats—microsatellites.

At this time, Bert had gained considerable prominence because of his work on multistep carcinogenesis, for finding the gene for FAP, and other work on cancer-related genes such as *p53*. He had been elected to the prestigious National Academy of Sciences, which gave him the privilege of publishing five papers of his choice each year in the journal the *Proceedings of the National Academy of Sciences, USA,* also called *"PNAS"*. In some instances, the member of the academy might select reviewers who would be more friendly to a novel and "out of the box" concept, which can reduce the time and hassle required for publication. Manuel knew that Bert might be able to help get this novel concept published. A few months after the Toledo meeting, Manuel sent a draft of his manuscript to Bert and asked him to support its publication in *PNAS*. Bert looked at the paper, and found it "surprising, intriguing, and potentially exciting", but suggested that the paper needed some editorial improvement, needed to be shortened considerably (as *PNAS* has strict word limits). He offered to hold one of his five prized allotted publication slots until Manuel could make these changes, and offered to discuss the best ways to address these concerns. However, Manuel interpreted this as a rejection, said that he was "shocked" by the response, and furthermore, accused Bert of giving Manuel's NIH grant application a poor score at a recent review. Bert had actually never seen Manuel's NIH grant application, but it was the beginning of Manuel's frustration in getting his novel concept published, and fueled antagonistic feelings towards Bert.

In October, 1992, Manuel submitted his manuscript to the journal *Cell*, and specifically noted that Vogelstein had provided helpful comments on the work in his cover letter. *Cell* is another prestigious journal, asks for a lot of data and proof in a manuscript, and it can take a long time with multiple revisions to publish there. This journal gets many of the best manuscripts for consideration, and the editor must make some difficult decisions—not all of them correct, of course. The editor, Ben Lewin, PhD accordingly asked Bert for advice with Manuel's novel concept, and again, Bert responded in writing that the work was "fascinating, unexpected and intriguing", and "appropriate for publication as a full length article in *Cell*". He made some comments about technical issues with the work but added that these could easily be addressed with additional controls—the same comments he had given Perucho previously, which indicated that Bert had been involved in this review as well. He gave the manuscript a very high rating—eight on a scale of ten—which was identical to the other reviewer's score. So far, so good.

But, new concepts can be hard to sell. The Editor of *Cell* rejected the paper on the grounds that he thought the paper did not have sufficient mechanistic evidence to call this a new "pathway" to tumor development, which was not actually a reflection of the reviews. Perucho was furious again, and suspected that Bert was being obstructionist about his concept. Manuel then sent Lewin an email containing a few choice profanities, and Lewin responded that he should probably never submit another article to *Cell*. Perucho responded by suggesting that the editor stick his journal in a safe, warm, personal hiding place. He showed me this email exchange, but propriety prevents me from reproducing it here word for word.

Vogelstein and his consortium were, at this time, very focused on discovering the basis of familial colorectal cancer (largely known as HNPCC to those who believed in it at all), and was not directly working on Manuel's concept of a novel pathway. Manuel's concept was recognizably novel and interesting, but tangential to their interests. However, an idea this rich and important will eventually be discovered by others who, just like Perucho, work carefully and then stumble upon it. Conversely, Manuel had no prior experience with or insight into familial cancer. Consequently, there was no good reason why Bert or his group would want to hinder or diminish Manuel's progress. Bert has always given Manuel credit for discovering microsatellite instability, and I have never heard him suggest anything else.

Time was slowly ticking by, and on November 13, 1992, Perucho finally sent his manuscript to *Nature*, which may be the most difficult journal of them all in which to publish. More than six months had passed since Manuel had first publically aired his new concept. The manuscript was returned for revisions on January 12, 1993. After more exchanges back and forth, *Nature* finally accepted the paper in mid-March, but with the provision that he cut the size of his manuscript (substantially) from a longer "Article" to a shorter "Letter". There is nothing second-rate about a Letter in *Nature*, but Manuel was furious once more, and put the manuscript aside for a week or so to settle down. Unfortunately for him, when May arrived, and he would become even more enraged.

First, Thibodeau (May, 1993)

While Perucho was being put to task by journal editors with his proposal of a novel "pathway" to colon cancer, two other groups were finding exactly the same thing. Stephen Thibodeau, PhD is a molecular genetics researcher at the Mayo Clinic in Rochester, Minnesota, and he had been using microsatellite analysis like everyone else to characterize allelic imbalance in colorectal cancers. Like the rest of us, he was using PCR on the panel of CA repeats that James Weber, PhD (the one from the Marshfield Clinic in Wisconsin) was discovering and sharing. Steve had access to a large number of tumor specimens at the Mayo Clinic, and selected ninety for analysis. Again, he was using markers that were linked to the *APC* gene on 5q, the *p53* gene on 17p, other yet unidentified colon cancer-related genes on 18q, plus a few other locations. By early 1992, Thibodeau found mutated CA repeats in a portion of colorectal cancers, and suspected this represented a novel process of tumor formation. He didn't submit his paper for publication immediately, as the Mayo Clinic wanted to secure a patent on the concept. He didn't know that other labs were finding the same thing at the same time, or the degree of competition going on silently.

When you read the articles that appeared in this time frame, it was clear that everyone was searching in the same places with essentially the same tools. However, Thibodeau saw something that others had not, namely that there were mutations within the CA repeats in about 28% of all tumors. (This is essentially what Perucho had found, unbeknownst to Thibodeau, although they used slightly different criteria to define the abnormal tumors, so Thibodeau's numbers were higher.) However, Thibodeau was not initially aware of the eventual implications of this finding for hereditary colorectal cancer. He tried to categorize the tumors based upon the magnitude of the mutational deletion within the microsatellites, and by the number of different mutations they found in each tumor. This detail ended up being relatively unimportant. However, he cleverly noted that the tumors with these mutations were more likely to be located in the proximal colon, and that patients with these tumors had a better chance at surviving their tumor. Incidentally, these are features of Lynch Syndrome. He concluded that the clustering of microsatellite mutations within a subset of the tumors indicated that something special was going on in that group, and like Perucho, suggested that this might be an "independent pathway" to tumor development. Better yet, he came up with the name that has stuck to this process: *microsatellite instability.* He submitted his paper to *Science* on March 3, 1993. It was initially rejected. However, he called the editor shortly after receiving the negative review, and the editor indicated that they had changed their opinion about the work. If he would respond effectively to the criticisms, they would reconsider publication. It was published in the May 7, 1993 issue of *Science.*

Then, Vogelstein and de la Chapelle

That was not the only landmark paper to appear in the May 7 issue of *Science.* Bert Vogelstein had established an international consortium that included the Finnish gene hunter, Albert de la Chapelle, MD, PhD. They had a collection of families with hereditary colorectal cancer, and their primary focus was to find the genetic basis of Lynch Syndrome. Instead of using microsatellite markers to look for more tumor suppressor genes, they were using them to map the genome to find the chromosomal location of the Lynch Syndrome gene. This involved the use of "linkage analysis", which generates the aforementioned LOD scores. Let's say that you have 300 microsatellite markers scattered evenly throughout the genome, you know where each is located, and these provide an individual fingerprint for each person, since the sequence lengths of microsatellites are variable throughout the population, and each individual will have a personal pattern. You could then record the variations at each of the 300 sites, and within a single family, you could link the DNA-based information with whether or not a person from the Lynch Syndrome family did or did not have the disease (assuming you could figure that out). If the gene you are looking for is located close to one of your microsatellite markers, then, within that family, one can calculate the odds or likelihood that the gene of interest is "linked" to the marker. CA repeats were favored tools for this type of gene hunting.

Linkage analysis goes like this. Let's say that you analyze a CA repeat in one hundred people, and you find that some people have 20 CA repeats at a particular microsatellite (that is, 20 CA pairs for a total sequence of 40 bases), but other people might have 21, 22, 23, 24, 25, 26 or more repeats. So, even though most humans' DNA is very similar, it is quite variable at microsatellite sequences. Let's give these "alleles" arbitrary names: "a" (for 19 CA repeats), "b" (for 20 CA repeats), "c" (for 21 repeats), "d" (for 22 repeats), and so on. We get DNA from both parents, so each person has inherited two copies of each CA repeat, and each person would have an individual pattern of alleles at that particular "locus". This could be aa, ab, ac, ad, bc, or any combination of alleles. It is quite easy to use PCR to characterize the combination of alleles at each of these microsatellite sequences, and then determine if a particular pattern corresponds to the disease process in a family. If a particular microsatellite locus used for mapping is located on a different chromosome from the true disease gene, the microsatellite fingerprint is not "linked" to the disease, and the relationships are random. However, if the microsatellite locus is (by chance) located inside the gene or very close to it, then there will be a very high concordance between the CA repeat allelic pattern and the disease pattern—in that family. The farther apart the gene of interest and the microsatellite are, less "linkage" exists, and the LOD score is lower. So, if you have enough genetic markers and you have a family that is large, and if you are very patient (and lucky), you can eventually map a genetic characteristic to a specific spot in the genome, and start looking for responsible gene, which should be nearby.

The person who was doing the linkage analysis for two large Lynch Syndrome families (one from Canada, one from New Zealand) was Lauri

Aaltonen, MD, PhD, with de la Chapelle's group in Finland. He recalled the moment of discovery very specifically to me. At 3:45 PM on the afternoon of Saturday March 13, 1993, he found that the gene responsible for Lynch Syndrome in one family was located on chromosome 2p ("p" indicates the short arm of the chromosome), which had previously not been on any cancer researcher's radar screen. The CA repeat that led to the discovery was called D2S123. He was particularly happy, as this was the 345th marker he had analyzed in this study of these families. Once he recognized that the gene was located somewhere near the D2S123 CA repeat sequence, the next logical experiment was to determine if this was a tumor suppressor gene, and look for LOH at this locus, using the same CA repeat marker. If the Lynch Syndrome gene were a tumor suppressor, one copy of the gene would have been mutated by inheritance, and there was some likelihood that the other copy of the gene would be deleted by LOH in the tumor cells that in this hereditary colon cancer family.

So, they did the experiment with D2S123. Instead of seeing a deleted gene, they saw mutations inside the microsatellite markers, just as Perucho and Thibodeau were observing. They recognized the importance of the finding, quickly wrote up their work, and submitted two papers to *Science* on April 8, 1993, just after the editors had rejected Thibodeau's manuscript. The first paper reported that a Lynch Syndrome gene had been mapped to the short arm of chromosome 2, and the second paper suggested that there were widespread mutations in microsatellite sequences in these tumors. They noted that 13% of all colorectal cancers showed these features, but this group did not find the differences in mutational frequency at *APC*, *RAS* or *p53* as Perucho and Thibodeau had noted, perhaps because of the small sample size.

Realizing that this work was similar to what they had just seen from Thibodeau, the editors at *Science* decided to take a second look at his manuscript. Therefore, the two papers from Vogelstein and de la Chappelle appeared immediately next to Thibodeau's paper in *Science* on May 7, 1993, just a month after the submission, and less than two months after Lauri's important finding. Vogelstein and de la Chapelle won the race to publish, but lost naming rights to Thibodeau. Their proposed term was the "replication error (RER) phenotype". Bert and Albert got the science correct, but needed better public relations and marketing consultants for naming rights.

So, by the end of this propitious day in May, 1993, we had a neighborhood address for the first Lynch Syndrome gene, and the tumors were linked to a novel pathway—microsatellite instability. At that very moment, I was sitting on a gold mine of microsatellite analyses from colon cancers and polyps in my own lab. Suddenly, I was in the middle of the story that I had longed to understand since the early 1970s. In a further bit of excellent (if accidental) timing, Henry Lynch and I had written a review of Lynch Syndrome, providing an overview of the clinical features of this purported disease, and provided suggestions for how we might find the genes at some time in the future. This article appeared in the May 1993 issue of *Gastroenterology*, and was cited repeatedly by workers in the field over the next several years as they wrote papers on this "new" entity. It became one of the most prominent articles in that journal for 1993, and has been cited subsequently over 1000 times. Most importantly, we would never again have to debate whether Lynch Syndrome was a distinct entity. That debate became history. The good luck just kept on coming.

Finally, Perucho (June, 1993)

Luck fell the other way for Perucho. When he saw the three articles in *Science* on May 7, his unpublished manuscript was still on his desk, and he naturally hit the roof. He had been "scooped" by two different teams. He feverishly complied with the demand from *Nature* that he revise and shorten his manuscript. He also contacted the Editor of *Nature*, and insisted that his paper be published as soon as possible after all the delays. So, even though his critical observation had been under review by one journal or another since early in 1992, his paper was finally published in *Nature* on June 10, 1993, more than a month after the three *Science* papers. Manuel still fumes about his bad luck, but those of us who know the story give him credit for his initial discovery of microsatellite instability. He just didn't know that he would have so much company on the winner's platform. Science is like this. What some fail to acknowledge is how many sets of shoulders are beneath the winner's platform.

The first Lynch Syndrome gene is cloned. Who are these guys?

The pace of discovery, which was white-hot in May, 1993 was to continue unabated for another year. I didn't even want to go home or to sleep, for fear of missing something. Perhaps the most surprising aspect of the discovery of microsatellite instability by multiple independent scientists looking for slightly different things was that not one of them initially understood the mechanistic basis of those aberrations. But, as soon as the primary data were published, many basic researchers in the world of yeast genetics took one look at the electrophoretic gel images of the PCR products in these publications, and almost immediately, several had a pretty good idea of what might be at the root of Lynch Syndrome.

In 1993, most basic genetics research was performed in bacteria (*Escherichia coli*), yeast (*Saccharomyces cerevisiae*), fruit flies (*Drosophila melanogaster*) and roundworms (*Caenorhabditis elegans*), in which the genomes are simpler and easier to manipulate quickly. One of the yeast geneticists who read the papers was Richard Kolodner, PhD, from the Dana Farber Cancer Institute in Boston. Richard studied DNA replication in yeast, and was an expert in a specific type of DNA repair activity called "DNA mismatch repair". He had recently cloned the DNA mismatch repair gene called *MSH2* gene from the beer-, wine- and bread-producing yeast *Saccharomyces cerevisiae. MSH2* was the second cloned homologue of the *MutS* gene in *E. coli* (so, it was called the *MutS Homolog 2*, or *MSH2*), and the protein made by this gene was essential for repairing mistakes that occur naturally during the replication of DNA. DNA mismatch repair is also an essential part of the cell cycle checkpoint apparatus that helps prevent the transmission of DNA replication errors to the daughter cells during mitosis. So, if the DNA synthesized during replication was damaged beyond the ability of the cell to repair it, the checkpoint controls prevent mitosis—a very important (and cool) function. At this time, people in the DNA repair field were considered a little off-beat, as their field seemed arcane to people in the medical field, and presumed to have little to do with human disease—or so we thought. Kolodner was about to change our perception of his field.

One reason to study *E. coli* or *S. cerevisiae* is that you can modify the DNA easily, and grow bacteria or yeast in bucket quantities. Kolodner knew that when the *MutS* (bacterial) or *MSH* (yeast) genes were inactivated by mutation or one of their manipulations, the resulting bacterial or yeast cells were hypermutable. These cells developed the "mutator phenotype" similar to what Perucho was proposing. The mutated PCR products shown by Perucho, Thibodeau, and Aaltonen looked a lot like the DNA from bacteria and yeast after inactivation of their DNA mismatch repair genes. Kolodner hypothesized in May, 1993 that the genes responsible for Lynch Syndrome would be mutated human DNA mismatch repair genes. He was correct.

Kolodner began by attempting to clone the human equivalent (or homologue) of the yeast *MSH2* gene. He was able to do so quickly because the human gene had a sequence quite similar to the yeast gene. In fact, he used the same approach to finding the human gene as he had used to find the yeast gene, by knowing the bacterial gene sequence. The high degree of similarity—or homology—between the human, yeast, and bacterial genes suggested that this might be an important gene that had undergone little evolutionary change over time. Cloning the human *MSH2* gene (which he called *hMSH2,* or the *human Mut S Homolog*) was the easy part. The hard part was finding a family that had a mutation in this gene, and determining the clinical result or "phenotype".

To achieve the cloning and move into human work, he teamed up with his previous post-doctoral fellow, Richard Fishel, PhD, who was on the faculty of the University of Vermont at the time. He also got help from several members of the clinical faculty at the Dana Farber Cancer Center, including Judy Garber, MD, who had identified putative Lynch Syndrome families to work with. Kolodner and Fishel split up the work, and did their best to keep their project a secret, since they predicted that other workers in the field would be stumbling in the dark for a while, and they might win this particular contest on the basis of their interest in yeast—which would be a relatively unique situation.

First, they discovered that the *hMSH2* gene they cloned mapped to human chromosome 2, the location (or "locus") where Lauri Aaltonen had mapped the gene in his Lynch Syndrome kindred. This suggested they were on the right track. They then screened a number of selected colorectal tumors for microsatellite instability and sequence variations in the *hMSH2* gene. They found that seven of twenty-six colon cancers had instability at CA repeat microsatellite sequences, and that two of the seven microsatellite unstable tumors had a sequence variation (a C to T change) in an intron six nucleotides upstream of one of the splice sites in the *hMSH2* gene.

We need to discuss some background on gene structure to understand what happened next. Genes are not encoded in a single long reading sequence in human DNA. The parts that ultimately encode for proteins are called "exons", and the exons are interrupted by longer non-coding segments called "introns" (*Figure 24*).

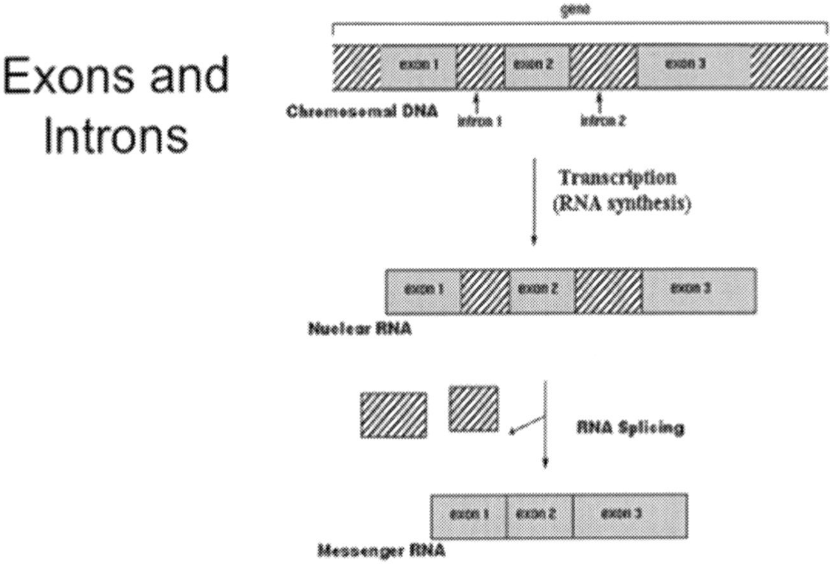

Figure 24: Schematic figure of exons and introns in a gene. The solid bars represent the part of the genetic code that results in the mature messenger RNA and for about 21,000 genes, a protein. The introns are represented by the hatched bars, which are edited out of the early RNA and do not appear in the fully spliced or processed messenger RNA. This format permits "alternative splicing" and can result in additional diverse forms of any gene with multiple introns. The earliest DNA sequencing strategies analyzed only the exons of each gene, as these make up only about 1.5% of all of our DNA, and ignore the other 98.5% of the DNA. This greatly simplified the process of DNA sequencing, but certain types of mutation—including some large deletions—were undetectable with this approach.

After DNA is transcribed into messenger RNA (mRNA), which is the working version of the gene for making proteins, the introns are spliced out, and the exons stitched together as the mRNA is "edited". Kolodner and Fishel are brilliant yeast geneticists, but they were inexperienced in human genetics in early 1993. They reasoned that this C to T sequence variation in the intron might interfere with the proper editing of the *hMSH2* gene—although they did not prove this. They erroneously concluded that this sequence variation was a "mutation", and found it in three affected members from one Lynch Syndrome family and two affected individuals from a second family. Also, it was not present in two unaffected individuals from the first family. They felt sure that they had found the first gene in which mutations would cause Lynch Syndrome. In fact, they had identified the right gene, but the sequence they called a mutation was actually a common variant that we call a "single nucleotide polymorphism", or SNP (pronounced "snip"). This is one of the big challenges in linking DNA sequence variations with human diseases. The SNP was located on the same allele as the mutation that caused the Lynch Syndrome in this family, and just as in a mapping experiment, this sequence would be seen in all of the affected people in this family, since the SNP and the true mutation were "linked" together. So, they found the right gene, but initially, didn't find the culpable mutation. Ordinarily, that would be a very good start on solving this problem. But, Kolodner and Fishel knew that time was critical here, and they made a leap of faith that this was it.

Kolodner's and Fishel's team had been working day and night since May, 1993, and by November 8, felt they had the correct answer and wanted to be the first to publish their findings. They sent the manuscript to *Cell*, and asked the editor that the manuscript not be reviewed by anyone in Vogelstein's group. They got their review back quickly, made the requested changes, and submitted a revision on November 18, which was accepted for publication in the December 3 issue—reflecting the journal's interest in capturing priority in the field, and currying favor with the scientists involved in important discoveries such as this.

Bert's group was also very close to finding mutations in the *hMSH2* gene, and was pretty sure that he and Kolodner were barking up the same tree—from scuttlebutt among people in the yeast genetics field, including a key cross-fertilizing, prominent yeast geneticist named Mike

Liskay, PhD, from the University of Oregon. In November, Bert called Richard Kolodner and proposed that the two of them could co-submit their papers (as occurred in the case of the *APC* gene, where multiple groups were working on the same project, and everyone could share the priority). Bert suspected that the two labs were essentially analyzing the same gene, and joint publications would strengthen their claims—and share the individual credit that might be handed out. Kolodner was in favor of this, but apparently Fishel refused to go along with the suggestion. Meanwhile, Kolodner and Fishel's paper was submitted first, got on the fast track, and was published just fifteen days after its acceptance. Once his paper was accepted, Kolodner gave Bert a "green light" to contact the editor of *Cell* (Lewin) about sending their paper to the same journal, which was immediately encouraged. Bert got his group's paper written and submitted to *Cell* on November 29 (just twenty-one days after the Kolodner/Fishel submission). They revised and resubmitted the manuscript *in one day* (November 30), and it was published in *Cell* on December 17!

After both papers were accepted, in the furious days just before publication, Bert called Kolodner, and the two scientists exchanged manuscripts. But when Bert read the Kolodner manuscript, he recognized that the sequence variation was unlikely to alter gene splicing, and that the data failed to prove convincingly that this was the cause of Lynch Syndrome. Bert had been looking at human genes for some time, and thought that changing the C to T in the intron, six nucleotides upstream of the splice site, would have no effect on gene function. Bert then called Richard Kolodner and pointed out the problem. Bert agreed that *hMSH2* was probably a Lynch Syndrome gene (since they had just found the same), but he didn't think that this SNP was a deleterious mutation causing the disease. Kolodner refused to modify his paper, and thought that Bert was being competitive. Over time, Kolodner and Fishel found the actual mutation in the *hMSH2* gene (but never published that), and in spite of the error, received the majority of the credit for that discovery.

So, on December 3, *Cell* published Kolodner's article, and *The New York Times* announced the finding of the first familial colorectal cancer gene on the front page. I had the newspaper in front of me at breakfast, and almost aspirated a spoonful of cereal when I read it (literally). This was one of the most exciting days in the annals of hereditary colon cancer research, and I had no clue whatsoever about the DNA mismatch repair genes. Moreover, who in the heck were Kolodner and Fishel? They were newcomers to the hereditary colon cancer story. Given the past six months, I was beginning to anticipate the unexpected.

hMSH2 and how causative mutations were finally found

Back to November, 1993, the Vogelstein-de la Chapelle partnership was very determined to make sense of microsatellite instability and the link to a Lynch Syndrome gene. They brought other collaborators into the study, including Henry Lynch, who had a freezer full of DNA from possible Lynch Syndrome families. They began mining for critical genes nearby D2S123 on the short arm of chromosome 2. They found many interesting candidate genes in this neighborhood, one of which was the homologue of the bacterial *mutS* gene. This finding also led them to look for additional DNA mismatch repair genes—but these others were not located on chromosome 2p, so they drilled down on *hMSH2.* In retrospect, the speed with which this group progressed was astonishing. They must have been foreswearing meals and sleep.

They cloned the *hMSH2* gene and began to search for mutations in families with presumed Lynch Syndrome. They had DNA from a patient who had colon cancer at age twenty-seven—which together with his family history suggested Lynch Syndrome—and he was missing forty-nine DNA bases from near the start of his *hMSH2* gene—an unquestioned disabling defect in the gene. This defect was also found in other members of his family who presumably also had Lynch Syndrome. They also found the C to T SNP in the intron within the *hMSH2* gene that had been reported by Kolodner's group, but this was also found in the DNA of two of twenty unrelated individuals who did not have Lynch Syndrome, so, they dismissed this as an innocent SNP, perhaps present in five to ten percent of the population, and without functional significance. They then discovered two more mutations in the *hMSH2* gene from putative Lynch Syndrome patients, one of which was another unequivocal inactivating mutation that created the code to stop protein production (a so-called "premature stop codon"). The mutation was also found in a similarly affected family member, increasing confidence in the conclusion that this was the culpable mutation. A third, somewhat more ambiguous mutation was found in a third Lynch Syndrome kindred. They concluded that they had found a Lynch Syndrome gene, and there was a high degree of plausibility that a defect in a DNA repair system would cause microsatellite instability. As described above, their paper was submitted to *Cell* just four days before the publication of the Kolodner article, and was published on December 17.

So, from May 7 to December 17, the field of hereditary non-polyposis colon cancer had gone from near total darkness to an understanding of the unique pathological process involved, and the discovery of what was the first of several disease genes. Kolodner had gotten the gene first, but didn't find the causative mutation in his first pass. Vogelstein and de la Chapelle's group nailed the whole process. Interestingly, Kolodner's group was given enough credit for their discovery to claim a patent for diagnostic purposes, but one could argue that the entire process moved at a breakneck pace because of the competition. In Kolodner's own words, the intellectual property arena is more like horseshoes than pure science. You only have to be approximately correct, and be closest to the stake when the measurements are taken. Frankly, from the perspective of the other hereditary colon cancer researchers at the time, we didn't really care who got credit. We were dazzled by how much had happened so quickly, and were ecstatic that the dark space surrounding this was being illuminated. Sitting on the sidelines was a treat, as the science was spectacular. It was irrelevant to most of us in the field who got credit for what. The accomplishments were real, and convincing. I didn't want this to end.

It didn't, and it didn't take long for the next wave to hit the shore.

Finding more Lynch Syndrome genes

Kolodner knew that there were other DNA mismatch repair genes and that the proteins worked together in a complex to repair defects in DNA. Therefore, inactivating mutations in other DNA repair genes might cause a similar problem as a mutation in *hMSH2*, and were candidates to be additional Lynch Syndrome genes. Earlier in 1993, a Swedish group led by Annika Lindblom, MD, PhD, a Professor of Clinical Genetics at the Karolinska Institute in Stockholm, did a linkage study on an affected family and predicted that a second Lynch Syndrome gene was located on the short arm of chromosome 3 (3p). After the successful linking of the *hMSH2* gene on chromosome 2p to Lynch syndrome, and understanding its role in DNA repair, the chase was on to find another DNA mismatch repair gene on 3p. It didn't take long, and this race to the finish was even closer than the first one.

The *hMLH1* gene

Kolodner teamed up with the aforementioned Michael Liskay, PhD from the University of Oregon, who was an expert in the mismatch repair genes in bacteria, and particularly the *mutL* gene (a bacterial gene that encodes a protein partner of *mutS* in the bacterial mismatch repair complex). They used a technique similar to what Kolodner had used to find *hMSH2*, which was to find something in the human genome that was the equivalent of the bacterial gene, and they found that a human homolog of the *mutL* gene was located on chromosome 3p. They cloned this gene, and using Lindblom's families, found mutations in the human homologue, the *hMLH1* gene (human Mut L Homolog) in one of them. The mutation this time occurred in a protein-coding exon, and the resulting amino acid change caused by this alteration occurred in a place where there is very little sequence variation among several different species (a so-called "conserved" region of the protein). Sequence conservation across species suggests that this part of the protein is functionally important, has been "selected" by evolution, and that a mutation in it might alter function. It was present in other affected members of the family and was not found in unrelated people in the general population. This manuscript was submitted to *Nature* on February 8 (just two months after the *hMSH2* paper had appeared), revised, accepted on February 28, and published on Thursday, March 17, 1994. Now there were two Lynch Syndrome genes.

Can you top this?

Not to be outdone, Vogelstein and de la Chapelle used a "bioinformatics" approach to seek genes from a database of "expressed DNA sequences" (technically, "expressed sequence tags" or ESTs), looking for a human gene that was similar to the bacterial *mutL* gene. Bert called one of the masters of this technique, J. Craig Venter, PhD, and jokingly called this "cloning by phoning". However, it was a tremendous shortcut to the answer. They found three homologous genes! One was on chromosome 3p (bingo), and the others were on chromosomes 2 and 7. The 3p gene was the *hMLH1* gene. Importantly, they found germline (inherited) mutations in multiple affected members of four Lynch Syndrome families. All of the mutations were convincingly damaging. Their article was submitted to the journal *Science* on February 22 (two weeks after Kolodner's), accepted on March 4, and published on Friday, March 18, 1994. *Nature* comes out on Thursday and *Science* on Friday, so their paper was published one day after Kolodner's, another virtual dead heat.

Kolodner used his insights into yeast DNA repair genes to provide critical insights into hereditary colorectal cancer. Vogelstein set up extraordinary collaborations and worked faster than anyone else on the DNA from well-characterized Lynch Syndrome families to relentlessly chase down the genes responsible for this disease. It was a unique time in the history of biomedical research when there was such a horserace, and the findings of these groups have revolutionized the care of patients with these hereditary predispositions.

In the fateful December of 1993, Vogelstein's group also reported microsatellite instability in a cultured human colon cancer cell line—grown in the lab. This was reported in a companion article in the December 17, 1993 issue of *Cell,* along with their *hMSH2* paper. Interestingly, they did not mention whether this cell line carried a mutation in *hMSH2.* In fact, it did not. They called this cell line "H6", and through yet another serendipitous event, was to become important to my lab. We called the same cell line HCT116, and it was to put our group on the hereditary colorectal cancer scientific map in a few months.

Two more genes?

In the paper published by Vogelstein's group on March 18, 1994, they indicated that their screen of ESTs found three homologs of the bacterial *mutL* gene in the human genome. One was the *hMLH1* gene, which they clearly linked to Lynch Syndrome in that paper. The other two were similar to the homologous yeast gene called *yPMS1* and were on human chromosomes 2q and 7p. They called the two human genes *hPMS1* (or human post-meiotic segregation-1 for the gene on chromosome 2q) and *hPMS2* (for the gene on chromosome 7p). Unfortunately for those of us keeping score, the human *hPMS1* gene was actually the homolog of the yeast *PMS2* gene, and visa-versa for the *hPMS2* and gene. Oh well, a rose by any other name....

We didn't have to wait long for the next shoe to hit the floor. On September 1, 1994, another paper was published in *Nature* from the Vogelstein consortium reporting that *hPMS2* and *hPMS1* were also Lynch Syndrome genes. Perhaps to demonstrate that no one is perfect, time has shown that *hPMS2* is indeed a Lynch Syndrome gene—but an enigmatic one—but that mutations in *hPMS1* do not cause Lynch Syndrome. They seem to have gotten that one wrong. One problem that has confounded our understanding of the human homologs of *mutL* and *yPMS1* is that the human genome contains at least twenty additional copies of the *hPMS2* gene that are not expressed as regular full-length genes. These are copies of the gene that have been duplicated in the human genome, and may or may not play any functional role in DNA repair. These DNA sequences are referred to as "pseudogenes". The presence of so many "false genes" creates a technical nightmare for those trying to develop diagnostic tests for Lynch Syndrome, since most of the pseudogenes have normal (called "wild type") sequences, which obscures our ability to see the mutant sequence in a diagnostic test.

One final gene

There was still one more Lynch Syndrome gene to be found, and this one was a homologue (with sequence similarity) of *hMHS2*, and located very close to *hMSH2*, suggesting that it evolved in that location through duplication and sequence drift. In 1995, a European consortium headed by Josef Jiricny, PhD found a gene that they initially called the *G/T binding protein*, or *GTBP*, which was similar in structure and function to *hMSH2*. The gene was defective in a cultured cell line with microsatellite instability, but they did not report mutations of this gene in any Lynch Syndrome families. Vogelstein's group was working collaboratively with Jiricny, and the two labs published joint papers describing defects in *GTBP* in the cell lines, in *Science* on June 30, 1995. However, it was not until December, 1997 that a group led by Michiko Miyaki from Tokyo, Japan reported in *Nature Genetics* convincing germline mutations in a large Japanese kindred with Lynch Syndrome, and called the gene *hMSH6*, because it was related to the bacterial *mutS* gene family, and was the sixth homologue of the yeast *MSH* gene family in humans. They reported a second family with a suspicious but not proven deleterious mutation in *hMSH6*. Waiting eighteen months for the last Lynch Syndrome gene seemed excessively long compared to the prior frenetic pace of discovery. We eventually found out that Lynch Syndrome caused by mutations in *MSH6* had different features that made it more difficult to recognize.

What genes cause Lynch Syndrome?

Now that sufficient time has passed, we have a clear concept of what causes Lynch Syndrome. Lynch Syndrome is an inherited disease caused by germline mutations in one of four DNA mismatch repair genes: *hMSH2*, *hMLH1*, *hPMS2* and *hMSH6* (*Figure 25*). Mutations in *hMSH2* and *hMLH1* cause the classic forms of the disease with a marked predisposition to early-onset cancers of the colon and endometrium. There is also an excess of tumors in the urinary tract, stomach, ovary, brain, and a few other organs. The tumors all have microsatellite instability. Certain type of mutations in the *EPCAM* gene, which is located immediately next door to *hMSH2,* can cause silencing of the *hMSH2* gene, and certain types of mutations in *EPCAM* act more or less like Lynch Syndrome of the *hMSH2* type. Lynch Syndrome can be caused by germline mutations in the *hPMS2* gene, but many people who carry these mutations do not get tumors for reasons that are not clear; we call this "incomplete penetrance". They still carry the mutation and can pass it on to the next generation whether or not they develop a tumor. Finally, Lynch Syndrome can be caused by germline mutations in the *hMSH6* gene, but there are some differences in this form of the disease. First, the tumors in these families occur later in life, and the family history may appear to be spuriously negative. So, the disease is similar but delayed in time, making it more difficult to detect. Second, women with Lynch Syndrome-*MSH6* type have a very high incidence of carcinoma of the endometrium, perhaps as high as seventy percent. Also, for reasons that involve some moderately complex (but understandable) biochemistry, some of these tumors will not have microsatellite instability.

Name of Gene	Clinical Features
MSH2	Classic Lynch Syndrome; common mutation in Lynch Syndrome; prone to large deletions; loss of the termination signal from the *EPCAM* gene silences MSH2 and causes Lynch Syndrome that can have predominantly colon cancers.
MLH1	Classic Lynch Syndrome; common mutation in Lynch Syndrome
MSH6	Lynch Syndrome with later-onset cancers; uncommon mutation (<10% of Lynch Syndrome). Affected women highly prone to endometrial cancer.
PMS2	Lynch Syndrome with lower penetrance (most carriers never get cancer). Prevalence uncertain, probably <25%, but might be the most commonly mutated DNA mismatch repair gene. There are >20 "false copies" of this gene in our genome, which complicates detecting mutations.

Figure 25: The Lynch Syndrome Genes

Type X Disease, hypermethylation of *MLH1* and Lynch-like Syndrome

We have learned a few more things about hereditary colorectal cancer. Nearly half of the familial clusters of colorectal cancer—which initially appear to be Lynch Syndrome—are not caused by mutations in the DNA mismatch repair genes. The tumors do not have microsatellite instability, the "penetrance" is a lower, and there is no excess of extra-colonic tumors in these families. This clinical mystery has the temporary name "Familial Colorectal Cancer, Type X", and is not Lynch Syndrome. We are beginning to learn that the Type X disease probably has many different genetic causes. This creates a diagnostic conundrum, since one may have to test many genes to be able to manage Type X families. This will complicate the lives of those affected, as well as those trying to diagnose and advise such families. These families can probably be managed with frequent colonoscopies.

Finally, there are two types of entities that produce colorectal cancers with microsatellite instability that are not due to Lynch Syndrome. One of these is the acquired silencing of the *hMLH1* gene (by a process called promoter hypermethylation). This is relatively common, accounting for about 12% of all colorectal cancers. Probably 90% of these tumors are in the right side of the colon (usually the cecum or ascending colon), and they tend to occur in older individuals. It is not familial. These tumors can be identified because they sometimes have a mutation in the *BRAF* gene (which is not found in Lynch Syndrome), and also, one can measure promoter methylation of the *hMLH1* gene, which is higher in tumors with the acquired methylation problem than in Lynch Syndrome-*MLH1* type.

Finally, there is a relatively uncommon phenomenon in which there are two acquired (somatic) mutations in one of the DNA mismatch repair genes, in which it is neither inherited nor caused by promoter hypermethylation. This is currently called "Lynch-like Syndrome", and it is not familial.

Summary: understanding Lynch Syndrome

In May, 1993, we got our first glimpse into what was previously a dark mystery, and the full story unfolded in an astonishingly rapid fashion. The pace of discovery was accelerated by the love of science, old-fashioned competition, overheated egos, and the desire to attract attention. Some of the discoveries were serendipitous; others were hammered out with the use of elegant thinking and scientific discovery. When microsatellite instability and the initial Lynch Syndrome genes were found, everyone in the field quickly acquainted themselves with this unexpected scientific party crasher: the field of DNA mismatch repair. Each time we thought we understood the story, something new would emerge to complicate the concepts we thought we understood, and we had to think and learn new things. As each new concept seemed to clarify itself, something new and disruptive came along as the next chapter. The period from 1993 to 2001 taught me in particular how complex and hazardous it would be to predict each new development in the field. However, I had now enough information to tackle the real problem that launched my medical career into research.

Chapter 14

The Transformative Years (1994-2001)

The events of 1993-94 were transformative in many ways. First, the colon cancer research community opened the lid on Lynch Syndrome, confirmed that it was a discrete disease, and we had a test to identify the tumors that were a result of this disease. We found out where the disease genes were located, which gave us an opportunity to determine which members of an affected family actually carried the mutation and which ones did not. We recognized that FAP and Lynch Syndrome were two driven by completely unrelated biological mechanisms, each of which led to familial forms of colorectal cancer, and this stimulated our imaginations to think about whether we might need to develop more individualized approaches to diagnosing and preventing cancer in each setting. For the first time, we had real scientific principles that defined the diseases, and we saw the way forward to learn more.

From a personal perspective, my immediate career direction was now very clear. By being persistent and open to where the answers might lie, I had taken a sabbatical at just the right time, pushed myself into a new area, and I was now able to think about tumor genetics and design meaningful experiments. It was particularly fortuitous that Andy and I decided to use microsatellite analysis to help characterize multistep carcinogenesis. However, it was mostly good luck that the non-FAP form of hereditary colorectal cancer was so intimately related to mutated microsatellite sequences. I was sitting on thousands of microsatellite analyses, and by early 1994, had more experience and data on microsatellite instability than any other gastroenterologist. This was a new and totally unexpected feeling. Importantly, there had been just enough time for me to transition and become comfortable with the techniques required in molecular biology. Whereas experiments involving glycoproteins would take months to execute, we could design and carry out experiments in genetics in a more compressed time frame. For the first time, there was a real trail to follow, and it was possible to dream about finding the source of the trouble in my family, and do something about it.

Koi's remarkable experiments

In December, 1993, Andy Feinberg accepted the Chair in Genetics at Johns Hopkins and returned to Baltimore. One of the people in his lab was Minoru Koi, PhD, who had befriended and helped me while I was on sabbatical in 1990. He preferred to be called just Koi. He was not going to Hopkins with Andy, and had been offered a job with a branch of the National Institutes of Health in Research Triangle Park, North Carolina, but could not start in January because there was a government shutdown at that time that resulted from a battle between Gingrich-led Republicans and President Clinton. Koi didn't know how long this would last, and needed a job, at least temporarily. We sat down together on December 27, 1993, and discussed the two papers that had just come from Vogelstein's lab in *Cell* on December 17. Bert's group had found that the cell line "H6" had microsatellite instability, represented a potentially valuable model for studying this process in mammalian cells, but curiously, they did not report that there was a mutation in the *hMSH2* gene in these cells, even though they had just reported finding this gene in the accompanying paper. He had been silent on the issue, raising the possibility that *hMSH2* was not mutated in this cell line, and that there was some other abnormality there to be discovered.

I thought it was time to invest the funds given to me by the Minneapolis family to study this disease, and Koi had a unique idea. He had the technical expertise to stably transfer an entire copy of a "normal" human chromosome into a cultured cell line. Very few people could do this. We knew that the *hMSH2* gene was on chromosome 2. But because of the previously mentioned paper from Annika Lindblom's group in

Stockholm, we suspected there might be another Lynch Syndrome gene on chromosome 3. If you read the papers coming out at this time, it is clear that we weren't the only ones thinking this way, and that is part of the reason that multiple groups published the same findings at the same time. These ideas were heavy in the air, and were ready to fall out of the sky like raindrops. Any of us might be the ones to properly seed the clouds. That was what made it such a stimulating time to work on this. Don't take any time off; just keep on truckin'.

Koi said he thought he could transfer a single copy of either chromosome 2 or 3 into the cell line. We had H6 in our lab, but called it HCT116—and if the critical mutated gene was on chromosome 2 or 3, we thought that we might be able to "fix" the microsatellite instability. We didn't know at that time whether it would alter the cell's ability to grow function like a cancer cell, but we could test that hypothesis with the gene-correcting experiment. The alternative approach would be to clone the working copy of the gene, put it into a "vector", transfer the vector to the cell, and see what happened. However, we did not have experience in cloning and manipulating a gene at that time, figured that Vogelstein was probably doing that experiment as we spoke, and I knew that you couldn't reliably put just one copy of the gene into cells this way, nor could one reliably regulate its expression. I thought that a transfected gene was likely to over-express the gene, and that too much of a protein that binds and works on DNA might be deadly to the cell. The cell needed just enough of the DNA repair proteins, and if an unregulated form of the gene were introduced, it would be hard to interpret whatever result you got. A gene on its native chromosome would be likely to have all of its regulatory elements attached. However, a chromosome transfer experiment would be messy in that we would be transferring ~3000 genes on chromosomes 2 or 3 into the cell along with the working copy of the mismatch repair gene. At least the gene of interest would be under its normal physiological control, since the principle control elements are located on either side or the gene—or inside it, in the introns. So, we thought our approach might be a better experiment, and we could do it in a short period of time. Koi agreed to work in the lab at least six months, and after that, he would be free to take the NIH position.

The JC virus interlude

Monday January 3, 1994 was the first work day of the New Year. Koi arrived and started to work on the new project. As a curious aside, on that very day I walked around the corner from my lab and met with a geneticist named James V. Neel, MD, PhD. I knocked on his door and he was in, and I tried to convince him to sponsor a manuscript for publication in *PNAS*, as he was a member of the National Academy. He wasn't interested, and he quickly changed the subject. Jim was seventy-eight, had seen a lot of science in his time, had been a leading figure in human genetics, found the second sickle cell disease mutation (Linus Pauling had found the first), and Jim had worked on radiation-induced illness in the Hiroshima atomic bomb survivors. He was also canny and wasted no time getting to the point.

He looked at me and said "you are a young fella—what is it that you really want to discover?" I told him that I had always wanted to know how cells became malignant. I reviewed the events of the past year, and said that everyone was heading straight into the microsatellite instability story, and that we had just started such an experiment that very day. However, I noted that most colorectal cancers didn't have microsatellite instability. Only about 15% did—although I was especially interested in a subset of those that had Lynch Syndrome. I told him that I didn't want to lose sight of the other 85% of tumors that had chromosomal instability (the initial Vogelstein concept). That would be important too.

He asked me what I thought might be causing chromosomal instability. We had a brief discussion, and after I gave him my hypotheses on the causes of chromosomal instability, he proposed a novel hypothesis. He had recently found that people who had been exposed to the human polyomavirus called "JC virus" (named after James Cunningham, from whom the virus was first isolated) had abnormal lymphocytes in their circulation that he called "rogue lymphocytes"; these cells looked like they had chromosomal instability. More importantly, the polyomaviruses (JC virus and a few of its friends) encoded the most dangerous gene imaginable to mammals, called "T antigen". This protein could fracture DNA and simultaneously silence the main cell cycle checkpoint proteins, which would permit the cell to divide even though it contained damaged DNA. This would be a monstrous gene to have in your cells.

I had never heard of that virus before. He asked me if I could look for JC virus in tumors. I asked if he had the DNA sequence of the virus, and he did. I told him it would be easy to find this, using PCR. I agreed to do the experiment, and left his office. I was impressed that he was able to make this link, and he was impressed that I knew immediately how to use PCR to address the problem. He had given me a lot more credit than necessary for this, as many researchers had learned how to do PCR by now, but it was the complementary information we shared that made a perfect match. This launched a fifteen year exploration into JC Virus, which we later found in most colorectal cancers. I won't describe that further. The curious fact is that we started critical experiments on microsatellite instability in HCT116 and experiments on JC virus on the same day, within a few hours of one another. One can go years without a really good idea and two were launched on the same morning, which ultimately led to twenty years of funding from the NIH.

In a slump

Koi is one of the most fascinating scientists I have ever known. He worked quietly alone, always doing every hands-on part himself. He had grown up and trained in Japan, married a woman (Mary) from Minnesota, and had two sons. He has an even-tempered and gentle personality, and the ability to make light of any hardship. You could never tell if things were going well or not, as he always had a smile on his face, and seemed to cruise over or around anxiety.

One day in February, 1994, I asked him how the chromosomal transfers were going. He said:

"I'm in a slump".

"A slump?" I repeated. "How long has this been going on?"

"About two weeks", he replied.

I laughed. "Most of us don't even know we are in a slump if we have had trouble for only two weeks." He carried on and within a few days everything started to work better again. By the end of February, he had successfully transferred both chromosome 2 and chromosome 3 into HCT116 colon cancer cells, and had multiple clones of each transfer. What would be the result? I had never been in a serious horserace before, and wondered who else might be doing the same thing. I was about to find out that we were racing Secretariat.

A bombshell in Baltimore

At that time, I was on a Data Safety and Monitoring Board (DSMB) for a study supported by the Veterans Administration evaluating the performance of colonoscopies to screen for colon polyps and cancer among US military veterans. A group of us who were independent of the study and not involved in the design or execution of the study were asked to look at the data and decide whether there were problems that necessitated stopping the study prematurely. We received no pay or credit for this. It was part of the research process. We had to fly to Baltimore for a one day meeting on Thursday March 17, 1994. We assembled, listened to the results, and found no problems. The meeting ended by noon, but my flight back to Ann Arbor wasn't scheduled until about 4:30 PM. I had the unexpected gift of a few hours to kill—in Baltimore, where Johns Hopkins University is located. I had never met Bert Vogelstein, although we had spoken on the phone, exchanged emails, and DNA samples, so I decided to give him a call. He invited me to come to his lab for a face-to-face meeting. I was delighted.

I took a cab to the designated location on the Johns Hopkins medical campus, and found that Bert's lab was a one-time strip-mall supermarket turned into one of the most important research labs in the world. I had to get through two layers of security, and was led to Bert's office. He was a few years younger than I, but very friendly, and he welcomed me as if I were a long-lost cousin. His hair had grown longer than I had seen in photos. He wore blue jeans and a T-shirt. His office door was covered by a curtain of beads and his office was dimly lit. It seemed more like going into a hookah shop than a researcher's office. Bert was completely unpretentious, and he asked me about my health and that of family members, as he knew about my familial cancer problem.

At first I thought that I should be discrete about our chromosome transfer experiment; but it was costing me a lot of money, and I figured that he must have been doing something similar. So I opened up, and told him what we were doing. I felt a strong sense of unspoken trust. He then told me that he had just cloned a second Lynch Syndrome gene on chromosome 3p, they called it *hMLH1*, and it was about to be published.

Little did I know, but as we sat there, Kolodner's *hMLH1* paper had just been published that day (March 17) in *Nature*, and Bert's paper would appear the next day in *Science*. I was so clueless at the time.

He then dropped the bombshell. The mutant gene in HCT116 was *hMLH1* (on chromosome 3), and not *hMSH2* (on chromosome 2). Moreover, they had cloned the wild type (normal) copy of *hMLH1* into a transfection vector, and inserted it into HCT116—the experiment that I knew would take us too long, and was beyond our grasp. Bert confessed that every time they put the *hMLH1*-containing vector into HCT116, it killed the cells. (Yes!!) Therefore, he suggested that I should keep trying the chromosome transfer experiment, that they would do their experiments, and if one of us completed the story first and the other was nearly done, we could share the limelight and submit parallel papers. Given my novice stature in the field, I thought that was a very reasonable agreement. He then reached into a file cabinet, and gave me complete information about the DNA sequence of *hMLH1* and other details that were about to be published. He showed me around their renovated supermarket, introduced me to several lab members, and sent me on my way. What an afternoon!

"Do I have news for you!"

I took a cab back to the airport, feeling like I was having a pretty lucky St. Patrick's Day. (I had no idea it wasn't over yet.) I got back to Ann Arbor about 6:30 PM, and drove straight to the lab. Koi was there, and seemed pleased with himself, as he usually did.

"Koi, do I have some news for you!"

"No, I have some important news for you", Koi countered.

"My news is more important", I suggested confidently.

"No it isn't", retorted Koi.

"OK, what's your news?" I was quite smug that I had the biggest news.

"Chromosome 3 corrects microsatellite instability in HCT116. I have just proven it. So, what's your news?"

"Never mind." He certainly beat me on that afternoon.

By complete coincidence, in the hours that I was learning that HCT116 was a Lynch Syndrome-*MLH1* cell line from Bert, Koi had just discovered the same thing. Kolodner's paper just came out that day, and by the next day, Bert's paper was to be published. I simply had no experience with this pace of discovery. Needed to blow into a paper bag.

Breaking into the big leagues of tumor genetics

We now knew that chromosome 3 carried a gene that corrected microsatellite instability in HCT116 cells, but we were a long way from a definitive story. Chromosome 3 contained a lot of other genes that might have been responsible for the result, and we needed to prove that we actually repaired the defective DNA mismatch repair system. That was going to require a new set of tools that we didn't have in the laboratory. So, I sent a post-doctoral fellow who had joined me from Rome named Giancarlo Marra, MD, PhD to the laboratory of Tom Kunkel, PhD, who was one of a very small cadre of people who could help us with this. He had a lab with the National Institutes of Environmental Health and Safety (NIEHS) in Research Triangle Park, North Carolina. He welcomed Giancarlo into his lab, shared reagents, and showed him how to directly measure DNA mismatch repair activity—a punishingly difficult assay. Giancarlo was there for just over a week, and returned to the lab to confirm what Koi had done.

We found that putting chromosome 3 and a functioning copy of *hMLH1* into HCT116 cells also restored the G2/S cell cycle checkpoint, which Koi had predicted from prior work done on bacterial cells. Specifically, he found that the original HCT116 cells were relatively resistant to the toxic effects of a DNA-damaging alkylating agent called MNNG, and that restoring the DNA mismatch repair system with chromosome 3 also restored sensitivity to MNNG, which now killed the cells. The original HCT116 cells tolerated the DNA damage induced by MNNG and went on replicating, whereas the "HCT116+chromosome 3 cells" either repaired the damage done by the agent (at lower doses of the drug), or signaled the cell to die (when the DNA damage was overwhelming and not fixable). That is what you want your cells to do of course; fix the problem, or stop replicating damaged DNA. This demonstrated that there was no honor among these cancer cells. They had lost their ability to repair certain types of DNA damage, and simultaneously lost their ability to sense the problem and shut down cells with damaged DNA. This is a deadly compromise for the host of those cells.

We were elated with these results, so I called Bert to tell him about it. He said that they had not been able to successfully transfer copies of the cloned *hMLH1* gene into HCT116 (or any other) cells, that we had won this round, and we should write up our manuscript and publish it. I was worried that others might have done the same experiment, so we quickly wrote the paper and submitted it to *Cancer Research* as an "Advances in Brief" article, which promises a quick decision and publication if you have a compelling story that you can present in a brief paper.

We sent the paper off on Friday June 24, and about a week later, I got a fax from the journal. It arrived in the morning, and I didn't even look at it, assuming that we had submitted the paper incorrectly or had some other problem. I was busy and didn't want to read about it. I put the fax on my desk, and didn't look at it until the end of the day. When I finally picked it up, I found that the paper had been accepted as written, with no requests for revision or additional data. This was unbelievable. We celebrated our first paper published in the area of tumor genetics, and experienced an incredibly rapid turnaround from submission to acceptance. The paper appeared in the August 15 issue of *Cancer Research*, and we were the first to publish this finding. What a start in the field for us. We continued to use Koi's model and he continued to advance the story even after he moved to North Carolina in September, 1994. I tallied up the outcome of our collaborative experiments a few years later, and we ended up publishing eleven manuscripts as a result of his work. Not the ordinary type of slump at all.

1994 was the watershed year for the lab. We had a high impact paper by developing the first laboratory model to study Lynch Syndrome. Since that time, probably 200 laboratories have asked for and gotten these cells. In 1995, we published the results of the work begun on sabbatical in *Nature Medicine*, in which we used microsatellites to confirm exactly where each of the mutational steps occurred in colorectal tissues as they progressed from normal, through the benign states to cancer. We formed a collaboration with a lab that was developing the first diagnostic approaches for Lynch Syndrome, and published the first result of its clinical application. Suddenly our papers were being accepted in top journals (*Science*, *Journal of Clinical Investigation*, *PNAS*, and others). I was asked to write reviews and book chapters, and my academic life seemed transformed. Between 1982 and

1994, I published an average of 5.6 papers per year. In 1996, we published twenty-two, and the impact of the articles was greater. Few people could read the glycoprotein papers I wrote because the material was dense and arcane; they just weren't interested. Once we got into tumor genetics, other cancer researchers noticed.

The University of California San Diego

One of the unintended consequences of being noticed is that other institutions want to recruit you to their place. Tachi Yamada was very generous in mentioning my name to departments who were looking for a new division chief. Of course, he would wait for me to come to him and then talk me out of it—like the flirtation with the University of Rochester. This continued, and I was collecting a folder-full of letters from various departments of medicine asking if I was interested in moving. I usually either didn't respond to general mailings or politely refused the personal requests. Ann Arbor was a great city for raising a family, and the UM School of Medicine rose to the top tier of research-intensive medical schools. Why leave?

In January, 1994, I got a letter from the Search Committee at the University of California San Diego (UCSD) asking if I was interested in being Division Chief there. Tachi was now the Chairman of Internal Medicine and Chung Owyang was the GI Division Chief at the UM. Both of them knew UCSD well and advised me that this was a difficult institution because the campus was split into two parts that were fifteen miles apart, and that there were some "difficult personalities" in the institution that would make it an unpleasant job. I declined to come out and take a look. I didn't think more about it, as letters of invitation were coming in regularly.

Then, in November, 1994, I got a call from Steven Wasserman, MD, who was the Chairman of the Department of Medicine at UCSD. The Search Committee had failed to identify a willing candidate, so he disbanded them and took it over himself. He asked what I thought and I told him that I had gotten advice from Tachi and Chung to not bother. I was very frank and told him exactly what I had heard. He felt that the rumors of dysfunction were exaggerated, and urged me to come take a look. I told him that Thanksgiving was coming up, that I had intensive clinical duties in Ann Arbor during December, so the earliest I could come out was in January. I told him that if he found someone else in the interim, I didn't care. He told me to plan on visiting in January, and we set a date for this.

So, in early January, 1995, I headed to the airport in Michigan for a trip to sunny San Diego. In the worst case, I had a two day respite from winter in the upper Midwest. There was a fierce snow storm on the morning of my trip. I was on the highway between Ann Arbor and the Detroit airport trying to stay on the snowy road and, for the first time, watched a tractor-trailer perform the difficult jackknife maneuver. (I had never thought previously why they called it a "jackknife" until I saw this.) I got off the plane in San Diego and it was sunny and about seventy degrees. Not a bad start. I met with Steve Wasserman and others in the Department of Medicine and GI Division, and I began to see the possibilities there. I called home and told Pat that the job there was a bit more interesting than I had initially anticipated. Interestingly, the VA Hospital was located on the main campus in La Jolla, and the main Medical Center hospital was located fifteen miles down Interstate-5 in the Hillcrest neighborhood. I had been working for the VA nearly all of my time in San Francisco and Ann Arbor, and had a research grant through the VA. So, if I came to San Diego, I would be able to keep a VA appointment (which was valuable because of the research grant system in the VA), and still have a lab on the medical school campus with other investigators. Plus, the UCSD School of Medicine was world-class. Steve mentioned that the amount of research funding from the NIH per investigator at UCSD was second only to Stanford. There were several members of the National Academy of Science and a few Nobel laureates.

I told them that I was possibly interested and Pat and I paid a visit together in March. She agreed that she could learn to be happy in San Diego. Curiously, eleven years earlier, we had visited Ann Arbor for the first time, coming from San Francisco in December. As we went to dinner in Michigan, it was about five or ten degrees, and I saw myself welcoming the brisk northern winters again. Now, I was seeing the benefits of leaving those winters behind again. When I discussed the job with Tachi, he told me that I had become "sun-addled" during my visits to the southern California.

Accepting the offer

During my second visit, they gave me a formal offer to come to UCSD as Professor of Medicine and Division Chief. I thought about it for a several weeks. One morning I would wake up and decide to go, and later that day would decide to stay at UM. Tachi offered me an endowed chair if I stayed, but the way the institution deals with endowments, it wouldn't have changed my life at all; just another line in my CV or on my letterhead. I typed up an acceptance letter, and twice went to the fax machine to send it to Wasserman. I backed off both times. Then one Saturday morning, Pat and I went on our morning jog, and we decided to accept the offer. So, I went into work and faxed the acceptance. Our two oldest daughters, Tara and Maureen were in college at Bowdoin College in Maine and Colgate University in New York. So, I sent emails to them indicating that we had finally made a decision on the UCSD offer. I then realized that they might call home to add their opinions or ask questions, so, I had to call Pat and let her know what I had done.

Brigid strongly disagrees

However, our youngest daughter, Brigid, was fourteen, just finishing eighth grade, and very much looking forward to starting high school in Ann Arbor. She was an excellent student, an excellent field hockey player, had a lot of friends, and loved her school. She had a vision of how things would work out for her over the next four years, and didn't want any changes or complications. When I called home, Brigid answered the phone. I asked to speak with her mother. Brigid said that she was outside doing some gardening. Brigid asked if she could take a message. I told her that I needed to talk with her mother directly.

She asked: "Does this have to do with San Diego?" with rising impatience.

I told her that it did. She continued "Did you take the job?"

Again, I said I did. With that, the phone hit the floor and I heard a loud painful wail from Brigid. Then the phone hung up. A few minutes later Pat called and said that Brigid was inconsolable over the suggestion that we would be moving to San Diego. We had some convincing to do. Actually, Brigid lives in San Diego at this time, and is a committed resident of the region. She got over it and the problem was self-resolving.

Moving the lab

In August, the entire lab moved to San Diego. I took two Italian post-doctoral fellows—Giancarlo Marra, MD, PhD from Rome and Luigi Laghi, MD from Milan. Giancarlo was the one who traveled to Tom Kunkel's lab and acquired the expertise to measure DNA mismatch repair activity, which was critical to our work and difficult to master. Luigi worked on JC virus, and was getting provocative data. Also, in my last two years at UM, a post-doctoral fellow named John Carethers, MD joined the lab. He grew up in a large family in Detroit and suffered through some of the worst years of rioting in the city. He lived at home while attending Wayne State University in Detroit and continued there in the medical school. He was very bright, had an unyielding work ethic, and ended up at the top of his medical school class. He then landed one of the most prestigious internships at Massachusetts General Hospital in Boston, and came to the UM for his fellowship in Gastroenterology. He was interested in studying colon cancer from the beginning, but hadn't had much prior laboratory experience. For the first month and a half of his lab fellowship, he attended a full-time course provided by the medical school to teach the principles and practice of molecular biology and genetics. He went in knowing very little, but six weeks later he emerged filled with new capabilities and his career was launched. He was one of those people who learned everything very quickly. He picked up laboratory procedures, it seemed, just by being nearby someone who was doing them. He had an upbeat and good-natured approach to life that was different than many lab-based fellows, who can sometimes feel overwhelmed by all they need to learn to be successful. John began applying for every grant he could, and even though rejection was a frequent result, he ended up getting well-funded by pure persistence. I think that people look back and think that it must have been easy for him once he got his grants funded and papers published, but I watched the applications and manuscript go out, and saw how patiently he took the bad news with the good. I knew I had a winner in John. Fortunately, he agreed to come to San Diego with me, and he was a crucial part of the move. Over time he rose through the ranks as Section Chief at the VA, GI Division Chief at UCSD, and now he is the Chairman of the Department of Internal Medicine at the University of Michigan.

They let him get away in 1995, but they thought better of it and brought him back to lead the Department fourteen years later.

Fast times in tumor genetics

The lab was productive during the UCSD years. Everyone was working well together, each person would bring some unique expertise, and the lab became well-known nationally and internationally. We weren't afraid to go after anything. At one point, a surgical resident named Andrew Zigman, MD entered the lab, and told me he eventually wanted to pursue additional training in pediatric surgery. (We also had a young pediatric gastroenterologist named Sherry Huang, MD in the lab about then.) I warned both of them that we were going to stay focused on colon cancer, and that children rarely got that disease. Andrew went to the dysmorphology clinic at the San Diego Children's Hospital and found a group of children who had a rare disease called the Bannayan-Riley-Ruvalcaba Syndrome. These kids also developed intestinal polyps. Someone had done karyotype (chromosomal) analyses on these patients, much as Herrera had done on the young man with FAP, and two of them had abnormalities that their parents lacked. By good luck, both abnormalities involved the loss of some portion of chromosome 10q. We did a mapping experiment (using microsatellites, naturally), and found that the two deletions overlapped with one another. Better yet, a potential tumor-suppressor gene lived right in the middle of the overlapping deletions. Just like that, we had mapped a novel disease gene to a specific location.

John Carethers was in charge of the project that Andrew was conducting. I told him that I had never been so certain that something would be published, and we sent it off to the most appropriate journal, *Nature Genetics*. In a week we got the decision—a flat out rejection. I was puzzled. It was quickly accepted by another journal, *Gastroenterology*. I couldn't figure out how we missed the boat with *Nature Genetics*, which is a top tier journal until I read in the *New York Times* less than a month later that another group had beaten us to that conclusion, and *Nature Genetics* had the paper in its hands when we submitted our work. We were in a new world, and found out that being first meant being good, fast—and importantly, lucky.

All roads lead to San Diego

Shortly after I arrived at UCSD, Richard Kolodner came from Harvard to the Salk Institute, which is virtually contiguous with the UCSD campus, for a sabbatical. In part, his interest was spurred by a romance that was developing between Richard and Jean Wang, PhD, who was a Professor in the Department of Biology at UCSD. Richard and I met one morning in mid-February, 1996 on the courtyard at the Salk Institute, where we were discussing collaborations regarding Lynch Syndrome. I had access to affected patients and families, and he was the man who cloned the first two genes for that disease. It was a beautiful sunny morning, and the Salk Institute courtyard overlooks the Pacific Ocean. The sky was deep blue, and the view was gorgeous. He said that either Jean would move to Boston (as Richard was still a Professor at Harvard and the Dana Farber Cancer Institute), or Richard would look for something in San Diego. Richard was raised in the Southwest, and was one of the most celebrated PhD graduates of UC Irvine. We both were looking at the view for a moment, then we glanced at each other and Richard started to laugh. We both knew he would be moving to Southern California. He was offered a position at UCSD and the prestigious Ludwig Cancer Research Institute. He arrived within the year, and we had a productive relationship at UCSD.

"So you're the one?"

Manuel Perucho had also been in San Diego for some years by the time I arrived. We got together occasionally, and at one point, discussed writing a collaborative grant. In November, 1997, the National Cancer Institute convened a workshop to come to agreement on what constituted microsatellite instability, how we would measure it, and to make recommendations on how to decide which colorectal cancers should be tested to uncover cases of Lynch Syndrome now that we had a test for these tumors. They asked me to chair the meeting.

Perucho was in a state of funk and decided he didn't want to go to the meeting. He claimed at that time that he had to go to Madrid for important business, but he later told me that he really had no important commitment. He was just annoyed at some of the people in the field. Although he didn't want to go to the meeting, he still wanted his presence felt. To be collaborative, I accepted his request that I show his slides to the assembled group. He came to my lab and we discussed what I would say on his behalf, and to explain that he had an unavoidable conflict preventing his presence. Somewhere in our discussion, I mentioned that our lab had done the stable chromosome transfer experiments and corrected microsatellite instability in HCT116 cells.

When I told him he blurted out "So, you're the one!"

"The one who did what?" I asked.

"Stole my idea!"

"What idea?"

"The idea that different genes were involved in Lynch Syndromes and that act in a complementary way."

His comment was totally nuts and he quickly realized it. I told him that we were working quite independently, I had no idea what he was doing at the time, and that our experiments were nothing like his. He immediately settled down and realized that he was thinking somewhat irrationally, but I realized that the close finishes and his fear of losing priority on microsatellite instability had been hard on him. He even smiled when I pointed out that our approaches to the problem were completely different, and that I couldn't have known about his experiments. I genuinely respect his intellect and accomplishments, and learned a lesson about keeping perspective on the issues of competition and cooperativity in science. He felt as though he had been burned a few times, and it had eaten up a piece of his soul.

We had the National Cancer Institute workshop on microsatellite instability in November 1997. I assembled the summary report of our deliberations in February 1998 and submitted it to *Cancer Research* for publication as a "Meeting Report". Even though it was more like a newspaper report than scientific article, it had to undergo peer review, but I didn't anticipate any problems. However, the review dragged on for months, and we got no reports from the journal about when it would appear. I contacted the editorial office repeatedly asking what accounted for the delay. My co-authors thought that I had failed to get the report written in a timely way and were getting impatient. Worse yet, as each week passed, someone would come up with a new idea or suggest another co-author, and I wasn't interested in pulling the manuscript back for additional rewrites at that time.

Finally, the manuscript was accepted—without revision. (What the heck…?) There were very few people in the field who were not at the workshop who could have reviewed the paper. The external reviewer was Manuel Perucho, who had all sorts of complaints, and the editors allowed him to write his own rebuttal "Letter to the Editor" to accompany our workshop report. His letter was a diatribe of his perception that he had been wronged by others in the field, and hinted that his wrath was mainly against Bert Vogelstein. It was a sorry day for the field, but sometimes that's what overheated competition brings.

Fortunately, better days were around the corner.

Chapter 15

Cracking the Mystery: Trudy, Rita, Bert and Yan (1994-2000)

It was time to solve the mystery and—for all times—find the genetic source of all of the cancers in our family. Since the Boland family was a large and well-documented Lynch Syndrome kindred, Bert Vogelstein and I had been collaborating on the problem since 1990. Shortly after the cloning of the four Lynch Syndrome genes, we were very interested in finding which one was responsible for the disease in our family. That was an absolute requirement for finding the specific mutation involved so we could test family members before they developed their first cancer. I had three siblings and twenty living first cousins at risk. Half of the at-risk family members would be expected to carry the mutation and the other half would not carry it (statistically, anyway), and the unaffected individuals would be spared a lot of anxiety and clinical testing. So, finding the specific mutation in the family was now my highest priority. The question was how to get there.

Getting back in touch with Dad

In 1985, I was visiting Endwell, NY, for a high school reunion. I was asked to visit Wilson Memorial Hospital, and gave a basic clinical lecture to the staff on colorectal cancer. My father had been the Chief of the Department of Pediatrics there, I had been born there, and he died there. I had accompanied my father there many times as a child, and waited in the car or inside the hospital as he did his rounds. It was home.

After the lecture, I visited the Department of Pathology to obtain my father's pathological records. I discovered that Dad had undergone an autopsy after his death, and there were about fifty tissue blocks created at the time of the autopsy, embedded in paraffin, sitting in their archives. I asked the chairman of Pathology what he would eventually do with these, and he admitted they would eventually be discarded. Under the circumstances, we reached an easy agreement that I would take them back to my lab with me. We put them into a plastic bag, and I took them home. Of course, in 1985, I had no idea what I might do with them.

However, in 1993, microsatellite instability was discovered, and this was the key to determine whether a tumor came from a patient with Lynch Syndrome or not. Bert Vogelstein knew the family was valuable because of its size, so I sent him one of the specimens of colon cancer from Dad's autopsy. He called back in a few days and say that Dad's tumors had an extreme version of microsatellite instability—wildly so, with one exception. Every microsatellite they tested was mutated but one. The non-mutated marker was called "CA5", and that microsatellite was known to be inside the *hMSH2* gene. I didn't know what to make of that, but I was not at all surprised that Dad's tumor showed hallmark features of Lynch Syndrome. One step forward.

A family reunion and genetic testing affair

In the summer of 1994, there was a Boland family wedding, and I flew from Ann Arbor to Reading for the celebration. With the number of cousins I had, there was usually at least one family wedding each year. Before going to Reading, I arranged for several in the family to get together for some genetic research. On the day after the wedding, we assembled at the home of my Aunt Marcella (who was the wife of my father's younger brother, Bob), and I explained what we were doing, obtained informed consent, and drew blood on a group of uncles, aunts, and cousins. Almost everyone was very interested in participating, but there were a few hold-outs. My Uncle Larry (who had five children) refused to be tested—"I don't want to be a guinea pig"—as did a cousin who was my age, but had no children. The cousin said he would "just continue getting colonoscopies" and didn't want to know whether he carried the mutated gene or not. I didn't agree with the logic, but didn't press the point. That was his call.

Cousin Trudy

One of my cousins who showed up was Trudy, the daughter of my Uncle Matthew, who had died of lung cancer in 1953, at age forty-nine. Uncle Matthew was the first-born son, was a surgeon in Reading, and had two children. Trudy was the oldest of the twenty-seven cousins. As far as anyone knew, Matthew did not have a Lynch Syndrome-related cancer, as lung cancer wasn't on our list. He was sixteen years older than my father, and I had not heard as much family lore about Uncle Matt as I had about some of the other aunts and uncles—like Larry Bob, and Alice, who were closer in age. Interestingly, some in the family said Uncle Matt was a heavy smoker but others said he wasn't. Also, he had served in the Pacific Theater in World War II, contracted dengue fever in Southeast Asia, and some in the family attributed his lung cancer to that infection. (I am unaware that there is any link.) At that time, we knew there was no excess of lung cancers among Lynch Syndrome kindreds that had been collected and reported, but we suspected that perhaps any tumor could occur as a consequence of a Lynch Syndrome mutation if you studied enough people—especially if there were additional environmental exposures such as tobacco. We just didn't know enough about the disease, and we were just starting to analyze large kindreds in which there was proof of Lynch Syndrome. Access to confirmatory genetic testing was very new.

Gertrude Ann Boland was born in May, 1935, the first grandchild of Thomas Sr. and Gertrude Boland. Her married name was first Foley, and later, Preissing. She and her brother Matt, Jr were more than a decade older than most of the rest of the cousins, as just five of twenty-seven cousins were born before the end of World War II. I had never met her before that Sunday afternoon in the summer of 1994. Trudy was fifty-nine at this time, and had never been to a family reunion, wedding or funeral that I had also attended. She had undergone prior (successful) surgery for endometrial cancer, but more recently had an operation for gastric cancer—both classic Lynch Syndrome tumors. Her brother, Matt, Jr, had not had a cancer at this time. I realized that Trudy might have been the first of my cousins to have identifiable Lynch Syndrome. I never saw her again after that one visit; she died in March, 1995 of metastatic gastric cancer. However, she left us a powerful legacy.

Aunt Rita

The other possible carrier of the family's Lynch Syndrome gene was Aunt Rita. She was seventy-nine in 1994, and in good health; however, she had developed two simultaneous colorectal cancers in 1980, at age sixty-five. Developing one colorectal cancer at age sixty-five is not a big surprise, but developing two cancers in my family meant Lynch Syndrome until proven otherwise. Both tumors were successfully resected, and Rita was doing fine fourteen years later. Rita had five living children as well, so there was a lot at stake in understanding her situation.

All of the other likely candidates for being carriers of the "Boland mutation" had died. My grandfather and seven of his thirteen children had died—and all seven had developed some type of cancer. Among the younger six siblings, three were living (Loretta, Rita and Larry—who had a total of twelve children among them), and the three youngest had already died of cancer (Alice, Clement and Robert). The two youngest boys had left seven children at risk for the disease.

So, Trudy was the only one of the cousins of my generation to have developed a cancer. I hoped that we would find something to work with in either cousin Trudy or Aunt Rita. Just one year earlier, shortly after the discovery of microsatellite instability, Vogelstein's lab had retrieved Rita's colon cancer specimen from the hospital where she had her colonic surgery—as the hospital was in Maryland close to Baltimore. Bert's lab had performed microsatellite instability testing, and reported that it was positive, but much less prominently than in my father's tumor. We didn't know what to make of that—but it turned out to be very important when we finally solved the problem.

Koi steps up again

I drew blood on all of my relatives, including some of the spouses (to serve as controls), put the blood into the appropriate test tubes (some for DNA extraction, and some for growing lymphocytes), and had the FedEx truck meet me in Aunt Marcella's driveway. Off went the cells to the lab in Ann Arbor. Back at our lab at the UM, Koi was waiting for the cells. He extracted DNA from some samples, and created immortalized cell lines from others, according to plan. Koi never missed.

Bert steps in again

We sent DNA samples to Bert's lab. Vogelstein is like Cher or Beyoncé, and is the only scientist in our field—other than perhaps Francis Collins—who can be recognized on the basis of a first-name reference. By the summer of 1994, his lab had the DNA sequence information on the *hMSH2* and *hMLH1* genes, and was working on the *hPMS2* gene. The first thing he found was there was no mutation in any of these genes in either Rita's or Trudy's DNA. We were disappointed of course, but knew from the start this could be a long haul and a complicated problem. Bert had a few more techniques in development in his lab that would get us over this speed bump.

Separating the chromosomes

Koi successfully immortalized Trudy and Rita's cells, which meant that we could grow the cells indefinitely and get as much of their DNA as we wanted in perpetuity. More importantly, with a living cell line, you can grow and manipulate the cells for more sophisticated analyses. At that time, Bert had a researcher in his lab named Hai Yan, MD, PhD. Hai was working on a technique called "conversion of diploidy to haploidy". Normal cells have two copies of every gene, and are consequently called "diploid". Yan was working on converting diploid cells to haploid ones. This was a novel concept to circumvent a problem in analyzing human DNA caused by the presence of two copies of each gene in each cell. If the mutation of interest happens to consist of a large deletion of DNA, when one does standard DNA sequencing, you get information from the unaffected normal gene, and the deleted genetic information is typically invisible. Finding something that isn't there is one of the bigger challenges in genetics. When there is a simple, small change in the DNA sequence such as a "point mutation" or a small deletion of just a few nucleotides in the DNA sequence, one detects the problem because the sequencing analysis overlays the sequence results of both genes, one on top of the other. Since DNA sequences are a string of the four DNA "letters", when you encounter a mutation at a single point in the DNA, you get two simultaneous results in the read-out; the result might look like: …AGTC(C/G) TTAA…, in which the middle "letter" represents a C on one DNA strand, and a G on the other, whereas the flanking "letters" were the same on both DNA strands. When this occurs, typically one sequence is the "normal" or "wild type" sequence (we all like that term "wild type"), and the other sequence result indicates a deviation or mutation. When there is a small deletion or insertion in the DNA sequence, this creates a "frameshift", as the two DNA strands are no longer matched up in length, so the sequences downstream of the deletion all appear to be mutated. It would be as if two singers were singing together, and one singer either added a beat or dropped one. Prior to the missed beat, they sing in unison, but after the missed beat, the subsequent song would sound cacophonous. One way of visualizing this is to consider that we have sequenced the DNA twice (each strand gives its individual signal), typed each sequence on a separate piece of paper, overlaid one sequence on top of the other, and held it up to the light to look through both sheets of paper for difference—as if you were looking for typographical errors between two paper copies. This is easy to interpret. But, when the altered DNA was a large deletion, the techniques of the 1990s were not powerful enough to tell that we were only looking at one copy of DNA, and the other was missing. That problem has been resolved through technical improvements. Conversion to haploidy meant separating the two chromosomes of interest and analyzing each one individually, which lifts the obscuring veil hiding the mutation (*Figure 26*).

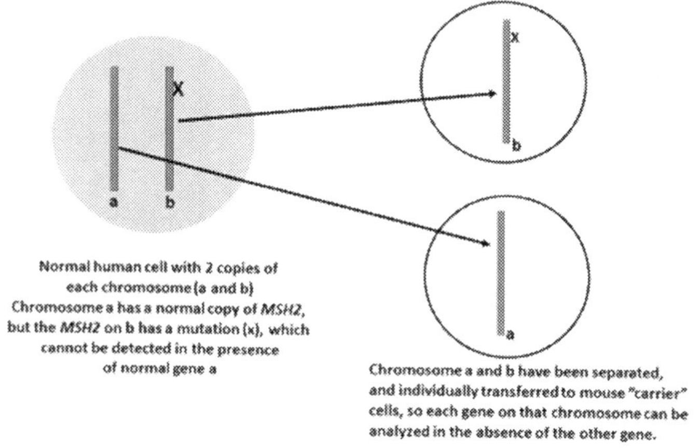

Figure 26: Schematic of conversion to haploidy. Trudy's mutation was a large deletion of about half of the *MSH2* gene, but it was masked and not detectable in the presence of the normal copy of *MSH2* that she inherited from her mother (*chromosome a*). The trick was to separate the two copies of chromosome 2 (a and b) from the cells we made from Trudy's lymphocytes so that the mutant copy (on chromosome b) could be evaluated by itself. Once the separation was accomplished, it was immediately apparent that the *MSH2* gene on chromosome b did not function properly, as it was missing exons 1-6.

It helped that we had some idea of which chromosomes might carry the affected gene. We predicted the mutation was on either chromosome 2, which carries *hMSH2*, or chromosome 3, where *hMLH1* lives, since these two genes were responsible for most of the Lynch Syndrome recognized at that time. We then needed a chromosomal marker that was different between the father's and mother's chromosomes 2 and 3—which was not difficult, because there were so many microsatellite markers available at that time. It didn't matter which chromosome came from mother or father; we just needed a way to tell whether one, both, or neither of the chromosomes were present in the DNA under analysis.

Armed with this information, Hai set out to separate the two copies of chromosomes 2 and 3 carried in Rita's and Trudy's cells, and determine if there were a DNA variation on one of the alleles that was being masked by the other gene. This required cell lines, and Koi's immortalized lymphocytes from Trudy and Rita provided this. Hai then isolated the nuclei from the lymphocytes, and coaxed the chromosomes to be transferred individually into cultured mouse cells. He was able to do this in a way that would transfer just a few of the human chromosomes at a time into the cultured mouse cells. If he did this enough times (which he did), he might eventually have a mouse cell line carrying just Trudy's father's chromosome and another carrying just her mother's chromosome.

This time, chromosome 2

On May 23, 1999, Bert sent me an email indicating that Hai had just separated chromosomes 2 and 3 from both Rita's and Trudy's cells. There is usually not much sequence variation within a gene among individuals, since there is only so much variability that can be tolerated in the synthesis of a critical protein. However, there is often considerable DNA sequence variation in the non-coding regions inside genes (introns) or in flanking sequences around the genes. These variations can identify which of two identical genes came from which parent, and can be used to determine relatedness between individuals or populations of people. We had DNA from the two family members most likely to provide the key to the genetic mystery.

By chance, Rita and Trudy had two different copies of both alleles of their *hMSH2* and *hMLH1* genes. That is, neither Rita nor Trudy had the same copy of either of these genes. This was a statistical fluke, but it raised a huge question. One explanation was that neither *hMSH2* nor *hMLH1* was the culprit gene in our family—which meant we had to go back to square one. A second explanation was that either Trudy or Rita didn't have Lynch Syndrome! It defied our expectation that one of these two—in the context of our family—could have something other than Lynch Syndrome. However, that turned out to be the case. In his news flash, Bert concluded that either Rita or Trudy was almost certainly a "phenocopy", which would be a Lynch Syndrome-associated cancer occurring in a Lynch Syndrome family—but not caused by that germline mutation.

Two days later, on May 25, Bert sent another news flash, with the apology that he wouldn't ordinarily send out such preliminary data, but he knew how important this was to me. Hai had created five cellular hybrids from the mouse cells that carried copies of Trudy's chromosome 2, and four that carried chromosome 3. All four of the hybrids carrying chromosome 3 expressed the *hMLH1* gene equivalently; that is, they were normal. However, among the five hybrids carrying chromosome 2, two expressed *hMSH2* robustly, but three didn't express it at all using a very sensitive RNA-based assay. This was strong evidence that the *hMSH2* gene was our villain, that Trudy carried a mutant, non-expressing version of it on the allele she inherited from her father, and that Rita had something else.

Understanding Rita's tumor

Later that day, Bert sent another email, after reviewing the microsatellite instability assay on Rita's tumor. When that assay was done in 1993, microsatellite instability was a new concept, and each lab used its own approach to measure it. We had been using our favorite tools, the CA dinucleotide repeats, because those were the tools initially used for gene mapping and the loss of heterozygosity experiments. However, at the National Cancer Institute Workshop in November 1997, we reviewed the scientific data and realized that there were two different types of microsatellite instability (MSI). One was called MSI-H (high), in which most of the microsatellites were mutated, and this was the distinguishing feature of a colorectal cancer that developed in the absence of DNA mismatch repair activity. This occurred in nearly all Lynch Syndrome colorectal cancers (about 3% of all colorectal cancers), and in another 12% of colon cancers, one found MSI-H because of the acquired silencing of the *hMLH1* gene. This latter situation was not Lynch Syndrome, and we soon had means to identify them specifically. Additionally, there was a second form of microsatellite instability that affected only a small proportion of the microsatellites tested, and this was called MSI-L (low). MSI-L mainly affected microsatellites consisting of di-, tri-, and tetra-nucleotide repeats, but usually not the mono-nucleotide repeats like AAAAAAA or TTTTTT, etc.). Once we recognized this, there was less confusion in classifying the tumors. In retrospect, Rita's colon tumor actually showed MSI-L, and with the new information, it was clear that she didn't have Lynch Syndrome; therefore, none of her five children was at risk for this. However, since she had two colon cancers that we couldn't explain, there might be something else going on there. Whatever genetic defect Rita had, she eventually lived to age ninety-seven, without another cancer. Rita's mystery was at least partially solved, and most of us would be pretty happy with Rita's genes.

Deletion of part of *hMSH2* is the culprit

So, the focus now was squarely on Trudy's *hMSH2* gene. In just a few more days, Bert wrote and said that Hai had analyzed the hybrids from Trudy that did not express the *hMSH2* gene, and that exons 1 through 6 of the *hMSH2* gene were missing. This was a huge breakthrough for us, as Trudy appeared to have lost half of the gene, including the critical "start" site. That copy of her gene would never work, and that was why she developed her cancers. Trudy had one of those large deletions that could not be seen when sequencing DNA from cells that also carried the wild type gene. The great news was that we now had a very good idea of which gene was causing Lynch Syndrome in the family. However, we couldn't use this information to make a diagnostic test, because of the problem of finding something that is *not there*. We would have to do the complicated "conversion to haploidy" on everyone in the family to do a proper test. Traditional sequencing the *hMSH2* gene would look the same whether you carried the mutation or not.

The explanation for Dad's unusual microsatellite instability

This finding also explained why my father's tumor showed microsatellite instability at every marker except BAT26 (*Figure 27*).

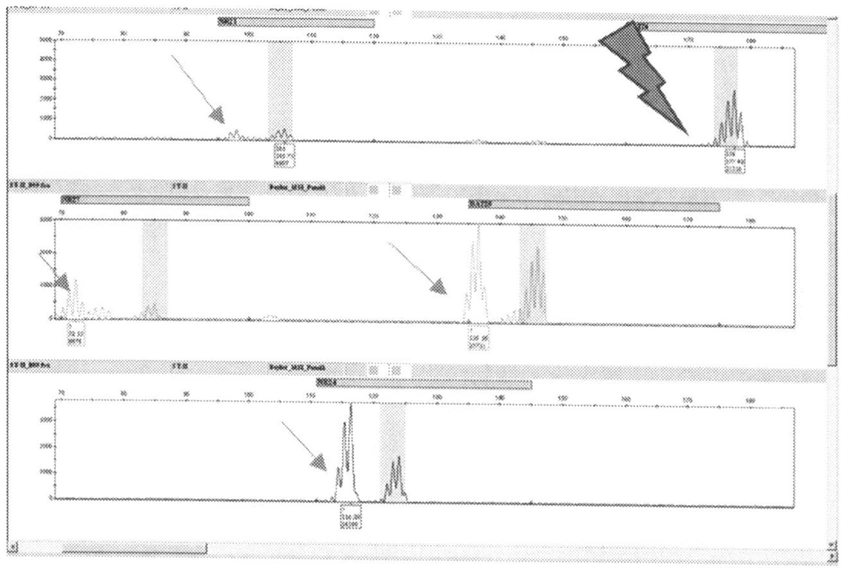

Figure 27: Testing for microsatellite instability (MSI) on Dad's tumor. The chromatographic tracing was run once, with multiple lasers, permitting three simultaneous analyses on the top, middle and bottom rows. There are two microsatellite analyses in each of the top two rows, and one on the bottom. The gray rectangular bands show where the "normal" PCR products should run (and there are always some normal cells in the tumor mass, so some of the peaks show up there), but for four of the five, addition mutated peaks are seen to the left of the expected peak, because they are shorter, indicated by the small arrows. However, on the top row, the tracing on the right is normal, and that is where the BAT-26 (previously called CA-5) microsatellite appeared. It is normal (with no mutant fraction, indicated by the lightning bolt) because both of the copies of this microsatellite were missing in the tumor, one of which was the germline mutation. Therefore, the only DNA being amplified was from the normal cells in the tumor mass. This told us that the germline mutation was likely to be a deletion in *hMSH2.*

That marker was located within the portion of *hMSH2* that was deleted in his DNA. Every cell in the body of a Lynch Syndrome patient contains two copies of the critical gene responsible for the disease; one is mutated and the other is "wild type". Each cell works fine with just one working copy of the DNA mismatch repair gene. A tumor doesn't develop until something happens to inactivate the wild type copy of the gene—in his case, the copy of *hMSH2* inherited from his mother. Both alleles must be missing for DNA mismatch repair activity to fail, and that is when mutations begin to accumulate at a very rapid pace. A common type of mutation that inactivates the second copy of the gene in this setting is an acquired large deletion—one of those "loss of heterozygosity" events that were the focus of attention in the late 1980s which we were all seeking using the microsatellite markers in the first place. Dad's tumor had an inherited deletion of the first half of his *hMSH2* gene, and then acquired an accidental loss of the other copy in one cell that eventually grew into the tumor. When microsatellite instability testing was done, both copies of *hMSH2* were missing from all of the cancer cells in his tumor. The marker BAT-26 looked normal because it reflected presence of a normal copy of *hMSH2* in the non-cancer cells in the tumor mass, which were also harvested and amplified doing that test. Curiously, this created a characteristic microsatellite "signature" in the family.

How do you make a test for a deletion?

Bert had his hands full with a number of other projects, and didn't have time to develop a diagnostic test for us. He told me that he would send back the hybrid mouse cells from Trudy's blood that carried the solitary mutant *hMSH2* gene, and advised me to "clone the breakpoint" in the gene. That would mean isolating the DNA sequences that immediately flanked the deletion, and developing a test for the place where the two pieces were spliced back together. The mutation was like a long series of beads on a string, in which a group of them had been removed, and the string tied back together. For now, there was no immediate way to test for this large deletion. We knew where the answer was hidden, but didn't have it in hand yet. My lab had never cloned a deletion breakpoint before. We were now about to try.

Chapter 16

MATT AND JENNIFER (2001)

In the fall of 2000, my sister Alice called me from Rochester, New York, said that her son Matt was considering a career in medicine, and wanted to know if he could spend some time working with me the next summer. He was a junior at Dartmouth College, and had taken introductory courses in biology, chemistry, and organic chemistry, but had no research expertise. I was spending most of my time in the laboratory, and was not in a position to give him much of a clinical experience. So, I suggested a laboratory-based research experience for Matt.

The American Gastroenterological Association (AGA) had a student research program. I had been on the Research Committee and knew about it. The student research award provided $1500 for students (high school, college or medical school) to spend about eight weeks, usually in the summer, getting an initial exposure to research in the laboratory of an AGA member. It had been noted that physician-scientists who chose careers in biomedical research usually had their initial exposures early—that is, before their fellowship training. This was a way to find the best and the brightest for our field. A grant such as this could make it possible for Matt to fly to San Diego and learn what we were doing in the lab. I didn't think he could accomplish that much on a serious project, but he would see how we approached problem-solving in a research lab, and it could trigger interest in more of it later. That would be good enough.

We had Trudy's cells in the lab, both her immortalized lymphocyte line and the mouse cells carrying her defective chromosome 2, but I didn't have anyone who was interested in dedicating a year to the project—which was what I figured it would take to clone the breakpoint and develop a diagnostic test for it. This was an intrinsic problem in characterizing something that isn't there.

The Human Genome Project

Fortuitously, the first draft of the Human Genome Project was about to be released in February 2001. Depending upon the level of detail in the report, we might be able to look at the genome map in February and get some idea of the genetic environment inside and surrounding the *hMSH2* gene, which would permit us to clone the deletion, characterize it, and develop a test for the family. Since we knew that exon seven of *hMSH2* was retained in the mutant gene (as only exons one through six were gone), we could possibly start with the first identifiably retained part of *hMSH2*, and then start "hopping" along the adjacent sequences of DNA upstream of exon seven using PCR and find the segment of DNA containing the place where the broken DNA pieces were joined back together, which would represent the "breakpoint". There were a lot of possibilities for how to solve the problem, once the framework of the "normal" sequence was known.

In early February 2001, I wrote a short research proposal outlining this approach, showing how we could be among the first to use the draft of the human genome to solve a clinical problem, and additionally, introduce a college student to the world of genetics research in gastroenterology. I wrote the basics of the science, Matt added his parts and we submitted the formal application for a student award. A little more than a month later, he was one of about twenty students funded for the summer of 2001.

Jennifer Rhees

At that time, I had a very talented Laboratory Assistant who rose to the level of Laboratory Manager named Jennifer Rhees, BS. A lab manager typically has a bachelor's or master's degree in biology or chemistry, runs the administrative functions in the lab, orders supplies, makes sure the equipment is running properly, keeps track of the finances, herds cats, and is the first go-to person for many details in the lab. That was enough to keep most people busy, but Jennifer did much more than this. She loved the genetics side of science, and was keeping up with the serial iterations of the Human Genome Project posted on the National Center for Biotechnology Information (NCBI) website. She was the first person I consulted to find out what DNA sequences were in any particular chromosomal location.

"What's going on in chromosome 2?"

A frequent conversation with Jennifer was "what's going on at the *hMSH2* locus on chromosome 2?" Once we found out that Trudy had a problem with *hMSH2*, Jennifer followed that gene on a regular basis. As the information obtained from the consortium of labs involved in creating the human genome gushed in, it was posted in an iterative series of "builds" or versions. Each one would presumably be a refinement of the last version based upon new data, getting a little more accurate and closer to the true sequence. The human genome had been divided up among different centers. One group might be working on chromosome 1, another on X or Y, and so on. The information was flowing into the NCBI site and the draft assembled in a massively parallel manner. Virtually no one knew what the big picture looked like, and everyone was waiting for the pieces to fall into place so that the formal analyses might begin.

Jennifer and I knew that a more detailed draft of chromosome 2 was imminent. But, week after week, Jennifer reported that something strange was going on in and around *hMSH2*. The sequences inside the gene, and the surrounding sequences, kept changing on the website as they reported the serial builds. The labs doing the sequencing were growing pieces of human chromosomes in BACs—bacterial artificial chromosomes—and the order of the exons continuously changed positions on the official site that was organizing the information. Jennifer couldn't explain it, but she kept telling me that "something strange is going on there".

PCR is a technique that permits you to amplify DNA sequences located between a pair of two primers. The sequence can be small (say, under one hundred nucleotides) or can be several thousand nucleotides long. There are limits to how much you can amplify on a very long template of DNA, and long amplifications require special approaches. However, as long as you know the DNA sequences in a general region, you can synthesize "primers" that will hybridize or stick to the target DNA—and you create them facing each other since DNA is read in a specific direction—and amplify the sequences between the two primers. Typically you start with a small amount of target DNA. The PCR reaction makes millions of copies of whatever is between the primers you have selected. If you then separate the resulting PCR products by electrophoresis, there will be one or more "bands" that are a million times more abundant than the initial template, and that is your result. If you select the primers poorly, you get an uninterpretable smear of results. If you get it just right, you get a single PCR product, which shows up as a single clear "band" on the purifying gel, which can be cut out and analyzed by a variety of approaches.

We decided that a simple approach to cloning the breakpoint in Trudy's defective *hMSH2* gene would be make one primer that would stick to the DNA of the remaining portion of Trudy's *hMSH2* gene on exon seven, orient the primer in the direction of the deleted portion of the gene (which was "upstream"), and then make serial primers at various intervals above the other end of the deletion (*Figure 28*).

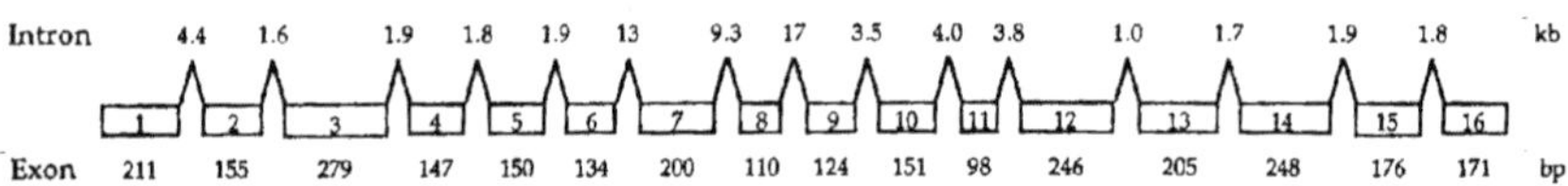

Figure 28a: Schematic image of the *MSH2* gene. The numbered rectangles are the exons, which are in the RNA after splicing out the introns. The *MSH2* gene has sixteen exons as shown here, and the number of DNA nucleotides is indicated beneath each exon. For *MSH2*, the first exon is made up of 211 nucleotides, the second 155, and so on. The introns between the exons are much larger, and their size is indicated in thousands of nucleotides. For *MSH2*, there are about 4,400 nucleotides in the first intron between the end of exon 1 and the beginning of exon 2. Many of the introns of *MSH2* are filled with Alu repeats.

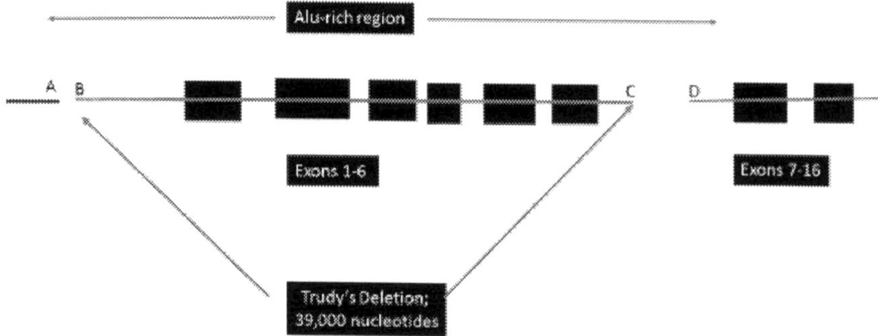

Figure 28b: *MSH2*, Alu repeats, and Trudy's mutation. The lower horizontal line represents the *MSH2* gene, and the upper horizontal line indicates that Alu repeats are found throughout the left side (so-called five-prime or 5') of the human *MSH2* gene. In Trudy's case, the first six exons of *MSH2* were missing, along with some span of the left side of the DNA sequence outside of the *MSH2* gene. The problem was that we didn't know just how much. In most people, DNA sequencing would find A, B, C, and D (as marked on the DNA) in that order, with the first six exons of *MSH2* between B and C. In Trudy's DNA, the sequencing showed that A was located immediately next to D, and the span between B and C had been deleted. This deletion inactivated that copy of Trudy's *MSH2*, and that was why Trudy had Lynch Syndrome. Our challenge was to identify the sequence of A, which would permit us to develop a diagnostic test.

What we needed to know was the normal sequence of the gene just above the start position of the gene, which the Human Genome Project data would presumably give us. We knew that any second primer (of the pair) located inside the deletion would give us no PCR product for that reaction—for the same reasons that this deletion was "invisible" during routine attempts to analyze Trudy's DNA in the first place. Using the Human Genome draft, we would be able to read what sequences were normally present in the presumed deletion, and eventually, we would land upstream beyond Trudy's breakpoint, and eventually, some primer pair would start giving us a PCR product—but this would be smaller than what was present in normal DNA. By determining how much smaller this PCR product was compared to the normal sequence, we could calculate the size of the deleted segment. We could then see what sequences were rejoined at the breakpoint, and calculate what had been deleted. Furthermore, as a confirmatory finding, one would not obtain the small PCR product from "normal" DNA, as this sequence would also contain the entire deleted portion, which would be too long for the PCR reaction. At least, such was our prediction.

We were pleased with this idea, and it would be soon possible to do this on the basis of the Human Genome data. Moreover, once we had two PCR primers that flanked the pathologically deleted portion of the gene, we would use this as our diagnostic test, since it would not be hidden by the other, normal copy of the *hMSH2* gene. Suddenly, the process of cloning the breakpoint seemed entirely tractable.

"We have a big problem"

In February 2001, the much-anticipated draft of the Human Genome was released with great fanfare, including television appearances by Francis Collins MD, PhD, J. Craig Venter, PhD, and President Bill Clinton. The data were freely available to all researchers. Jennifer dug into *hMSH2* to find the sequences that would solve the genetic mystery for my family. Jennifer just about croaked when she viewed the draft sequences. "Rick, we have a big problem".

The sequencing consortium had completed about 99% of the genome, because about one percent was at that time—and to some degree still is—unsequencable. What makes PCR possible is the uniqueness of the sequences of our genome. If you create a primer that is about twenty nucleotides long, it is likely to stick to a small number of places in our entire genome, perhaps just one place once you optimize the hybridization conditions. Furthermore, you design your primers using a program that attempts to guarantee that you will be amplifying a unique site.

What Jennifer saw was that the deleted portion of Trudy's *hMSH2* was in a swamp of *Alu* repeats. There are over one million *Alus* in our genome, all over the place, and frequently in clusters. *Alu* sequences make up over ten percent of our entire genome! They are non-coding and are thought to represent the result of an ancient attack on the primate genome by a retrovirus, which amplified itself over and over. Only primates have these sequences, and they probably facilitate some "jumping around" or rearranging of our genetic material.

This was just about the worst possible outcome. The draft of the genome more or less said "swamp here", and we couldn't even tell how many *Alus* were there. Worse, the number of *Alus* was variable from person to person. It would be very difficult to find a unique sequence in the neighborhood of the deletion for a PCR primer, because the genome groups couldn't find or publish the precise sequences in this region. If we made a primer that would stick to an *Alu* sequence, it would prime all over the genome, and would generate millions of uncharacterizable PCR products. It was the presence of these sequences that resulted in the changing reports about the structure of the *hMSH2* gene. The sequences were jumping around in the BACs used by the sequencers—art imitating life. For us, it was like Indiana Jones and snakes.

The presence of all these *Alu* sequences appeared to explain a lot. First, *Alu* sequences are nearly identical (not exactly, but close), and when the chromosomes wind up around one another, during mitosis (cells dividing) or meiosis (when the sperm or egg cells undergo their own conversion to haploidy), the *Alus* naturally stick to one another and "recombine", which can result in chromosomal rearrangements. So, the first thing that came to mind was that, if each end of the breakpoint in Trudy's *hMSH2* gene consisted of *Alu* sequences, that would give us a possible explanation of how the mutation had occurred in the first place in one of my ancestors. A similar problem had already been reported in a large Finnish kindred, and resulted in the deletion 3,500 nucleotides, including one of the exons of *hMLH1*, which resulted in Lynch Syndrome. In any event, our initial plan hit the garbage can.

Matthew B. Yurgelun

In late April, Matt made his way to San Diego, unaware of our conundrum. I hadn't known Matt that well prior to his arrival. I knew he was an outstanding student, and when he arrived I found that he had a wonderfully relaxed and unassuming air about him. Nothing seemed to bother him. Some days he would say "good morning" well into the afternoon as we passed in the hallways, and I thought he must have lost track of the time. Actually, it was just his sense of humor at work. He didn't look to see if he got a rise out of me; he just went on about his business. I had to get used to his droll style, but it wasn't hard, as he was so likeable.

We began each morning together in San Diego with an early morning jog, went to and from work together, and became quite close over the summer. His parents came to visit, and were impressed that he had settled in so effortlessly and seemed so excited about the lab experience. He was quite unlike any other student I had encountered. He took in everything I told him, and it seemed that no matter how fast I dished it out, he absorbed it all—and remembered everything. It was especially unusual because he made no attempt to impress me preemptively with what he knew. But every time I asked him something, he had the answer.

On his first day in the lab, Matt, Jennifer and I sat down and reviewed the problem that the *Alu* swamp had created with our initial plan. We needed a different approach. How do you find something that isn't there? Jennifer suggested that we try an approach called "inverse PCR". This was a technique that involved cutting the DNA with a restriction enzyme, which are DNA-cutting enzymes made by bacteria to protect themselves from invasion. With this approach, one can create ends of the DNA pieces that are "sticky". With proper enzymatic manipulation, you can coax the ends to rejoin. When you cut DNA with a restriction enzyme, both ends of each fragment have complementary features. So, under the right conditions, some of the ends of a single strand will join itself, and form a circle. If you isolate one of these circularized pieces of DNA that contains a known landmark (like the portion of exon seven that was possibly near Trudy's breakpoint), you can then use the known sequences from the newly created circle as a starting point, and sequence the DNA around the circle, finding the unknown portion in the middle. This allowed you to sequence DNA through a "back door", and jump over the missing sequences. Matt nodded that this sounded like a good idea.

I asked Matt, "Have you ever cut DNA with a restriction enzyme before?"

"Yes".

"How many times?"

"Once."

"OK, have you ever done PCR before?"

"Yes."

"How many times?"

"Once".

"Sequenced DNA?"

"Once."

We went on for a couple of minutes, and he had done most of the lab procedures we were planning on doing—once each time. Well, that was a start.

Inverse out, panhandle in

Matt worked on the inverse PCR experiment with Trudy's DNA for about two weeks, and we didn't think we were making any progress. Matt and I would discuss his results when we jogged at 6 AM, while in the car, and each day in the lab together with Jennifer. We decided that he needed to try something different. He disappeared for three days in the library, and had discussions with some of the post-docs in our lab and other labs. Then he came back to me.

"Uncle Rick. I have an idea of how to improve the inverse PCR approach. I found a new technique called 'panhandle PCR'".

"What's that?" He tried to explain that it involved some manipulation and extension of the ends of the cut DNA before circularization that would improve the efficiency of the technique. The technique was specifically designed to find sequences in the middle of unsequencable stretches of DNA, which was our challenge. One started with a cut fragment of DNA that you knew you wanted (like inverse PCR), used the known "sticky" ends as a place to start, and gradually added extensions to the cut ends. Under the right conditions, the extended arms would stick together, and the DNA segment would, theoretically, look like a pan and handle (*Figure 29*).

Panhandle PCR

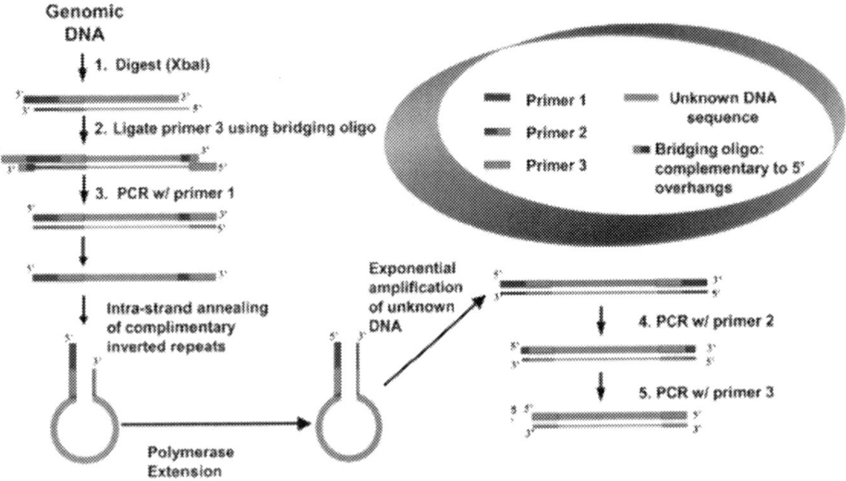

Figure 29: Panhandle PCR. This is a sketch of the strategy used to clone the sequences of DNA that flank something that isn't there, by cutting the DNA into random fragments, extending the ends of the fragments using routine genetic techniques that permit a specific fragment to be amplified a million fold using PCR. By analyzing the PCR product, if you are lucky, you can see where the sequence "jumps" over the deleted segment of DNA.

Once you had a "panhandle" of DNA with known extensions, you use those as starting points for cycles of PCR to amplify the fragment a million-fold. Then, one could start sequencing from the known retained part of *hMSH2*, and work into the previously unsequencable region.

"OK, give it a try". I was impressed with his independence, and he seemed impervious to anxiety or doubt, without a hint of swagger. Two weeks later, he showed me an autoradiogram from a Southern blot (a way of characterizing fragments of DNA) suggesting that he had isolated at least one fragment of DNA that was an appropriate size for "panhandling", and that also contained Trudy's important exon seven sequence. He then launched into extending and amplifying that fragment, and prepared it for DNA sequencing.

At this point, we would be doing DNA "walking", which was a more tedious approach in which you get as much of a DNA sequence as possible from a known starting position (such as the extension sequences from the "panhandle" fragment), create a new primer from the sequence at the other end, and keep walking upstream toward the putative breakpoint. You may have to slog through a swamp along the way, so the result was not predictable. Off Matt went, under Jennifer's able guidance.

"We Got It!"

One evening, it was about 7 PM in late June, 2001, and Jennifer and Matt were at Jennifer's desk, reading a DNA sequence they had just obtained. My office door was open, and I could turn my head and see Jennifer's desk from where I was working. Jennifer was reading the A's, C's, G's and T's out loud, and Matt was following along and comparing the sequence they had obtained with the recently published sequence in the sixth intron, where the breakpoint would presumably be found. This had become a late afternoon-early evening ritual, to assess the day's progress.

On this particular evening however, as they "walked" along the intron towards a possible breakpoint, they found an abrupt change in the expected sequence, and they were now in a DNA sequence that was from somewhere else. They had just jumped the deleted gap. The new place, they discovered, was 31,000 nucleotides upstream from where they should have been. Essentially, they had just walked across the breakpoint in Trudy's DNA, which permitted them to jump over the entire missing sequence of *hMSH2*. Moreover, each end of the breakpoint was in one of the dreaded *Alu* repeat sequences.

Matt calmly said, in a slightly excited tone of voice, "We got it". I heard it, and dared not to assume what they had gotten.

"What do you have, Matt?"

"The breakpoint".

"Really?"

"Yes, and it's an *Alu*-mediated recombination, as we anticipated".

We looked at the sequencing results together and exchanged hugs all around. It had been a landmark day. Jennifer went home to her family. Matt and I went home, told Pat what had transpired that day, and proceeded to have a nice meal, and the best bottle of wine in the house. Matt was clearly happy, but never giddy. He was, quite simply, amazing.

The next morning, we were jogging together, and I told Matt that he had accomplished something very important in the past six weeks. However, to be fully successful, he still had two more weeks to create a diagnostic test for the family. The problem was that the breakpoint was still situated in the *Alu* swamp. We couldn't necessarily pick any random place in this sequence to design PCR primers. Matt and Jennifer had to find a sufficiently unique sequence that would give just one PCR product in the entire human genome. That was essential. Both primers had to represent completely unique sequences not found anywhere else in the genome, otherwise, we would get "false priming" and spurious PCR results, and both ends of the breakpoint were in the middle of the *Alu* swamp.

However, this challenge played right into Jennifer's expertise, and I was beginning to recognize Matt's incredible way with luck. Matt and Jennifer picked what looked like a promising pair of primers and tried it out on DNA from the mouse cells carrying Trudy's mutant gene, plus her lymphocytes that we had in great numbers, as well as a number of negative controls. One try and one successful result. The test worked as planned. We had a small and identifiable PCR product that contained the sequences flanking Trudy's deletion, and this product was not present in any of the control samples. Furthermore, Jennifer engineered another PCR reaction (carried out in the same tubes) that would give a product in all normal or mutated samples to make sure that the DNA being tested was intact and that the PCR reaction was working properly. This would ensure that a negative result indicated the absence of the deletion, and not a problem with the assay. Everything worked perfectly. By July, Matt was heading back to Rochester thinking that research wasn't so hard after all, and in the fall he went back to Dartmouth for his senior year. His life was filled with remarkable possibilities, and I marveled at what he might do and become.

In a period of just eight weeks, Matt had flown to the West Coast, bonded with his uncle, learned how to do PCR, designed new PCR reactions, figured out how to overcome obstacles, and developed a novel test that was critical to changing the course of history for our family. I have never heard him boast about this, and whenever I bring it up, he just smiles contentedly, and thanks me for letting him stay with us that summer. Matt eventually went to Columbia Medical School, trained in medicine and oncology at Harvard Medical School, and is currently a GI Oncologist on the faculty of the Dana Farber Cancer Institute and Harvard Medical School. Jennifer stayed on as Lab Manager for another twelve years, and solved two more problems at least as complicated as Trudy's was. Matt and Jennifer had quite the summer. The combination of superior intelligence and really good luck is hard to beat.

Chapter 17

THE TEST AND ITS IMPACT (2001-PRESENT)

By the summer of 2001, we had found Trudy's mutation, developed an assay for detecting it in blood, and assumed that this was the mutation that was responsible for Lynch Syndrome for the rest of the Boland family. However, we hadn't proved that yet, and we didn't know if the test we developed would work properly on everyone. Furthermore, I didn't know if everyone would agree to take the test or how each person would respond to the result. Would knowing change things?

Who gets tested first?

We had DNA in the lab previously obtained from myself and my three siblings, which was where we would start. Jennifer was appointed to run the assays. She started with me and one sibling on our first day of running the test on living people. It was an anxious day for both of us. We weren't sure what to expect. It was a pretty simple test, now that we knew where to look and how to do it. Just a few PCRs done in a single tube. No autoradiograms, x-ray films, or other more complicated assays that take a lot of time and handling, which is where things can go wrong. We had the DNA purified and ready to go. We had the PCR primers waiting to be put into the tubes. All would be completed in a few hours. Jennifer ran the test and the internal controls. Everything seemed to be working as anticipated.

Jennifer had the results in hand and slowly came into my office, looking at the bands obtained from the agarose gel. The results had been run side by side. One was positive, and one was negative. We looked at each other without additional words, just a shrug. Oh well, here it is, now we finally know. We also concluded that the test worked; it wasn't just an idiosyncratic problem with Trudy's gene. On to the other two.

The next day, she ran the other two siblings' test. We didn't want to have too many samples open on the bench at the same time and possibly mix them up. That would be disastrous. We had more anxious moments as we awaited those results. Again she brought me the PCR results without a word. Once again, one positive, one negative. Just like flipping coins. She had written on the image who was who. Just like that, the mystery of so many years was over. We knew who carried the mutant gene, and who did not. Two had to continue with specific preventive care, and two were off that hook. Two had the deletion and two didn't, just as the bookmakers would have predicted. Also, the deletion fit exactly with the "fingerprint" microsatellite instability result we had found in Dad's DNA. This was it. We had just moved from the era of assuming into the era of knowing.

I took the two sets of results of the four of us, sat them on my desk and looked at them for some time. It wasn't an easy day. I called all three sibs, and everyone knew everyone else's situation. We then had to make arrangements for the appropriate children to be tested as well, since many had reached the age where they would begin to experience the risk of cancer. Everyone was calm about this, and we felt as though we were all in the same boat, regardless of who was a carrier and who was not. Moreover, in our situation, we knew there were very effective preventive measures. At that time, we were recommending colonoscopies every two years beginning at age twenty-five, with very careful removal of all polyps. Women needed to consider having their uterus and ovaries removed after childbearing was complete. Against all odds, our ages ranged from fifty to fifty-six, and no one had suffered a cancer. None. Both sisters had their uterus and ovaries removed some time back for reasons not directly related to Lynch Syndrome—although that risk was taken into account at the time. Both sisters had complicated diverticulitis that required colonic surgery. After a lot of consideration, both had a small section of their sigmoid colon removed, but that left the proximal colon in place, which is where about 70% of Lynch Syndrome colon cancers occur. We needed to keep up with the colonoscopies. As you might imagine, we shared a lot of colonoscopy and colon prep jokes in the family. Laughing can get you through a fair number of stressful situations.

Can you have Lynch Syndrome without cancer?

One thing struck me as I gazed at the results. When I was researching my MD thesis in New Haven in the 1970s, I was in the basement stacks of the Yale Medical School library, all alone, doing a statistical "doodle". I was unconsciously doing calculations of the likelihood of whether a theoretical fifty-fifty proposition might occur in all four of us, or in none of us. This was the same as calculating the likelihood that you would flip a coin four times and come up with four heads or four tails. The most likely outcome was that two would inherit a Mendelian dominant genetic trait, and two would not. How likely would it be that all four of us would have the same result? There was one chance in sixteen that either all four would carry the mutation, or that none of us would. All four of us had a barium enema shortly after Dad's death in 1970, when our ages ranged from nineteen to twenty-five. We continued those periodically, at no precise interval. They were messy, unpleasant, and involved considerable exposure to x-rays. I had no idea how dangerous that amount of x-ray exposure might be for a Lynch Syndrome patient, since we had no idea what the disease was about, or whether we might be more susceptible to x-ray injury. (We now think this is the case with hereditary breast cancer, but not hereditary colon cancer syndromes.) When we got together, we would remind one another. "Had your test lately?"

Here was the mystery. I didn't have my first colonoscopy until June 30, 1978, when I was thirty years old. My siblings eventually started colonoscopies at some time thereafter. All of us were older than age twenty-seven by the time we had our first colonoscopy, and by that age, our father, grandfather and Aunt Alice had already developed their first colon cancer. Colonoscopies are important because you can remove premalignant polyps and prevent cancer from developing. A barium enema has no such value. But we had all been spared. What was happening? Were we just lucky? The chance that we were really lucky was one in sixteen. Now, some thirty-one years after Dad's death, we found out that there had been a fifty-fifty split on inheriting the gene, but no one had been sick from it (discounting the many colonoscopy preps we all had). What did this mean? Was the disease in the Boland family more complicated?

Once microsatellite instability was found (and instantly confirmed in three labs) and the Lynch Syndrome genes were discovered, it was possible to look at all familial clusters of colorectal cancer and confirm that diagnosis. Did every familial cluster of colorectal cancer represent Lynch Syndrome? This analysis was performed, and to my surprise, nearly half of all familial clusters of colorectal cancer did not have a mutation in a DNA mismatch repair system gene, and therefore, did not have Lynch Syndrome. This was first reported by a large consortium that assembled over 160 familial colorectal cancer clusters that met the criteria for Lynch Syndrome (which included the requirement of at least three affected members in a family and one person under age fifty), and forty percent of those familial clusters definitely did not have a DNA mismatch repair problem. After much discussion at the national and international Lynch Syndrome meetings, we decided to call those families with a proven germline mutation in a DNA mismatch repair gene Lynch Syndrome. So, the name that I came up with in 1984 now had a more specific connotation. That name meant the "real thing". So, what was happening in the other forty percent of families, those with a cluster of colorectal cancer, but no microsatellite instability and no mismatch repair gene mutations?

"Syndrome X"

Laney Lindor, MD, a geneticist from the Mayo Clinic sent me an email one day in 2004 and told me about the newly recognized 40% problem. She said she was sure that they didn't have Lynch Syndrome, but they were likely be confused with the real disease, and perhaps be given inappropriate counseling and management. Moreover, we didn't know what might constitute appropriate management of these families. She suggested the moniker "Familial Colorectal Cancer-Type X". I thought that was a reasonable placeholder name until we figured out what was going on in those families. Of course, I later found out that some geneticists found that name unacceptable because there was an X chromosome; apparently, no copyright had been claimed by its creator. So, there we were with another familial colorectal cancer disease. It was like pre-1993, all over again.

I wondered why some people with Lynch Syndrome—such as my father, grandfather and aunt—got colon cancers between ages twenty-five and twenty-seven, and others, like myself and my siblings, got into our sixties without cancer? Also, my Aunt Rita developed two colon cancers at age sixty-five, and her tumors (in retrospect) did not have microsatellite instability. This was confusing. We had tested Rita's DNA for Trudy's *hMSH2* deletion, and (as expected, based upon what Bert and Yan had told us), she didn't carry it. Suppose both Lynch Syndrome and Familial Colorectal Cancer-Type X were in the family? Suppose Dad, grandfather and Aunt Alice all had both problems, and the others who developed cancers later had just the Lynch Syndrome gene, and Rita had the Type X gene? Rita lived to age ninety-eight without another cancer. Furthermore, none of her five children has had a cancer. Whatever she had, it was nothing like Lynch Syndrome.

This made the interpretation of the Lynch Syndrome results tricky. By 2001, in my father's sibship of thirteen, ten had died, and three were living and could be tested. Two were tested (Aunt Loretta and Aunt Rita), and both were negative. Uncle Larry refused to be tested. Loretta, Rita and Larry lived to ages ninety-two, ninety-seven, and ninety-four respectively. In my generation ("the cousins"), twenty-four of twenty-seven of us were living and presumably at risk for Lynch Syndrome (*Figure 30*).

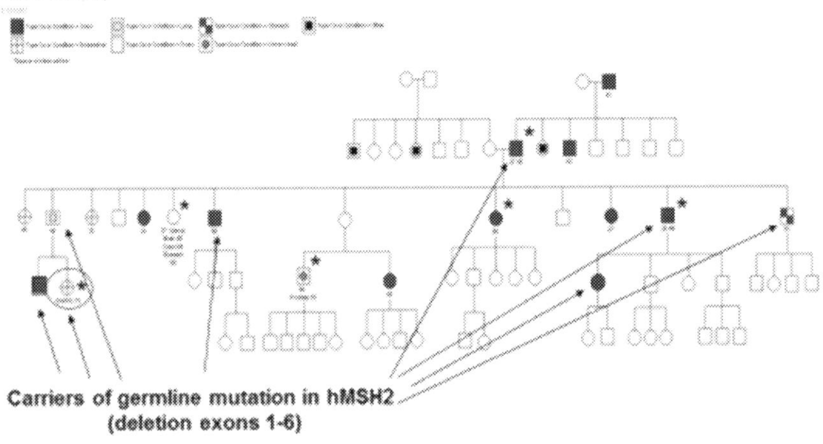

Figure 30a: Finding the mutation carriers. Once the test was developed, we found by direct measurement (Trudy) and inference (relatedness or microsatellite instability) who were the carriers of the Boland family deletion in the *MSH2* gene, as indicated by the arrows. Those mutation carriers who are still living are not listed, with the exception of Suzanne (Chapter 18).

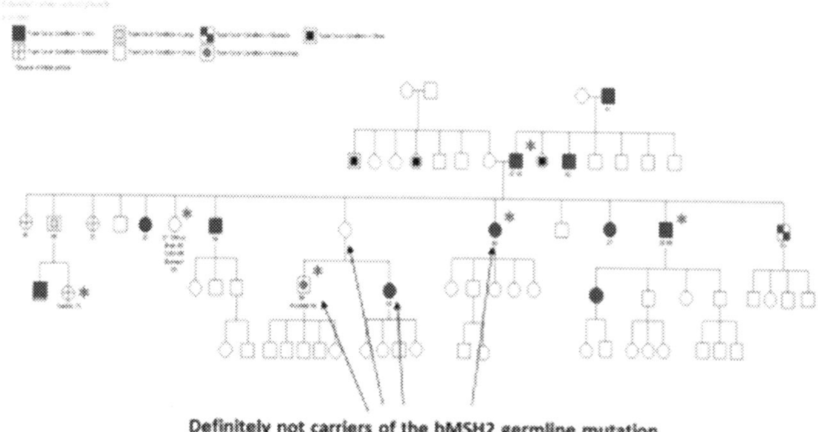

Figure 30b: Excluding those who did not carry the mutation. Nearly as important, we are able to exclude several members of the family from having Lynch Syndrome. Most notably, Rita—who had suffered two colon cancers—definitely did not have Lynch Syndrome, so none of her five living children will have it either. Likewise, Loretta, whose daughter Mary Anne died of colon cancer, was not a mutation carrier, and none of her grandchildren can either. This saved a considerable amount of confusion, anxiety and unnecessary colonoscopies and surgeries.

We knew exactly who in my sibship inherited the risk gene, but for the two living aunts and one living uncle, there were twelve living offspring, and a substantial number of grandchildren. Also, Trudy had an at-risk brother, and Bob, who died of gastric cancer, had three living at-risk children.

Assigning risk and preventing cancer

Getting negative test results on Loretta and Rita immediately removed seven cousins from the risk pool. I tested three of the cousins who were children of Larry, and all tested negative, and they were home free. We figured out Uncle John's and Uncle Bob's situations, and got those parts of the family properly advised. Cousin Matt (Jr), Trudy's brother, refused to be tested or talk about his situation. He had no children, claimed that he was taking care of his health as he saw fit, and that was all he wanted to know about the disease. I don't know what surveillance regimen he was following. However, he developed two colon cancers, the first in 1995—a detail that he withheld from me (and everyone else)—and eventually died of a second cancer in 2009. Along the way, he had a malignant sebaceous tumor removed in 1999 (indicating that he had the type of Lynch Syndrome called Muir-Torre Syndrome), and a prostate cancer had been successfully treated. Whenever I spoke with him, he politely declined to discuss his disease possibilities, or how to respond to it. Although I don't understand it, that was his choice, and I respected his desire to not get involved with the solution to the problem.

Every one of the cousins who tested positive started the prevention program I recommended, and only one has developed a single colon or gynecological cancer since 2001 (see the next chapter). Moreover, none of their children has developed a tumor. Also, about half of the group tested negative for the mutation, and they have been advised to take "usual" preventive measures that anyone in the general population should follow. Importantly, the possible intrusion of a "Syndrome X" problem meant that there might still be an unexplained family history of colorectal cancer mixed in with the Lynch Syndrome mutation. I could only deal with the *hMSH2* problem and give appropriate advice for that problem. I had no way to deal with the Syndrome X possibility.

That problem notwithstanding, this was a remarkable turn-about for the Boland family. We could carry the mutation, and live a normal, long life. Furthermore, those aunts and uncles who were not carriers of Trudy's mutation tended to live a very long time, and had very productive lives. So, the decision that Pat and I made in 1974 to start a family, long before there seemed to be a chance that we would ever solve the problem, was a sound one. Furthermore, I am very grateful for my father's decision not to undergo radiation therapy for his Stage III colon cancer in 1946. It would have harmed him, and I would never have walked on planet Earth.

Mary Anne Stitzel's puzzling and lethal cancer

Aunt Loretta had two children—cousins Ed Kuhn and Mary Anne Stitzel. Loretta was eighty-seven at the time we developed the test, and she had never had a tumor of any kind. As expected, she tested negative for Trudy's mutation. I had suggested to Ed and Mary Anne in the 1990's that, given their mother's favorable health circumstances, they probably were not at risk for Lynch Syndrome. If mother does not carry the mutation, they cannot. The presence of a tumor can skip generations, even in the presence of a mutated gene because of "incomplete penetrance". Mary Anne was a nurse, and I knew from prior discussions that she was clinically perceptive. She had been the first one to suggest (to her mother, Loretta) that my mother appeared to be taking steroids when she was in the early stages of her Cushing's syndrome problem that led to her death.

One day in 1999, Mary Anne developed rectal bleeding, which she ignored for some months. Eventually she had the problem evaluated, and in May, 1999, her physicians found a large adenocarcinoma at her rectosigmoid junction; she was age fifty-five. The tumor was moderately invasive, and two lymph nodes were positive for cancer at the time of her operation, making it a Stage III tumor. There was no evidence of microsatellite instability, and it had normal expression of *hMSH2* and *hMLH1*, confirming with certainty that this was not Lynch syndrome. She then received post-operative adjuvant chemotherapy.

Unfortunately, she developed a metastatic lesion in her liver. She underwent resection of the liver lesion at Johns Hopkins, but her tumor was relentless, and continued to recur. She died of liver metastases in November of 2004. She had four children, and I have told them (repeatedly) that they do not have Lynch Syndrome. I am not sure that they all believe it, given what happened to their mother. At least one tells me that he is getting regular colonoscopies. How strongly could I tell him that he might be overdoing it? The problem is that there is still a lingering possibility of a Syndrome X gene running amok in the family—just to confuse and terrorize all of us.

The impact of the test

At the time of this writing, it has been over fourteen years since we developed a test to let us know whether or not we carry the dreaded Lynch Syndrome gene. Most of those at risk were tested, and a few did not, which is rather surprising, since the refusers were my uncle and a couple of my cousins. I have had patients refuse testing for a variety of reasons. Most are unwilling to give a cogent reason, and every refuser has been a male. Go figure. Must be something on the Y chromosome.

Among those who have tested positive for the mutation, annual (or in some instances, semi-annual) colonoscopies have not only prevented cancer deaths, that has also prevented the occurrence of colorectal cancer, since removing benign adenomatous polyps is an effective means of preventing colorectal cancer. It appears that the growth from the small benign lesion to a larger malignant tumor occurs more quickly in Lynch Syndrome than in sporadic situations. Thus, whereas annual or semiannual colonoscopies would be overdoing it for a typical family history of colon cancer, it appears to be necessary—and apparently very effective—in this setting. I don't expect this approach will be perfect forever, but it has been very good thus far.

There has been only one exception to the cancer-prevention rule. Sister Sue.

Chapter 18

Suzanne (2006-2015)

Lead me not into temptation; I can find the way myself." Rita Mae Brown

Sue is my older sister, and we have been very close all our lives. My three siblings and I each have three unique relationships. Sue and I have a special closeness as the older two—just as Alice and Jim have as the younger two. Jim and I have the special relationship as the "two boys"—and boys will be boys, of course. Finally, Alice and I have a special relationship as those in the middle, and I am pretty sure that Alice and I have never had a serious argument or fight. Ever. I am writing one chapter focused on Sue because her circumstances—and her response to them—have earned her a special place in this book.

I have specifically not called out any living person in my extended family who is a carrier of the Lynch Syndrome mutation out of respect for their privacy. Sue gave me permission to do so as she is an extraordinary survivor, and anyone who knows her would immediately recognize that she was one of the anointed ones in the family, even if I hadn't written this chapter. She has already had multiple cancers, and survived them all. She talks about it freely, and has declined the cover of privacy over this. After all, none of it is her fault.

At the time we discovered Trudy's mutation and developed a test to detect those who carried it, none of the four of us had ever developed a tumor, in spite of the fact that we were well past the typical age of cancer in the Boland family. Sue got the unwanted call from me in the summer of 2001 that she was a carrier of the mutation. When a person hears that news, a series of psychological responses and defenses immediately kick in. "I knew I would be the one". "I looked the most like Dad". Maybe some of us thought "I can take it better than you others". Sue didn't say that, but it would be a common response, especially for the eldest sibling. No complaints, no drama. "Just tell me what to do, and I will do it."

Sue then began a regimen of colonoscopy every two years, which was an accepted preventive program at the time, and still is. She had already lost her uterus and ovaries for a prior problem. Women with Lynch Syndrome have a 40% lifetime risk of endometrial cancer, and we had three aunts and a cousin who had that disease, two of whom died of it, a long time ago. Sue had previously undergone the removal of a segment of her colon for diverticulitis, but still had all of her proximal colon, where most of the cancer risk resides. So, she started her prevention regimen, and we traded on-line video jokes over the years about the awful preps that were required. On a few occasions, she privately told me that her prep hadn't been perfect. I would scold her for this, and she would make a joke out of it. It was part of our brother-sister dynamic.

In 2005, Sue retired as a guidance counselor in the public school system at age fifty-nine. Her husband, Charlie, was seven years older, had been a high school history teacher, a spectacularly successful high school basketball coach, and had retired a few years earlier, in part because he had developed a meningioma deep in his brain, and the attendant surgery had left him with some residual problems. So, they started their joint retirements together.

How to lose a lot of weight without really trying

In 2006, Sue lived in Binghamton, New York and I was in Dallas, Texas, and we spoke on the phone regularly. A few months after retirement, she proudly announced that she had lost five pounds. I congratulated her for this. A couple of weeks later, she gushed that she had lost five more pounds. I told her this was great, and asked what she was doing to lose the weight. She thought that perhaps she was eating fewer cookies or snacking less since leaving the workplace. Eating was an important part of her life. She was a beautiful child, young woman, and is still attractive and lively (*Figure 31a, 31b*). But, over the years as she became an excellent cook (and as her husband was Italian, she became particularly accomplished in that style of cooking), and a few pounds gradually accumulated year after year. "I don't know why I got fat, and I don't know why I am now getting skinny, but I like it", was her analysis of the situation. A month or so later it was fifteen pounds, then twenty pounds. It just kept coming off. I was a little worried. In my family, weight loss is not an unmitigated gift.

Figure 31a: Suzanne Boland as a child

Figure 31b: Suzanne, October 2014

By April, 2006 Sue had lost forty-five pounds, and suddenly became ill with right lower abdominal pain and spiked a high fever. She saw her primary care physician, and he thought she had the flu. I called him and suggested that, in her situation, the flu was not a reasonable diagnosis. Sue had undergone a colonoscopy eighteen months earlier that was negative, but Sue had admitted to me that she had not had a perfect prep that time, and her proximal colon was not entirely clear. So, I recommended that she either have a colonoscopy or a CT scan of the abdomen. Her physician ordered a CT scan, which was read as negative.

"Who read it? Was the appropriate contrast agent used?" I asked. "Take it to the best radiologist in town", I suggested.

He did, and it was still read as negative. She then developed a urinary tract infection with an organism that is known to occur in people who has colon cancer—Group D Streptococcus. I called her gastroenterologist and told him that I thought he needed to look at her colon again. I told him I thought she either had a cancer in the proximal colon (where the pain was), or in her right renal collecting system (a relatively rare tumor that is greatly over-represented in Lynch Syndrome caused by the *hMSH2* gene.) He agreed reluctantly because of the negative test eighteen months earlier. I remembered Sue's description of the prep, but also knew that tumors in

Lynch Syndrome could grow from an overlooked small lesion into a big one in a short time. I was never sure that her physicians necessarily believed that she had Lynch Syndrome or understood what that meant, even with my reminders. I felt I had to push.

Colon cancer (2006)

Finally, Sue was scheduled for a colonoscopy. She had a five centimeter tumor (which is quite large) in her cecum (proximal colon), right beneath the pain, and in the same place her father and grandfather developed their first tumors. She was advised to make an appointment with a colorectal surgeon. I flew to Binghamton immediately. I was sitting in the living room with her when she called the surgeon's office and was told by the receptionist that she would have to wait several weeks to see the surgeon. I told her—while she was on the phone—that she was coming back to Dallas with me immediately, where she would get her surgery in one day. The person on the other end of the phone heard me say that, and asked her to wait a moment. She was then told they would see her sooner. Fortunately, she was seen and taken to the operating room forthwith, and had the rest of her colon removed. The tumor was large, there were fifty lymph nodes in the resection specimen, some quite large, but fortunately, none of them contained cancer. The lymph nodes were actually chock full of lymphocytes—immune cells that can kill tumor cells.

The return of the microsatellite signature

I asked the pathologist to send me one of the paraffin blocks of Sue's tumor tissue for microsatellite instability testing. Jennifer ran the assay as soon as we got it. She came to me with a knowing smile. Sue's tumor had the exact same microsatellite signature that our father had. The first four microsatellites were wildly unstable, but BAT-26 was as stable as a rock. The result in Jennifer's hand confirmed three things simultaneously—once again. The tumor had microsatellite instability (MSI-H), a germline deletion in *hMSH2* was the "initial event", and the loss of the other *hMSH2* gene occurred in the tumor as the "second hit", leaving the BAT-26 marker standing proudly non-mutated in the tracing because of the normal cells in the tumor mass. A perfect trifecta result. Jennifer, myself, and perhaps about half a dozen other people in the world could look at the tracing and recognize exactly what it was saying to us. I sent the results and an explanatory letter to her surgeon and gastroenterologist, wondering if they would find this interesting. I found out later that her surgeon, Michael Barrett, MD, had done some research in the field of hereditary colorectal cancer, and he was very interested. Because Sue had a Stage II tumor and the tumor was MSI-H, there was no need for adjuvant chemotherapy. The likelihood of a cure from the surgery alone was better than 90%, and it has not recurred.

Skin cancers

Sue did fine for several years, but had a series of skin tumors including basal cell carcinomas, squamous cell carcinomas, a melanoma and at least one sebaceous neoplasm (which comes with the Lynch Syndrome territory, giving her the Muir-Torre variant). In her earlier years, Sue spent a little too much time seeking out the meager sunshine available in upstate New York, and with her fair skin, there was enough exposure to do the trick—probably because of the Lynch Syndrome background. None the less, she has survived these, and didn't complain as her dermatologist has gradually skinned her. I advised her once to completely avoid the sun as she headed to Florida for a winter vacation, and she said that she would only take in "a little bit". Sometimes, even your closest friends or family members can be incorrigible.

Breast cancer (2012)

In October 2012, six years after the successful colon surgery, Sue was now sixty-seven, and had a routine screening mammography. It revealed a one-centimeter mass in her breast, which was removed surgically. None of the lymph nodes contained metastatic cancer and the surgical margins were clear, so this was an early stage lesion. Microscopically, it was a poorly-differentiated, infiltrating, ductal adenocarcinoma. Her breast oncologist in Binghamton, Joseph Readling, MD, was interested in the phenotypic features of the tumor to guide therapy. It was negative for the estrogen and progesterone receptors (ER and PR), but positive for the EGF-receptor (Her2-neu) a somewhat unusual combination. They prescribed radiation and an cocktail of chemotherapy to match the tumor characteristics.

I was interested in something else. Breast cancers are quite common in all women, but there is no apparent increase in risk for breast cancer in women with Lynch Syndrome. So, I did the immunohistochemistry test on the tumor, and the tumor cells failed to express *hMSH2* protein (and its partner *hMSH6*, as expected). The microsatellite analysis showed that the tumor was MSI-H, which is unusual in a breast cancer, but in this instance, did not show the "fingerprint" that we had seen in Sue's and our father's colon cancers. Microsatellite instability can serve as a type of "molecular clock", and one can roughly estimate the age of the tumor by the extent of the MSI. In the case of this tumor, it clearly came from the mutated *hMSH2* gene (by virtue of the unmistakable immunohistochemistry), but the weaker version of the MSI probably reflected the early stage of the tumor. Chalk up a victory for mammography.

Chemotherapy for the breast cancer

Sue then began many months of chemotherapy. We spoke very regularly during that time. As a cruel twist of fate, her husband Charlie had died of his brain tumor just a year before the breast cancer appeared, and she was without her biggest supporter. Alice, Jim and I all pitched in to help Sue through this period. Alice stepped up particularly, driving from Rochester to Binghamton on a regular basis, and saw Sue through some of her toughest moments. Also, Sue's son Frank was constantly attentive, and would come by in the evenings, and have regular Sunday dinners with her. Frank probably should be considered for canonization for his patience and attention, especially after the death of his father. Sue was quite stoic about the cancer issue, and there was no sense of existential angst about her fate or the bad luck of inheriting this high risk gene. However, the chemotherapy sapped much of her strength, dampened her mood as one would expect, and in addition, made her slightly anemic. Again, I got worried. In our family, you can't settle for ordinary explanations of anything.

Sue completed her nine months of chemotherapy, and for a second time, she felt that she was probably cured of cancer. However, near the end of her chemo, she had been getting abdominal pains, had occasional vomiting, had periodic diarrhea (but was missing most of her colon), and the anemia persisted. In spite of all these problems, there was a plausible explanation for each of them, largely because of her prior surgery and the recently completed chemotherapy. Sue had plenty of things to complain about—and dearly missed Charlie, which only added to the issue. But I never heard her complain that, through no fault of her own, she had inherited a gene that greatly increased her risk of cancer. I exchanged emails and phone calls with her breast oncologist now, just as I had with her gastroenterologist and colorectal surgeon in the past, and we were just going to wait and see what happened. I had long conversations with Sue, and asked about weight loss (none), symptoms of gastrointestinal obstruction (none), or other problems that might point to a new gastrointestinal tumor. She denied them all. I couldn't always tell if she was actually free of these symptoms, or whether her profound ability to deny trouble swept these things under the carpet. Her colorectal surgeon examined her residual colon (actually, just a rectum at this point), and there was no cancer.

Is there more going on?

Finally, I got worried that something was being overlooked. I didn't know for sure just what, as Sue denied specific symptoms that might have pointed to another intestinal tumor, or any other cancer one can get with Lynch Syndrome. The anemia was persistent, and there was no certain explanation for this. So, in early November, 2013, I had Sue fly to Dallas so that I could make sure she was getting the best care. As a matter of simple bad luck, Sue arrived during a fierce ice storm that nearly paralyzed Dallas. I had my favorite cab driver, Ray Hodges, pick her up at the airport, as the freeway was completely iced over, and Texas has essentially no equipment for removing snow or ice. He had no problem with the ice, and saved me an hour of terrifying driving.

Sue arrived, and she looked pretty good, so we went out and had a sumptuous dinner together. She ate with gusto, and I began to think that perhaps I was over-reacting, and that she just had just some residual anemia from her chemotherapy. I had arranged for the gastroenterologist who took care of my Lynch Syndrome patients in Dallas, Elizabeth Odstrcil, MD, to start her evaluation. I took Sue to the hospital the next morning for an upper endoscopy, and I stayed in the room to watch. Sue had a moderate amount of gastritis (inflammation in the stomach), which can ooze blood. This is it, I thought. The chemotherapy inflamed her stomach, and her bone marrow couldn't keep up with gradual blood loss. I had initially planned to follow the endoscopy with an abdominal CT scan looking for a tumor somewhere, but I decided this finding was enough to explain the anemia, and I canceled it.

We had a second wonderful meal that night, and Sue looked and felt good. Sue's early morning flight back to upstate New York was postponed—fortunately—which obviated a four AM pickup for the harrowing trip to the airport over the persistent ice. She made it back home the next day.

A small intestinal cancer (2013)

However, Sue's anemia continued, and when she went to see her oncologist, he thought that more was going on, and he wasn't convinced that this was the end of the story. He gave her a blood transfusion and decided to get the CT scan that I had not done in Dallas. To my absolute horror, they found a tumor mass, this time at the end of her small intestine, just above the anastomosis to her rectum. I had totally blown it. I had her come all the way to Dallas, got 'this close' to getting the right diagnosis, but got it wrong. I was very upset that this might be a disaster. However, Michael Barrett operated again, found a large but removable tumor, and resected it with no evidence of metastatic disease. He saved the day for Sue.

Another colon cancer! (2015)

After the small bowel surgery—which was a large but self-contained cancer—Sue was looking forward to some clear sailing for a while, and a year without any cancer problems. However, in the late spring of 2015, she underwent a routine sigmoidoscopy. At this point, all of her rectal tissue was intact, and a small bit of sigmoid colon linked the top of her rectum to her residual small intestine. Unfortunately, a small (one centimeter) polyp was found, and it contained invasive cancer. This clearly developed in less than a year's time, she was being followed by a knowledgeable colorectal surgeon, and she only had a small bit of colon left. The imaging studies showed no evidence of metastatic disease, and Sue gamely gave up her summer for yet one more laparoscopic surgery to remove the polyp and surrounding sigmoid colon tissues. Again, there was no evidence of metastatic disease, and she came through this operation with flying colors. Sue was more than a bit disgusted to have to return to the operating room again, but these procedures have been life-saving. Moreover, her surgeon,

Mike Barrett, MD, has figured out how to work around all of the prior surgeries she has had, and has brought her through each one successfully.

Small world: Michael Barrett, MD

I had discussions with Mike Barrett about Sue's multiple cancers of the colon and small intestine. He had been the surgeon who took out Sue's colon cancer in 2006, the small bowel tumor in 2014, and the sigmoid polyp in 2015. I was wondering if he knew much about Lynch Syndrome. Indeed he did. He had been in colorectal surgery training at Harvard Medical School in the fateful months of 1993 when Richard Kolodner's lab had been hunting for the *hMSH2* gene. Mike had taken tumor samples to Kolodner's lab, and had briefly done some cancer research. We had a long talk about where the field had gone in the twenty years since he was involved in research, and I thought I heard a wistfulness in his voice about leaving the heavy science behind. I was mostly reassured that Sue was in very capable hands, and that the letter I had sent explaining the microsatellite signature some seven years ago had been appreciated.

Most importantly, Sue is doing fine without evidence of recurrence of her many tumors, and I have never heard her make the slightest complaint about having inherited one of the defective Boland genes. You take the good with the bad, and make the best of what you have.

Auto-immunization in Lynch Syndrome

How has Sue survived all this? Part is her attitude of course. It has long been known that people with psychological depression also depress their immune systems, and that can lead to infections and other illnesses. There is a less well-documented or understood relationship between an upbeat approach to life and a stronger immune response. Maybe that is part of Sue's success.

However, there is another important issue that has been appreciated in the past few years. It has been shown by a group of researchers in Paris, France—led by Jerome Galon PhD and Franck Pages MD, PhD—that colorectal cancers have a lot of tumor-infiltrating lymphocytes, or "TILs" in the tumor mass itself and in the 'stroma', or background non-cancer cells in which the tumor grows. Depending upon the specific identity of the TILs and their location in the tumor, one can predict the clinical outcome of the cancer even better than the traditional pathological staging, which involves the depth of invasion and involvement of the regional lymph nodes by cancer. The more tumor-killing TILs, the better the outcome.

Second, it has been noted that colorectal cancers in the setting of Lynch Syndrome have lots more TILs than sporadic, non-MSI colorectal cancers. I have noticed that colorectal cancers that are MSI-H are particularly likely to have numerous, large regional lymph nodes in the resection specimen that is removed with the primary tumor. This is probably a reflection of how a colorectal cancer develops in Lynch Syndrome. These tumors are "hypermutable" and cannot repair errors that ordinarily occur during the replication of DNA. It has been demonstrated that tumors with microsatellite instability contain ten-fold more mutations than sporadic, non-MSI cancers. One unique aspect of the MSI tumor pathway is that certain genes incur the exact same mutational sequence repeatedly in the any Lynch Syndrome tumor that develops. If you were to add a carcinogen to a mouse or group of cells in a culture dish, the resulting mutations are random and non-reproducible. Not so with Lynch Syndrome tumors. The same mutations occur over and over.

It has been demonstrated by a pair of researchers from Heidelberg, Germany—Matthias Kloor, MD and Magnus von Knebel Doeberitz, MD—that the MSI-associated mutations create antigenic proteins in the tumor that the immune system can detect and respond to. The immune system recognizes that these cells are "foreign", dangerous, and should be killed. These two investigators have also demonstrated that the colons of Lynch Syndrome patients harbor hundreds of microscopic DNA mismatch repair-defective colonic glands (or "crypts"), almost all of which somehow disappear, never causing cancer. One interpretation of this is that the colons in people with Lynch Syndrome continuously "immunize" that individual against the mutant proteins that are characteristic of the disease process. This process of "autoimmunization" and "immunoediting" may prepare the body to mount an effective immunological response to the tumor. This would explain the increased numbers of TILs in Lynch Syndrome colorectal cancers and the substantially better likelihood of surviving surgical treatment of the tumor. This may be why Sue, who has had four Lynch Syndrome tumors is still alive, and her cousin Mary Anne developed metastatic disease from her non-Lynch Syndrome colon cancer.

It is obvious that the immune response is only partially able to fend off these tumors. Historically, most people who developed these tumors died of them. But, in the newer world of early detection and effective surgery, this may change.

How bad is it?

The bottom line is that one surely would not wish to inherit a mutation that causes a disease like Lynch Syndrome. However, if that's what you have inherited, you could take the stance that fate could be worse, and that these are curable tumors. In any event, I tell my patients with Lynch Syndrome, if a tumor is found, don't panic. There is a lot that can be done to manage the cancers. More importantly, beginning in 2015, new therapies that stimulate the immune response to cancer (actually, it removes an inhibitory mechanism that the tumor mounts) is especially effective in colorectal cancers with MSI. Curiously, this therapy is of no value in the absence of MSI. It appears that the unique hypermutability tumors with defective DNA mismatch repair and MSI attract a lot of immunological attention, and this often leads to the killing of tumor cells. The tumor then responds with a "cloak" to hide its antigenic abnormalities, and the lymphocytes become less able to find and kill the tumor cells. The new class of immunological "check-point" therapy lifts the cloak, and unleashes the power of the immune system, allowing the body to resume tumor cell killing. This will be a focus of research for many years to come, and is reason to have additional optimism over our ability to deal with these tumors.

Sue is a good example of having benefitted from her body's ability to kill hypermutable tumor cells. I strongly suspect that her positive attitude has added to the benefit. Her explanation is: "I just came this way".

Chapter 19

WHERE IS EVERYONE NOW? (2001-2015)

La-La how the life goes on.

Pat

So what came of all this? The most important part for me was to have found and married Pat, and having made the decision to have children. Pat and I made a decision to marry in 1970, which was "part one" of the marriage pact. In 1974, as I was finishing up my internship and we were about to head onto the Navajo Reservation for two years, we thought it would be a good time and place to start a family, and it was time to cross into "part two" of our lives together. We made the considered decision to have a family, assuming that we might never have a means of determining who was a mutation carrier. However, I was confident that we were close to developing effective measures to prevent death from Lynch Syndrome cancers. That was an article of faith that was not based on any facts; it was based upon my own personal sense that life was worthwhile, and that even if I were to die young, my experience of life was valuable, and I was able to contribute to the overall welfare of my community—just as my father and grandfather had. I wanted to pass that on to my children. Most importantly, Pat put no conditions on our marriage or children. She never hesitated on this issue, and we never had a difficult discussion about it. Pat made another decision to split her time between being an attentive mother, and continuing to work as a nurse practitioner. She is one of my heroes, because she figured out how to do both. Her three daughters worship her.

Tara

While we were in the Indian Health Service in Gallup, New Mexico, our first daughter Tara was born on that bitterly cold night when I was on call in the hospital in the midst of an influenza epidemic. Tara was a wonderful child, was easy to raise, hit all of her emotional milestones early and was a mature child, adolescent and adult. She was a very good student, the captain of her field hockey and soccer teams, co-President of her senior class, and continues to be a leader. She was named to the Michigan All State Field Hockey team her senior year, and continued to play field hockey in college. She went to Bowdoin College in Maine, where she was an English major, and after graduation, she started out in the business world, spending a couple of years in New York City and Boston. She found the business world relatively uninteresting, so she changed direction and found a job teaching at a girls' boarding school in Connecticut—Miss Porter's School—where she taught two courses and coached two athletic teams. She met the man who would become her husband, Richard, at the wedding of another Bowdoin classmate, and after a whirlwind romance, she moved to San Francisco, where she lives now. Along the way she got Master's degrees first in English from Middlebury, and then in Educational Leadership from Columbia. She has two sons, Elliott and Nicholas, and she is teaching and counseling in a boy's elementary school in San Francisco. I cannot imagine life without this daughter, and I am continuously impressed by her dedication to teaching and enhancing the world around her.

Maureen

Before we left New Mexico, Pat became pregnant with our second daughter, Maureen, who was born just after we arrived in San Francisco, in August, 1976. She was also an excellent student, played field hockey as well, and was also named to the Michigan All State team. She went to Colgate University and majored in Sociology and Anthropology, graduating with Phi-beta-kappa honors (probably the first in the family to accomplish this). After college, she and her best friend from high school (in Ann Arbor) went on a US road trip together. When she arrived in San Francisco, she said "I've just come home". She has lived there ever since. After working in several different jobs, including some very challenging social work, she went to the University of North Carolina to get a Masters of Public

Health. She then returned to San Francisco and got a job with a firm that developed public service advertisements for healthy behaviors. This was particularly important in the gay men's community, which was so severely affected by the AIDS epidemic. After a number of years with that firm, she took over as manager of a free Women's Health Clinic, where she has been for many years. She met the man of her dreams in the city, Will, whom she married, and lives just north of the city. We consider Maureen to be the "soul" of the family, she is very committed to making the world a better place—as is her husband—and she pursues activities and a life style that are healthy, non-intrusive, easy on the earth, and sustainable. She is not afraid to speak up for someone who is being picked on or scapegoated. My life, and the world, would be diminished without Maureen's presence.

Maureen had a daughter, Camilla, in 2015.

Brigid

Nearly five years after Maureen was born, good fortune brought us a third daughter, Brigid. All three girls have different temperaments; inexplicably they are all totally different. Brigid was high-spirited in her earliest years, which required Pat and me to develop additional child-rearing skills. In Brigid's case it was all worth it. She started field hockey at a young age—because of the example of her sisters—and was a first team All-County field hockey player her senior year of high school in San Diego. She was the top student in her high school class, and was recruited to play hockey at Yale. She majored in Cellular, Developmental and Molecular Biology, performed research as a student, and graduated with honors. She took a year off after graduation to work in a research laboratory at UCSF, a move that was abetted by the fact that her two sisters lived in San Francisco at that time. One day she walked over to Young Kim's laboratory at the San Francisco VA, and when the secretary took one look at her, she said "You must be Dr. Boland's daughter". Apparently, it was that recognizable.

After the interval year, she entered medical school at UCSF, and after graduation moved to San Diego for her medicine residency and GI Fellowship. I have to say that she surprised me with two key decisions, first for medical school, and then with gastroenterology. She kept her plans to herself until she was completely ready to commit. She has continued to do medical research, and joined the academic faculty at UCSD in 2015, focusing on mucosal inflammation and inflammatory bowel disease. She married Jeremy, who had been the Chief Medical Resident when she was an intern; he is also on the UCSD faculty as an endocrinologist. They live in one of the beach communities of San Diego popular with young people.

Brigid had a son Cooper, in 2015.

Sue, Alice and Jim

Without a doubt, it would have been a terrible mistake for me not to have had my family. I am glad my father made the same decision. All of my siblings made the same choice. Sue, her two children, their spouses and children all live in upstate New York, and everyone is alive and well. Both children, Frank and Colleen, have been essential parts of Sue's survival, and they show up whenever needed on short notice, even when she has been a little grumpy.

Alice has been a Special Education teacher since college, raised two boys, one of whom was Matt, who developed the test for Lynch Syndrome in our family. Where would we have been without Matt? After Dartmouth College, he graduated from medical school at Columbia, did his residency and fellowship at the Beth Israel-Deaconess Hospital in Boston, and he is currently on the faculty at the Dana Farber Cancer Institute and Harvard Medical School. He is a GI Oncologist, and continues to do research on Lynch Syndrome. As a cruel irony, Alice lost her husband Gary at age fifty-eight to pancreatic cancer. We haven't been as clever in preventing these things in our spouses as in ourselves. Alice and her family are all doing fine.

Jim went into the pharmaceutical industry after college and Master's work, and has had a successful career in sales. Jim has a terrific wife, Nancy, and three sons—Pat, Ryan and Corey—who have become a physician, a lawyer and an engineer respectively. (There must be a name for having one of each of these, but I don't know what that is.) Jim and his wife live outside of Philadelphia where all three of his boys lived for most of their adult lives. Their eldest son, Patrick, is a GI Oncologist (like Matt), and works at the Roswell Park Memorial Cancer Institute in Buffalo, where his grandfather underwent a heroic, but failed final attempt to have his cancer removed in 1970. Patrick is involved in research into chemotherapeutic approaches to gastrointestinal cancer. His grandfather would have been proud of him and all his cousins, which includes three physicians. Jim and the boys are all doing fine.

Aunts, uncles, and cousins

Alas, before I started writing this book, the last of my father's siblings died. With just one exception, those who didn't have the Lynch Syndrome problem lived well into old age. In fact, Uncle Tom was the young one to die at age eighty-five, whereas Loretta, Rita and Larry lived into their nineties. The only exception was John, who survived his colon cancer, only to be stricken by a fatal heart attack at age fifty-seven.

There were twenty-seven first cousins on the Boland side of the family—whereas I had only three cousins on the Armstrong side. The oldest two Boland cousins, Trudy and Matt, both fell to Lynch Syndrome cancers. Since then, no one has. I had one cousin who died on the day of his birth, one was killed at age twenty-three in an automobile accident, and my cousin Tom Gery, who was four days younger than I, died suddenly of a cerebral hemorrhage in 2002. One cousin, Kevin, died of complications of cystic fibrosis in 2001. There is obviously a cystic fibrosis gene in the family, but only one has ever had the disease—because this is a recessive disease that requires a genetic contribution from both parents. Mary Anne had the fatal colon cancer that was unrelated to Lynch Syndrome. So twenty of us are still alive and well, and Sue is the only one to have had a cancer. The median age of the living group is just over sixty. This disease looks very different in the twenty-first century than it did in the twentieth.

Jennifer

As mentioned, Matt and Jennifer had just one productive summer together, and Matt's career is now launched and is rising. Jennifer has continued to be a valuable Laboratory Manager, and has solved two more previously unsolved Lynch Syndrome mysteries related to the *hMSH2* gene. In one instance, we had a large family that been taken care of by Henry Lynch himself, and he had sent the DNA all over the world in a fruitless attempt to find the culpable mutation. Jennifer noted a paper (which the rest of us missed) indicating that a specific type of *Alu*-mediated deletion involving the gene adjacent to *hMSH2* (called *EPCAM*) could lead to the silencing of *hMSH2*, and act just like Lynch Syndrome. She ordered the required reagents from Europe, optimized the technical approach to the assay, and found the mutation in this family. I contacted Henry about this and he was enormously appreciative. The family was quite large, and through the use of his database, we were able to determine that this mutation resulted in Lynch Syndrome with colorectal cancers but none of the other cancers we expected in this disease. This was one of several publications that Henry and I have had together.

Another time, we had found a family that we were sure had Lynch Syndrome. The tumors all showed MSI-H, and the tumors failed to express the *hMSH2* and *hMSH6* proteins in the tumor. We were pretty sure this could be nothing but Lynch Syndrome. Jennifer then went deep into the genetics literature (much easier with a computerized literature search than in the old days thumbing through *Index Medicus*), and she found the report of a single family with an inversion within the *hMSH2* gene that totally inactivated that gene, but left it with a normal diagnostic test using the conventional commercially available approach, because all of the exons were present, but just in the wrong order. She developed new assays for that inversion, and found it in ten individuals who had been collected in our familial cancer registry. Even more surprising, we realized when putting together the pedigrees that some of our patients came from two different families who were distantly related, but no health connection had been made between the two groups. This created a sticky issue of confidentiality, since we are not permitted to divulge the genetic results of one person to another without specific safeguards for privacy. The problem resolved itself when we were involved in a free lecture program for patients with hereditary colorectal cancer syndromes. Both sides of the family showed up for the same program, and they started asking questions. Quite the family reunion. Jennifer is a rare individual, and my family owes a lot to her.

Professional mentors and colleagues

Yale

Over the years, I had a lot of people teaching me how to be a physician, how to do research, how to do everything. Everyone in biomedical research stands on multiple shoulders. My initial two mentors at Yale Medical School were Howard Spiro, MD and Frank Troncale, MD. Howard stayed on for many years as GI Division Chief, but never fully accepted that Lynch Syndrome was a specific disease. He was the last person to be the sole author of an entire GI textbook, and in spite of my repeated reminders, Lynch Syndrome never appeared in his book. To be truthful, Howard was somewhat suspicious of molecular biology and genetics, and was more of a psychiatrist than a scientist. He was the last of the old guard. He had been the founding section chief of gastroenterology at Yale, continued in that position for many years (until the year I was trying to apply for fellowship), and he died in 2012.

Frank Troncale decided against a career in laboratory-based academic medicine not too long after we worked together in the lab, and set up a successful clinical practice in New Haven. He still practices gastroenterology, and I occasionally see him at GI meetings where we exchange pleasant greetings. He was the last person to perform a rigid sigmoidoscopy on me, or to take a giant biopsy from my rectal mucosa. For some life experiences, once is enough.

UCSF

I got my start in academic medicine due to mentorship at UCSF, and the freedom that Young Kim, MD and Marv Sleisenger, MD provided. Young continued to have a long and productive research career at the San Francisco VA after I left. He won the Distinguished Mentor and Distinguished Achievement Awards from the AGA over the years. Marv continued as Medicine Service Chief at the VA for many more years, and has been a constant source of support when I see him at the research meetings. Young and Marv were always keen to ask about how Pat and the girls were doing. I felt a bit like a son who was bringing rewards back to the fathers as I passed through each phase of my career. I last saw Marvin in 2012 when he stayed at my home for the birthday party of his close colleague, John Fordtran, MD. Also, I have been amazed that Holly Smith, MD, who had been the Chairman of Internal Medicine at UCSF when I had my first faculty appointment, always recognized me and asked about the colon cancer research when I saw him at meetings. He is one of those "remarkable men" one rarely meets. Rudi Schmid was promoted from Division Chief to Dean at UCSF while I was there in 1983. He was considered a successful Dean, and he clearly relished holding the reins of that medical school. UCSF has remained at the top of the rankings by every measure of US medical schools since that time.

Michigan

Over the years, I have stayed closest to my University of Michigan colleagues, where we were as much a family as a GI division, mainly due to Tachi Yamada's leadership style. Tachi rose from Division Chief to Department Chairman in Ann Arbor, and left there shortly after I did in February, 1996 to take a top executive position with the company that became GlaxoSmithKline, one of the largest pharmaceutical companies in the world. After a reorganization, he was named the Director of Research and Development, with a four billion dollar global annual budget. He had a successful run with them, and then became Director of the Global Health Program of the Bill & Melinda Gates Foundation. Along the way, he became president of nearly every professional organization he was part of. He now lives on the west coast, and has taken on yet one more job as Executive Vice President and Chief Medical and Scientific Officer of Takeda Pharmaceuticals, in Japan. He is perhaps the most multitalented person I have known. I had the opportunity to run in the morning with him for about 10,000 miles while we were neighbors in Ann Arbor, so I had plenty of opportunity to learn from him. He repeatedly recommended me to others looking to recruit leaders to their faculties, waited for them to contact me, and then talked me out of going.

Chung Owyang, MD, who was Division Chief in Gastroenterology at Michigan when I left in 1995 is still successfully ensconced in that role. His division has the highest level of loyalty of any I know, and his faculty are the most difficult to recruit away. He has a magical rapport with his faculty and lab workers. He may be the longest continuously sitting Division Chief among all the US medical schools.

Andy Feinberg, MD, MPH left the University of Michigan and returned to Johns Hopkins in 1994, which is how Koi came to work with me. Andy has been very successful, made a number of important discoveries in the field of epigenetics, and holds an endowed Chair at Hopkins. He continues to win honors and awards around the world.

UCSD

I spent a total of just eight and a half years at UCSD. My colleagues there were terrific, and San Diego is the most pleasant place in North America for living. The lab obtained multiple research grants, wrote papers, and lived up to the expectations of the recruitment. We got a grant to study Lynch Syndrome just after arriving in San Diego. This was initially based on Koi's cells, but has continued on the basis of Jennifer's findings and much more. It has been repeatedly renewed, and based upon a renewal in 2014, will extend at least into its twenty-third year.

There was relatively little turnover among senior faculty at UCSD, so people tended to stay for extended periods and fell into factions. I was probably considered a neutral player politically being one of the newer senior faculty members, and consequently was appointed to a number of committees, chaired the Search Committee to select the Dean of the School of Medicine in 1999, and eventually, I agreed to become Associate Director of the Cancer Center.

Unfortunately, about six months after Steve Wasserman recruited me to San Diego, the Department of Medicine underwent a financial meltdown and was considered to be in debt to the Dean for the rest of the time I was at UCSD. Consequently, the promises to me of financial resources to recruit additional faculty into the GI Division were not there when I needed them. I was able to function fine within the confines of my own lab, but the GI Division had no chance to grow. After Steve Wasserman was replaced as Department Chair, his successor had his own agenda, and GI wasn't on the list. After a while, this became less acceptable, and I thought about making myself available to move somewhere else. I was periodically asked if I wanted to become a Department Chairman at various institutions, but felt that I didn't have that skill set. Moreover, being Chairman might have converted me into a sort of middle-manager for the rest of my career, and I would probably have lost grasp of my research if I made that move. I moved into academic medicine to solve the problem of hereditary colorectal cancer, not to rise through the ranks and collect titles. I thought that the most interesting and enjoyable parts of my job were working with the fellows and technicians, looking at raw data, interpreting the findings, deciding the next steps, and writing papers and grants. I genuinely have enjoyed that part. The least interesting part of my job was dealing with personnel issues, behavior problems, conflicts between individuals in the lab, and administrative issues. If I were to have become a Department Chair, I would have lost most of the former, and gotten a huge dose of the latter, so I never sought it. I kept the letters of invitation for department chairmanships in a folder, in case I ever wanted to look at them and feel important. I did make one final move to Dallas in 2003, described below.

The discoverers

It is fascinating to follow the careers of those who contributed most to the discovery of the secrets about Lynch Syndrome. Each one had a story to tell.

Henry Lynch

Henry Lynch was the person who put Lynch Syndrome on the map. He gathered families into a massive registry, drew blood samples, saved specimens of DNA from these families, and interacted with basic research laboratories involved in the discovery of familial cancer genes. I had my first contact with Henry by phone and mail when I was a medical student, and he could not have been more encouraging or helpful. I cannot remember when I met him face to face for the first time; he seems to have been always a part of my research. There was a regional GI meeting in Omaha, Nebraska in the late 1980s, and Henry invited me give a presentation of our laboratory data on colon cancer tissues from putative Lynch Syndrome patients. We would see each other at the national and international meetings, and he introduced me to a wide range of scientists as if I was his hand-picked protégé. He is engaging, inspirational, and never misses an opportunity to congratulate someone on a new discovery, no matter how minor. He continues to work at Creighton University, and curates one of the world's largest registries of familial cancer. He recognized many of the now classic familial cancer syndrome associations long before the genetic bases were established.

Bert Vogelstein

Bert was by far the single most important person involved in solving the hereditary colorectal cancer story. Collecting the affected families will only take one so far; you need to find the genes involved and understand the processes behind tumor formation. Bert was making seminal discoveries about the nature of colorectal cancer in the early 1980s, he cloned the gene that causes FAP, established the first linkage for a Lynch Syndrome gene on chromosome 2p, accidentally found microsatellite instability while doing the experiments to explore that link, and was in a near dead heat with Kolodner in finding the initial human genes for Lynch Syndrome.

Various labs were making many of these discoveries at approximately the same time with Bert, but he was the constant figure through all the discoveries. That was no accident. It is important to acknowledge that he didn't personally make all of these discoveries, and he is the first to credit his students, techs and fellows for their contributions. However, he recruited and directed the people in his lab, created the consortium agreements to pull powerful labs together, kept his focus in spite of all sorts of distractions, and has been very dedicated to this work. He is the one with the vision and drive. He rarely travels so he can stay in the lab and work. He is quick to acknowledge the importance of his close colleague at Hopkins, Kenneth Kinzler, PhD, and has had a key collaboration with Albert de la Chapelle and his group of geneticists in Finland—including more important collaborators than I can mention here.

Bert and I have exchanged many emails over the years, and although his family story is not as hair-raising as mine, he had plenty of reasons in his own family to want to study and understand cancer. Periodically, I mused to myself that cancer picked on—and got the attention of—many smart people, and I hope we will finally put this disease in its place, and demote it to a minor disease. Someday cancer will be considered like a nasty infection. They will occur, we will know that they can cause trouble, but we will also consider it to be something that is usually cured, including metastatic disease. This will probably happen before the end of the twenty-first century. That is unfortunately too late for me, but I am confident that is what the future will bring for my grandchildren. I keep wondering why Bert hasn't been called for a trip to Stockholm for a Nobel Prize. He deserves it, and it will be a happy for all of us in the field when he gets a phone call early some October morning from the Nobel Committee.

Manuel Perucho

Manuel is the most passionate in this group about this work, but sometimes his passion boils over the top of the pan. He is the undisputed discoverer of microsatellite instability, regardless of the dates on the articles in 1993. He has continued to make important contributions to the science of cancer. He is a particularly astute scientist, and saw something very important that no one else saw, even while it was under our noses. It was simply a hard sell in 1992, and unfortunately, Manuel had a short stretch of bad luck with journals that has created a constant burr under his saddle. We all know how important he was to this field. He has partially given up his laboratory in La Jolla (where many of his discoveries were made), became Director of the Institute of Predictive and Personalized Medicine in Barcelona in 2007, and commutes back and forth between San Diego and Spain. He has recently remarried and started a new family with two daughters. This latest undertaking proves that he is, above all else, a very brave man.

Steve Thibodeau

Steve Thibodeau discovered microsatellite instability independently of the others, and I have never heard him raise his voice in defense of his discovery or make a case for his own importance. He is a classy fellow, has stayed at the Mayo Clinic ever since his discoveries in 1993, and has been part of many advances in our knowledge of Lynch Syndrome in conjunction with his clinical partners in Rochester, MN. He is one of our relatively unsung heroes in this field.

Richard Kolodner

Richard Kolodner is a scientist who had a decent reputation for his work in basic genetics before 1993. He woke up one morning and realized that he may have had the key to the secrets of microsatellite instability and hereditary colon cancer in his yeast culture dishes. He worked very quickly to clone the *hMSH2* gene first, and then the *hMLH1* gene, and these were eventually shown to be the most important Lynch Syndrome genes. This work was done at the Dana Farber Cancer Institute in Boston, but shortly after that, he moved to San Diego as a Professor at UCSD and an investigator in the Ludwig Cancer Research Institute. Richard was a good colleague while I was at UCSD, but essentially, his heart was in the basic biology of yeast genetics, how DNA is replicated and repaired, and what happens when various components of the DNA replication and repair apparatuses go awry. When the immediate applicability of his work to human disease settled down, he returned to his yeast cells. However, without people like Richard—and his colleague Rick Fishel, PhD—progress in clinical medicine would run out of steam and stall. You need excellent basic science to fuel the clinical sciences/ Basic and clinical scientists need to find a common language and you never know where the next hero might come from. So, Richard and Rick went back to their basic research after the smoke cleared. Perhaps they will rise again depending upon where the science goes next, or maybe it will be some other unexpected basic scientist who holds the key to the next discovery. Because of the link between yeast DNA repair and Lynch Syndrome, Kolodner was inducted into the National Academy of Sciences, and he continues his work in San Diego.

After finding Trudy's mutation

In the summer of 2001, shortly after we had found the problem in Trudy's *hMSH2* gene, I got a phone call from John Fordtran, MD, who is a gastroenterologist at Baylor University Medical Center (BUMC) at Dallas. He was a close friend of Alan Hofmann, MD, PhD who was in our GI Division at UCSD, and co-editor of a popular textbook on gastrointestinal diseases with my mentor from UCSF, Marv Sleisenger. John was looking for a colon cancer researcher to come to Dallas as Chief of their GI Division at BUMC. Alan told me to expect a call from John to help with their recruitment, and suggested that John then would try to talk me into that job. I told Alan that I would help but that there was "no chance" I would take the position there.

John asked me to come to Dallas to meet with him and the Search Committee. At his request, I drew up a list of thirty-three potential candidates with complete descriptions of their work, their personalities, and where I thought their research was headed. My name was not on the list. He wanted me to come in the fall, but events occurred on September 11, 2001 that postponed my visit for a month. In October, I flew to Dallas, met with the Search Committee, and presented my list to them. We were at dinner, and I was reviewing the candidates, but John wasn't interested. He said "we want you to consider this position". I told him that there was "no chance". He asked why, and told him that his I was committed to my university appointment, and I wouldn't leave San Diego for Dallas in any event.

I thought that was it, but they invited me back a couple of times, and I finally returned in the spring for an endowed lectureship. After giving a Medical Grand Rounds lecture and a seminar for the residents, I was taken to a meeting room for a presumed lunch, where the Search Committee was waiting once again. I politely declined to discuss the job again. John said he would send me a formal offer anyway, and he did. I took a look at his letter, and realized that it represented a chance to focus all of my effort on research, and I would have limited administrative or clinical responsibilities. Just research. He didn't care whether I saw patients or not. I realized that I could set up a clinic and see people in the Dallas-Fort Worth region who might have hereditary cancer syndromes, something that was not going to happen in San Diego.

Suddenly, it seemed like an attractive idea. I didn't think Pat would go along with this, but when she recognized the degree to which this would stoke my passions and permit me to continue what we had started with the discovery of Trudy's mutation, she agreed to take a look. It was a huge issue for the family, as all three of my daughters were in San Francisco. After a lot of discussion, we agreed to take the plunge. I then got Jennifer to agree to come, and a critical associate, Ajay Goel, PhD, who was a rising star in the lab, also agreed to join in. I recognized that Ajay was a brilliant scientist with passion and an intense work ethic. The three of us could do it. It would have been very difficult alone. We all moved to Baylor, Dallas in February, 2003.

Baylor University Medical Center, Dallas

Some of my colleagues thought I had taken leave of my senses to move from UCSD to a community hospital in Dallas. However, when each visited, they recognized what had attracted me. Baylor was a large, thriving clinical center and provided us with a large amount of space, renovated it to a state-of-the-art molecular genetics lab, and provided all the equipment we needed. Fordtran was constantly looking out for us, and unwaveringly supportive. I hired more people, including a research nurse to handle the interactions with our familial cancer patients, who I knew would need extra attention, and to establish a familial cancer registry. I was fortunate to find Millie Arnold, RN, who was a warm and understanding advocate for our patients. Almost every patient I saw became a research subject. We could follow the clinical outcomes of the patients in whom we had an accurate diagnosis, and hunt for the genes in those patients who confused us. Jennifer, Ajay and I were in heaven.

During the decade after arriving, there was a tremendous growth in the industry involved in genetic diagnosis, and we went from having individual genes selected for sequencing to the development of panels that could analyze multiple genes, and eventually to the technology called "next-generation" sequencing, which permits the sequencing of hundreds of targeted genes, or even sequencing the entire genome. I was in just the right place as all this developed, and had very few committee or teaching assignments to interfere with my work. It was just the right move at just the right time. The administration loved the attention from the world of research that our lab brought to the hospital, and the Baylor Foundation regularly stepped up at critical times to get us new equipment that kept us out in front technologically. The philanthropy in Dallas was tremendous.

The American Gastroenterological Association (AGA)

During my time in Dallas, I became increasingly involved in the AGA, was elected to the Governing Board, and in 2011-12, served as its President. That was one distraction from my research that I welcomed, and it also provided me with opportunities to increase exposure of gastroenterologists to the concept of familial colorectal cancer, which was no longer a controversial entity. The AGA had outstanding staff, and two of the most important people I worked with were the co-Executive Vice Presidents, Lynn Robinson and Tom Serena. Both were very committed to the field and brought two different and wonderfully complementary personalities to the organization.

In the summer of 2011, when I started the AGA Presidency, I flew to Bethesda, Maryland, to meet with the AGA staff, which numbered about ninety. Lynn and Tom asked me to address the group, and they knew about my family history, research, and why I was doing it. They urged me to open up and discuss the reasons for my research passions to the AGA staff. I had always been quiet about that subject, told a few people privately, and never, ever discussed this publically. But, this was a different time, and perhaps it was time to come out of the closet. Lynn and Tom were particularly persuasive and convinced me that the AGA staff would appreciate my reasons for doing what I did. So, I took a deep breath and faced the assembled staff, and opened up about my family, my concerns, my initial failings, and my determination to understand this disease. I nearly panicked just as I began, but got it out. I cannot say that I felt a catharsis, as this was the first time. It wasn't the last.

That winter, the AGA and the US "Liver Society" hosted a joint Academic Skills Workshop, in which there are two days of presentations from leading gastroenterologists and hepatologists directed towards graduating GI fellows and junior faculty members who were just starting their academic careers. The president of each society traditionally gave a lecture to the group, historically explaining the value of their organization, and attempting to convince them to become more deeply engaged in our professional societies.

I was asked to give the after-dinner talk following the first day, and the AGA staff asked me to prepare a lecture. I wondered what would be most valuable to this young group. About a week before the meeting, I watched a movie called *Hugo*, which is a period piece set in Paris in the 1930s about a thirteen year old boy who lived with his widowed father until the father was killed in an accident. The boy, Hugo Cabret, began living alone secretly in a train station, loosely supervised by an uncle who was a clockmaker. Hugo brings with him an automaton—a mechanical robot—left by his father, which he toils to restore. However, he is missing the heart-shaped key which is necessary to make the robot work. He encounters a girl who has the key, and when they activate the automaton, it reveals the secret from his father. I was moved to tears by the film—a children's film at that—and of course I realized what had triggered my emotions. So, I started to write a lecture for this group of young researchers, and asked them to look into their souls for passion, and to choose something that matched their skills and would permit them to do something special. I suggested that there were secrets for all of us to find out there; we just had to look. As I was about to start the talk, my mouth was suddenly dry, I felt a wave of anxiety, and had to take a long quaff of water to get started. I had given plenty of lectures to bigger groups than this, but the topic was obviously more charged this time. Once I got started, I was fine.

In May 2012, I gave the President's "farewell address" at the annual meeting of the AGA. I took the Academic Skills workshop lecture, added some professional issues that were pertinent for the membership, then transitioned to my family pedigree, showing exactly where I was in the tree, and what we had done to address that problem. Again, I urged my colleagues to use their considerable talents to do something important as physicians. Finally, I was able to stand up before a crowd and admit the terrible secret about my family. I had the same disappearance of saliva as I started my remarks, but with one sip of water, I was ok. I think that no matter how many times I do this, my body will have to deal with the "fight or flight" decision. Of course, the only answer is fight. It took me the first thirty years of my life to discover that, and to start seeking the secret my father had hidden for me to find.

The AGA continued to be generous to me. In 2011, one of the "Sections" of the AGA—the GI Oncology Section—gave me the "Distinguished Mentor Award", to acknowledge the successes of the people I mentored over the years. In 2015, I was given the "AGA Beaumont Prize in Gastroenterology" for my research on Lynch Syndrome. That is the top research prize given by the AGA, awarded once every three years. Two prior winners were Nobel laureates. Later in 2015, the Collaborative Group of the Americas on Inherited Colorectal Cancer gave me their "Lifetime Achievement Award" for this work. It was quite a year.

Dyslexia

It is probably important to mention what happened to my dyslexia problem, even though I don't understand how. By age thirty, the problem simply resolved itself. Pat and I were living in San Francisco, I had my persistent frustration about reading, and Pat signed us up for a "speed reading" course taught in a man's home. I desperately wanted help. He started with a hand-advanced film strip that showed a couple of words, then a phrase, and progressively longer phrases or sentences. We would read these silently to ourselves, and he would advance the film strip. The technology was strictly out of the 1950s. He showed us a few of these, and then tested us for content and comprehension. He progressively advanced the slides faster and faster. Finally, he reached full speed, and I discovered that I was able to read and comprehend all of it, no matter how fast he advanced the slides. I was shocked. I went home and started reading and haven't stopped since. The problem had disappeared, and I hadn't realized it. I don't know why I had the problem, or what made it go away, but I didn't have it anymore. I had a huge amount of pent up demand to read everything. Bad luck followed by good luck, I guess.

Luck, the good and the bad: *"Life is full of misery, loneliness and suffering—and it's over much too soon". Woody Allen*

A recurring theme in my life and this book is the issue of luck. I've had good luck and bad luck. I don't believe in a benevolent providence; at least if there is anything guiding our fates, it appears to be more malevolent than benevolent. Most of what happens on earth represents responses to the forces of nature (gravity, atomic forces—physics and chemistry) and of biology (cellular structure, DNA, evolutionary forces, etc.). Then, there is luck, which is random. We can barely describe what influences most of our lives, and have relatively limited means of changing or manipulating the big picture. Plague swept through the world in the Middle Ages and wiped out one third of the human population. Children are born in Sub-Saharan Africa by a simple twist of fate, and twenty percent of them die of infections before they reach the age of five. Someone is walking on a sidewalk, and a car runs out of control and kills the innocent walker. A meteorite from outer space falls to earth and leads to the elimination of an entire planet-full of reptiles who were perfectly happy to eat plants and each other forever. Stuff happens.. Our understanding of these events gradually is increasing, but we can only do so much to change the trajectory of the world or our lives.

But, we are not helpless. It may seem that way because progress is slow. The life expectancy of an American in 1900 was forty-six years for men and forty-eight years for women. It will soon be over eighty for everyone. It would seem to have been a bit of dumb luck to have been born in 1947 as I was than in 1920 or 1880 as my father and grandfather were. I know how to deal with Lynch Syndrome—whereas my father didn't even know what it was. It was a curse or a terror in the night. Now it's simple issue of a variation in the DNA code, and there are ways of dealing with it. I initially thought that being my father's son was an issue of luck. It was. Very good luck.

Epilogue

GENETIC VARIATION AND ADAPTATION

"So, what's our superpower?" Uyen, a Lynch Syndrome patient.

Genetic variation is a natural consequence of imperfect DNA replication, imperfect mitosis, mutagenesis, inflammation, and other disruptors of the integrity of our genomes. Each one of us probably brings one hundred new mutations into the world that neither parent had. Most of this genetic variation is silent, but over time, the genome experiences "drift". In any event, the appearance of a new or "*de novo*" disease-causing mutation is a relatively uncommon event. In the case of some diseases (achondroplastic dwarfism, familial adenomatous polyposis, many others), the mutant gene in the affected individual is not present in either parent, and the disease was an unpredictable accident. So, things happen, and life is dynamic and ever-changing. It is not possible to pass a perfect copy of your genome to the next generation. Replication is a messy, imperfect biological process, and apparently, evolutionary pressures favor this situation. It fact, zoo-keepers and animal breeders fear the consequences of inbreeding and the lack of diversity among their animal populations, since that leaves the herd potentially susceptible to the introduction of a single variation in the environment—a new microbe or a change in the climate for example.

Importantly, some genetic variation is adaptive. It confers a survival or reproductive benefit to the host. However, adaptability is context-dependent.

For example, a substantial proportion of people who live in parts of the world affected by malaria have one of several genetic variants that protect them from dying of malaria in childhood. Two such examples are the sickle cell genes, and thalassemia. If you are a *carrier* of one of these genetic variations (that is, you have *one copy* of the variant), you are more likely to survive in an environment where there are malaria-bearing mosquitos than someone who does not have this. However, we have two copies of each gene—one from father, and one from mother. If both of your copies encode for the sickle cell or thalassemia genes, then a serious disease results, childhood disease ensues, and life expectancy is reduced. There is no apparent benefit from either gene outside of surviving malaria. So, some variants are beneficial in one setting, and neutral or detrimental in another.

In the case of germline mutations in a DNA mismatch repair gene, there appears to be no advantage for humans. These mutations seem to have been genetic accidents, and were neutral when humans had lifespans ranging from thirty to forty, and the mutations were simply carried passively as silent passengers from one generation to the next. Once we began to live for more than fifty to sixty years, the situation changed, and they became "disease genes".

This situation can look different, however, in bacteria. A microbiologist created strains of *E. coli* bacteria that could tolerate toxins that damage DNA. He referred to these as "mutator" strains of bacteria, because they also had elevated mutation rates. These bacteria could survive higher doses of DNA-damaging agents, and could generate more diverse populations of bacteria because of the diminished ability to repair altered DNA. The broader diversity made the colony of bacteria more robust, since, some of the bugs in a mud puddle (or someone's gut) might have a genetic variant that permits adaptation to the next "new" change in the environment. All things considered, this might have provided some survival or reproductive advantage to the affected bugs. However, the inability to completely repair all DNA damage has some disadvantages as well. A lot of mistakes are made, and most will be deleterious. In the case of a colony of bacteria, the presence of diversity in the population enhances the speed by which the colony can adapt to change. When there are millions or billions of bacteria in a colony, this is an acceptable price. Everything depends upon the environmental context.

I once cared for a Vietnamese-American family with Lynch Syndrome in Dallas. There were five siblings, and one developed colon cancer in her forties. It would be somewhat unusual for a Vietnamese person to develop colon cancer, and especially at that age. We found the germline mutation responsible for her Lynch Syndrome. One day, two of the sisters came in to discuss appropriate preventive measures. They were bright, energetic, upbeat, and had a well-developed sense of humor.

They sat across from me, looked briefly at one another, smirked, and Uyen spoke up. "We have the mutation. So, what's our superpower?"

I loved the question. I told them the story about the bacteria, and told them that adaptation and survival all depended upon context. I just wasn't sure what the superpower was. I agreed to let them know when I figured it out.

I was born into a family that has a genetic disease going back as far as I can see in our pedigree. It killed too many of my ancestors, and it made me angry. I ended up going to medical school, and was forced by fate to confront this situation. The challenge dictated my career path. Eventually, many of us together figured out the puzzle, and we now have means for diagnosing this disease, and very effective means to mitigate the likelihood of dying of the cancers caused by this disease. I was motivated initially by fear and anxiety. I found myself in a position where I had a chance to solve the question. It's all a matter of context and finding the right adaptation to the situation. The circumstance that didn't kill me made me stronger. If I had had a different father, nothing would have been the same. We all have something. I was just lucky enough to be born into a Lynch Syndrome family.

Appendix

The History of Lynch Syndrome (1895-2013)

(*The following is a revised version of an article I published in 2013, upon the centennial of the first published report of Lynch Syndrome. The broad strokes of this medical review have been covered in the prior chapters. This had been written for those in scientific fields, is somewhat redundant of prior material, but has the details that some will want to read. Consider it supplemental, and not essential, information. Some of the figures from the original article have been deleted. Adapted from: Boland CR and Lynch HT. The History of Lynch Syndrome. Familial Cancer 12:145-57, 2013. PMID: 23546821. NIHMS462896.*)

The Early Years: 1895-1937

A.S. Warthin and Family G

In 1913, Aldred Scott Warthin, MD, PhD, Chairman of the Department of Pathology at the University of Michigan in Ann Arbor (*Figure 32*), reported the first family with the disease we now call Lynch Syndrome [1]. In 1895, a woman who worked as his seamstress reported distress over the fact that many of her family members over several generations had succumbed to cancer, and she feared the same for herself. Indeed, she developed endometrial cancer, and died of that disease as she predicted. Warthin dryly noted that "the statistical study of carcinoma …

[has] been carried as far as it can be profitable; and certainly but little that is new has been gained by this method during the last decade". Throwing a statistical approach to the wind, he undertook a "fairly complete survey" of the family, and created a pedigree, showing which family members had developed cancer, and their relationships.

Figure 32: A.S. Warthin, MD, PhD as a young man about 1900 (A), and later in his professional life, dates uncertain (B-D).

The seamstress' immediate sibship included ten members; two had uterine cancers, two had stomach cancers, and one had an "abdominal cancer". The descendants of all five of those with cancer also had multiple cancers. Among those in the family without cancer who had children, none of the progeny had developed cancer. Warthin concluded that there could be, at least in this instance, a familial predisposition to cancer. The family had emigrated from Germany to Michigan before the Civil War; Warthin called them "Family G".

Warthin also reported that, in 3,600 cases of neoplasia that had come through his laboratory at the University of Michigan from 1895-1912,

1,600 of these were carcinomas, and that "about 15%" of those had a family history of carcinoma. Reinforced by a report in 1912 from a German investigator named Levin, Warthin concluded that there were "cancerous fraternities", and that there was "some influence of heredity on cancer". He presented a series of pedigrees to illustrate his case.

Warthin wrote a "further study" of cancer family "G" in 1925 [2]. By now, he had concluded that the familial susceptibility to cancer was particularly true for carcinoma of the gastrointestinal tract and uterus. He recognized the early age of onset of the cancers, and suggested that the tumors might be occurring "at an earlier age in successive generations"—a phenomenon we now call anticipation, but which has not been substantiated in further studies of Lynch Syndrome. He also noted that three young members of the family presented with appendicitis, but at operation were found to have advanced cancer—presaging the proximal colonic tendencies for the colorectal cancers (CRCs) in this disease. Among 146 family members, almost 32% had developed cancer, at a median age of 37.9 years. He also commented that his observations had been met "with little favor among surgical writers". Some things never change. As was typical for scientists of his era, I was told by James Neel, the geneticist from the University of Michigan, that Warthin was a proponent of eugenics and voiced his opinions in his writings, but did not intervene in the lives of "Cancer Family G".

Warthin died in 1931, but his colleagues I.J. Hauser and Carl V. Weller issued a "further report on the cancer family of Warthin" in 1936 [3]. As more time passed, and more individuals were followed for a longer period, mitigating one type of ascertainment bias, the average age for death from cancer in Family G rose to 48.3 years. They noted that there were no cases of cervical cancer among those with uterine cancer, that there were many gastrointestinal cancers, and few breast cancers. They provided detailed pathological analyses of the tumors from each branch of the family. As more data accumulated, they concluded that there was a "diminishing incidence" of cancer with successive generations. These authors proposed that this family provided more evidence for an "inheritable organ-specific predisposition to carcinoma".

Twentieth Century Insights

From Warthin to Lynch

The story grew cold during the period from 1937 until the 1960s. Occasional case reports of this disease came from the Mayo Clinic in 1941[4], England in 1956[5], and a variety of locations in the 1960s[6-11]. None the less, the existence of a familial form of colorectal cancer that was not familial adenomatous polyposis remained in considerable doubt. One person who noted these familial clusters of cancer was Henry T. Lynch, MD (*Figure 33*), who reported several families in detail in 1966-67[12-14]. Lynch was aware of Warthin's "Cancer Family G"; therefore, he arranged for a family reunion near Ann Arbor, MI, to learn more about this family. He conducted a detailed medical genetic investigation of the family, obtained data on >650 family members (among whom ninety-five had now developed cancers), and found a predominance of cancers of the colon, uterus and stomach in the kindred in his iconic "Cancer Family 'G' Revisited" manuscript of 1971[15]. Once more, progeny of affected individuals continued to be at risk for early-onset cancers. He recognized the autosomal dominant nature of inheritance. A variety of hypotheses were proposed to explain the disease, but the time for discovery of the basis of hereditary cancer had not yet arrived. He used the term "Cancer Family Syndrome" in this report.

Figure 33: Henry T. Lynch, MD

This would not be the final report on Cancer Family G. In 2005, Douglas et al. (from the University of Michigan) provided additional confirmatory follow-up of the family with data on 929 descendants of the original progenitor, and reported on the specific mutation in the *MSH2* gene [16]. This work verified the risks for cancer of the colon and endometrium, showed that the risks for gastric cancer which were initially prominent had gradually disappeared through the twentieth century, and provided standardized incidence ratios for cancers of various organs. There is probably no other instance in which one family has contributed so much to the understanding of an important genetic disease such as this.

Giving "Cancer Family Syndrome" a more specific name

In 1973, my medical school thesis was entitled "A Familial Cancer Syndrome", recognizing the same disease; this led to the publication of two papers describing additional families with Lynch Syndrome. In the first of these, I reported the details of my own family, and used the term "Cancer Family Syndrome", based upon Lynch's initial nomenclature [17]. However, when I wrote up a second family in 1984 and reviewed the literature available, I noted that some families had developed only CRCs, whereas other families had the characteristic non-colonic cancers we now associate with this disease. I thought it was important to point this out, and called Henry to ask his permission to attach his name to the syndrome. He agreed. The terms Lynch Syndrome I and II were coined to distinguish those families with a CRC-only vs. the full spectrum of cancers [18]. There is now evidence that some germline mutations can produce a colorectal cancer-predominant syndrome[19], although the designations of Lynch Syndrome I and II are no longer used or necessary. Interestingly, in 1985, Lynch first used the term "hereditary non-polyposis colorectal cancer" or "HNPCC" for this disease, which was the accepted term for many years [20, 21]. It would not be until the genetic basis of the disease was discovered, and more importantly, the recognition that not all familial clusters of colorectal cancer represented one disease, that the term Lynch Syndrome was finally applied to those families with documented germline mutations in DNA mismatch repair genes [22]. HNPCC was a mouthful, and occasionally, people who had a partial familiarity with this entity would scramble the letters. Also, the name drew inappropriate attention to the unrelated disease familial adenomatous polyposis. It was my opinion that we needed to get rid of the term HNPCC once and for all. Ironically, it still persists, and has been used to specifically refer to hereditary clusters of colorectal cancer that are *not* Lynch Syndrome.

The Amsterdam criteria

In this general time frame, Hans Vasen, MD, a clinical geneticist from the Netherlands, emerged as a major leader and contributor to the field. Hans was one of several key members in the formation of the "International Collaborative Group on Hereditary Non-Polyposis Colorectal Cancer" (or ICG-HNPCC), which was conceived during a colorectal cancer meeting in Jerusalem in 1989, and had its first formal meeting in Amsterdam in 1990 [23]. Meetings were held on a regular basis thereafter, particularly as the understanding of hereditary colorectal cancer grew, and the biological basis of the disease was uncovered.

While some observers doubted the existence of a hereditary non-polyposis colorectal cancer syndrome, Hans and other interested clinicians accumulated and characterized familial clusters of CRC, and developed the "Amsterdam Criteria", which were valuable for finding families who had Lynch Syndrome [24, 25]. Gathering "reagent grade" families for analysis and the concomitant evolution of molecular genetics soon led to the discovery of the genetic basis of Lynch Syndrome [26]. Ultimately, the ICG-HNPCC merged with the Leeds Castle Polyposis Group [27] to form the "International Society for Gastrointestinal Hereditary Tumours", or InSiGHT, which continues to have semi-annual meetings and research initiatives.

Microsatellite instability and CRC

From the late 1960s until 1993, progress in understanding Lynch Syndrome was slow. The clinical features were refined, but there were no features useful in diagnosing the disease until a person developed a cancer, and there were few clues about the nature of the tumors that could lead to a genuine understanding of the disease. There were multiple attempts to understand the basic mechanism responsible for the disease; all failed.

Thing changed dramatically in the early 1990s, which set off one of the most impressive scientific "horseraces" in the history of medical investigation that involved established figures in the field and some unexpected newcomers. By way of background, in 1989-90, the laboratory of Bert Vogelstein, MD proposed that colorectal neoplasia developed through multistep carcinogenesis, and that the sequential loss of specific fragments of chromosomal DNA was a key part of this process. Loss of DNA in a tumor was termed "loss of heterozygosity" or LOH, because of the genetic techniques used to detect it. The losses, which were being identified on a regular basis in many types of tumors, led to the discovery of "tumor suppressor genes" at those locations. Whereas simple mutations (such as those that alter one nucleotide) in a gene might or might not change its function, deleting a gene is a certain way to inactivate it.

Laboratories developed progressively more inventive ways to discover all the genetic deletions that could be found in a cancer that were present in the normal tissues of a cancer patient. One laboratory, that of Manuel Perucho, PhD, was looking for chromosomal losses in CRC tissues using a technique called "arbitrarily primed PCR" to amplify randomly selected genetic targets from paired samples of CRC and normal tissues. Members of his lab literally threw dice to ensure that a large number of random DNA segments would be analyzed. He didn't care where the DNA targets were; there just needed to be a lot of them scattered throughout the genome. When they used the technique, they obtained the exact same "fingerprint" of PCR products every time from the same sample. The way they analyzed the results was to separate the PCR products (the DNA fragments of interest that had been amplified over a million fold by the technique) based upon their size using gel electrophoresis. He put the normal DNA and the colorectal cancer DNA products side-by-side, and the initial plan or hypothesis was to find genetic deletions (or additions) in the cancer DNA compared to its normal counterpart [28].

There were plenty of these to be found, but he cleverly noted that there were also subtle changes in the lengths of some of the amplified DNA fragments in CRC tissues, specifically those that happened to contain simple repetitive sequences called "microsatellites" [29]. He then analyzed the PCR products, and discovered the nature of the simple repeated sequences (they were repetitive series of A's or CA's, etc. that are very common in the human genome). Something unexpected was going on, and there were many, many mutations in these microsatellite sequences. Only some CRCs showed this, but those that did had an estimated 100,000 such mutations. He proposed that this subset of CRCs was different from the rest, and that this represented a unique "pathway" through which colorectal tumors could evolve.

There is a little back story here. In May, 1987, the laboratories of Vogelstein and Perucho simultaneously published in the journal *Nature* that a substantial portion of CRCs had mutations in the oncogene *Ki-RAS*. This was one of the first reports in which a member of the newly discovered oncogenes (a concept that won the Nobel Prize for Michael Bishop and Harold Varmus in 1989) was involved in a common human tumor. It is definitely the case that both Perucho's and Vogelstein's laboratories were working on this project independently, but it may have been the case that Perucho's laboratory was "tipped off" about Vogelstein's submission, and hastened to submit their work quickly.

Perucho had previously shown his preliminary data to a group of scientists in a meeting in Spain in the spring of 1992. This was clearly his discovery, but it was not at all clear how this occurred or what it actually meant. Perucho specifically withheld a key piece of data from his presentation, namely that the mutated sequences were microsatellites. But when picking up his slides, he divulged the key to Bert Vogelstein, who was now a powerful influence in the scientific community. Perucho claimed that he felt he needed the support of others in the field for his finding to gain acceptance. Perucho sent a draft of the manuscript to Vogelstein for consideration of publication in *The Proceedings of the National Academy of Science, USA*. Bert was a member of the National Academy of Sciences, and could get a paper published by obtaining appropriately positive reviews. According to Bert, the reviewers were intrigued and interested, but asked for more data and supporting evidence before it could be published. When Bert reported to Perucho that he would have to do additional work, revise, and resubmit, he was upset, and thought that there may have been some obstructionism in the reviews. He then sent the paper to *Cell*, where it got essentially the same positive reception for the concepts, but with requests for more data and clarification. Most importantly, the editor, Benjamin Lewin, PhD, was not convinced that these findings were sufficient to prove that this represented a "novel pathway" of carcinogenesis, as Perucho had argued. Manuel was particularly upset at this rejection, and sent a profanity-laced response to Lewin, who suggested that Perucho not submit future articles to his journal. (And, he hasn't).

Perucho decided to send his manuscript to the most prestigious and difficult journal, *Nature*. This gave him an opportunity to have the work read by new reviewers in Europe. After some delay, the editor told Perucho that *Nature* would publish this manuscript, but it had to be cut down in size and published as a "letter" instead of as a full "article". Perucho said that this made him despondent, and he put the manuscript on his desk for several days to get over the disappointment. Interestingly, Perucho gave his observation the tongue-twisting moniker "ubiquitous somatic mutations in simple repeated sequences", and insisted it was a "new mechanism for colonic carcinogenesis". In spite of the frustration, he was about to have his day in the sun. However, it was now May, 1993, and something remarkable happened that month.

While Perucho was muttering about his difficulty in getting his new story accepted, two other laboratories independently discovered microsatellite instability. Given the techniques available and the number of excellent investigators working on this, the discovery was becoming inevitable. I had seen it in my own laboratory, but didn't have enough samples or insight to recognize what it meant. I literally said to the post-doctoral fellow, named Juichi Sato;

"There are three billion base pairs in the genome, we chose a 150 base pair DNA sequence to analyze, and there was a two base pair deletion in the middle of it. What are the odds that this is real? There must be a mix-up of samples." I asked him to repeat the experiment. He did, and showed it to me. I had no idea what we had in our hands.

One of the laboratories that figured out what this meant was that of Stephen Thibodeau, PhD, from the Mayo Clinic. He had used PCR to analyze his tumors, and coincidentally noted that some of the tumors had mutations at microsatellite sequences, and he coined the term "microsatellite instability", or MSI. He noted this was mainly seen in CRCs from the proximal colon, survival was better in the patients from this group, and the presence of microsatellite instability correlated inversely with the LOH events described earlier by Vogelstein's group. He suggested that this might represent a novel mechanism for tumor evolution compared with other CRCs [30].

At approximately the same time, an international consortium that included Vogelstein from Johns Hopkins, together with Albert de la Chapelle, MD, PhD, Lauri Aaltonen, MD, PhD and Paivi Peltomaki, MD, PhD from Finland (and others who provided the appropriately identified families), were completely focused on the familial CRC problem, and were trying to identify the gene responsible for familial clusters of CRC. To do this, they used a type of genetic mapping marker—dinucleotide repeats—which are microsatellite sequences that were the most widely used genomic mapping markers at the time. These were useful since the chromosomal location of each marker was known, and there was a high likelihood that the mother's and father's sequences were different in length, which provided a facile approach for tracking the inheritance of each parent's allele through the family. When you use enough microsatellites that are widely spread throughout the genome as genetic mapping markers, it is possible to localize the chromosomal position of a genetically-based disease within a family. This group was doing a lot of PCR analyses of microsatellites for completely different reasons than Perucho or Thibodeau. On one afternoon in the spring of 1993 (specifically 3:45 PM on Saturday March 13), Lauri Aaltonen localized a gene for Lynch Syndrome in one family to a specific location on chromosome 2p, using the microsatellite marker, D2S123 (which was the 345th marker analyzed in this exhausting study) [31]. For the first time, it was going to be possible to find the gene that was responsible for Lynch Syndrome. Whatever it might be, we now knew where it lived. The move from complete darkness to light occurred with an astonishingly quick stroke of discovery.

Not knowing what the gene might be, one presumption was that a tumor suppressor gene was located in the vicinity of D2S123, and the logical experiment was to look for LOH in the CRC tissue from Lynch syndrome patients. So, PCR was done using the D2S123 marker on several Lynch Syndrome-associated colorectal cancers. However, since these tumors evolved through a different cancer "pathway", instead of LOH they found the deletion mutations in the microsatellites, which changed their lengths, resulting in altered electrophoretic mobilities [32]. They recognized that there were a lot of mutations at these repetitive sequences, and called it the "replication error" (RER) phenotype. Most importantly, they closed the loop between microsatellite instability and

Lynch Syndrome, and recognized that the Lynch Syndrome CRCs all had microsatellite instability. Remarkably, three papers (one from Thibodeau and two from the international consortium) all appeared in the same issue of *Science* on May 7, 1993. The entire world of hereditary colorectal cancer was enlightened, as there was, for the first time, a clue regarding the molecular basis of this disease.

Perucho saw these papers, and hit the roof. He imagined that Vogelstein's group had stolen his idea, but the fact is that the international consortium came to their conclusion through an independent line of reasoning, and were focused initially on Lynch Syndrome, not the new pathway. However, Perucho knew that Vogelstein had prior knowledge of his ideas, and assumed the worst. Just to add insult to his perceived injury, Perucho's paper was published five weeks later, in *Nature*, on June 10, 1993 [29]. Although everyone knows that Perucho was the first to make the observation about microsatellite instability, he had no clue about its link to Lynch Syndrome. He had the opportunity to see the three papers in *Science*, and then flew to London with his hasty revision to demand that his work be published as soon as possible. He mentioned in the final sentence of his paper that his finding could be used to detect tumors that might be occurring through this pathway on a hereditary basis. However, at least one of his co-authors acknowledged that he did not recall reading about that concept in the prior versions of the manuscript. So, this particular horserace had a curious finish. But the main event was yet to come, and some of the next round of horses arrived from a totally unexpected direction. What was the Lynch Syndrome gene, and how did it create this newly-discovered phenomenon of microsatellite instability and a novel cancer pathway?

From MSI to DNA MMR genes

The speed of discovery increased substantially from that point. Interestingly, none of the initial discoverers of microsatellite instability recognized exactly how the gel electrophoresis autoradiograms they produced were the key to understanding the disease. Laboratories studying genetics in bacteria and yeast had previously discovered the DNA mismatch repair system, and knew that if mismatch repair genes were inactivated by mutation in microorganisms, it resulted in widespread mutations at microsatellite sequences. These groups took one look at the data in these papers, and knew it was time to become cancer researchers!

In May, 1993, several laboratories previously involved only in yeast and microbial genetics abruptly entered into a race to clone the human homologs of these genes, and determine if there were germline mutations in DNA mismatch genes in families with Lynch Syndrome. The first to do this successfully was the laboratory of Richard Kolodner, PhD, who was an established investigator in yeast genetics, and had just cloned the *MSH2* gene in yeast, but had not previously ventured into human disease or cancer. On December 3, 1993, less than six months after the initial linkage of microsatellite instability with hereditary colorectal cancer, his lab, together with several collaborators prominently including Rick Fishel, PhD, cloned the human homolog of the DNA mismatch repair gene *hMSH2*, and found a sequence variation in a family with Lynch Syndrome that was present in those who had developed cancer [33]. Even more astonishing, just two weeks later, on December 17, 1993, the international consortium led by Vogelstein and de la Chapelle found three additional kindreds with inactivating mutations in the *hMSH2* gene [34]. Moreover, they identified a CRC cell line, HCT116, that had microsatellite instability, and this created the first *in vitro* model in which to study the basics of the process [35]. For those interested in Lynch Syndrome, this was like the first step on the moon.

The race was far from over. Earlier in 1993, a Lynch Syndrome family had been characterized in Sweden, but in this instance the genetic linkage pointed to chromosome 3p, rather than 2p, where *hMSH2* had been found [36]. This launched yet another race to identify the gene. Again, the Kolodner group cloned the human *hMLH1* gene, in collaboration with R. Michael Liskay, PhD, who like Kolodner, had been working on MutL-related genes in yeast. They reported germline mutations in this gene in different Lynch Syndrome families on March 17, 1994 [37]. Not to be outdone, the international consortium reported the same result on March 18, 1994 [38]. They also found that *hMLH1* (rather than *hMSH2*) was mutated in the HCT116 cell line. By September, 1994, the human *hPMS2* and *hPMS1* genes were cloned, and linked to Lynch Syndrome [39]. So, in an incredible period of about sixteen months, Lynch Syndrome was firmly put on the scientific map, linked to microsatellite instability, which led to the identification of the human DNA mismatch repair genes, and it was possible to think about developing tests to diagnose the disease. Over the next several years, it was found that *hPMS1* was not actually a Lynch Syndrome gene, and *hMSH6* was brought into the fold as the fourth Lynch Syndrome gene, first by its involvement in cell lines with microsatellite instability [40, 41], and finally via germline mutations in affected patients with different types of family histories of cancer, with later characteristic onset of cancer than seen in classic Lynch Syndrome [42].

Evolution of diagnostic tests for Lynch Syndrome: from Amsterdam, through Bethesda, to Jerusalem

The ability to determine which patients and families actually had Lynch Syndrome permitted a refinement of the diagnostic approaches during the last decade of the twentieth century. Antibodies were developed to the DNA MMR proteins hMSH2, hMSH6, hMLH1 and hPMS2, and the diagnostic approach to microsatellite instability was standardized in a National Cancer Institute-sponsored Workshop in Bethesda in November, 1997. The Workshop manuscript reported a standardized diagnosis and panel of microsatellite markers, and the published paper has been cited in >3,250 other papers since then [43]. This manuscript also developed and reported the "Bethesda Guidelines", which were intended to identify CRC tissues that should be targeted for analysis, either looking for microsatellite instability or abnormal immunohistochemistry (IHC). The Bethesda Guidelines were revised in 2004[44], much as the original Amsterdam Criteria [24] had been in 1999 [25]. All of these recommendations have been supplanted by our current understanding that many true Lynch Syndrome families do not meet the Amsterdam Criteria (initially intended to identify families from whom the genes could be found), that many individuals with Lynch Syndrome do not meet the Bethesda Guidelines, and conversely, many who meet these criteria or guidelines do not have germline mutations in any DNA mismatch repair gene [45]. This problem ultimately led to a workshop in Jerusalem in 2010, in which it was recommended that any CRC in a person <70 years old should be screened by microsatellite instability testing or IHC for possible Lynch Syndrome [46].

Lynch Syndrome in the 21st Century

"Syndrome X"

The identification of the genes responsible for Lynch Syndrome gave those working in the field a euphoric sense that the problem had been substantially solved. However, as more details emerged, it became clear that only the surface had been scratched, and there was much more to be learned about the disease. First, it had been suspected (perhaps naively) that once the genes causing Lynch Syndrome were identified, we would be able to characterize all familial clusters of CRC. The Colon Cancer Family Registry (C-CFR), a large international consortium of research groups, collected 3,422 individuals from 161 families that met the Amsterdam Criteria for Lynch Syndrome between 1997 and 2001. DNA from affected individuals was subjected to the best available efforts to find germline mutations in DNA mismatch repair genes. Only 60% of these families had a germline mutation (i.e., actually had Lynch Syndrome). The other 40% had CRCs that did not have DNA mismatch repair deficiency. Therefore, they did not have Lynch Syndrome [22], and a new disease entity was identified, and tentatively called Familial Colorectal Cancer-Type X [45]. These families had a lower penetrance for CRC, later onset of the cancers, and did not have an increase in the non-CRC tumor spectrum as seen in Lynch Syndrome. There are genetic diseases such as Peutz-Jeghers Syndrome, Juvenile Polyposis, Cowden's Disease, Li-Fraumeni Syndrome, and others in which there is an increase in the risk of CRC, but "Syndrome X" does not fall into any of those groups, and remains an important research challenge at this time [47].

Interpreting the genetic analyses of the DNA MMR genes

Next, as more data came in and genetic tests became widely available commercially, it became apparent that it is not always simple to determine which DNA sequence variations in the DNA mismatch genes cause Lynch Syndrome, and which are silent sequence polymorphisms. Premature stop codons were easy to interpret, but many of the sequence variations altered gene splicing sites (not too hard to interpret once the "rules" were learned), or missense mutations that change the amino acid in that position in the encoded protein. It is not always possible to predict changes in protein folding and function based upon the change in the amino acid sequence alone. So, many genetic tests return with clinically uncertain or uninterpretable results [48]. This created new challenges for the clinician and genetic counselors.

One of first insights occurred when it became apparent that the *hMSH2* gene was often mutated by large deletions that were not detectable using the standard sequencing techniques. Over one third of the mutations in this gene responsible for inactivating mutations were large deletions within *hMSH2* in a key Dutch study, and they accounted for a substantial proportion (>6%) of all Lynch Syndrome in their registry [49]. One approach to identify large genomic deletions was to separate the paternal and maternal alleles for individual analysis—a labor-intensive technique called "conversion to haploidy", but this was not widely embraced [50]. Eventually, techniques became available that permitted an estimation of the number of alleles present at each exon (multiplex ligation-dependent probe amplification, or MLPA), which permitted the detection of large genomic deletions, and helped resolve this confusion.

A second insight into perturbations in the *hMSH2* gene was the discovery that deletion of the stop codon of the *EPCAM* gene, which is immediately upstream of the *hMSH2* gene, results in epigenetic silencing of *hMSH2*. Therefore, although no germline mutation was present in the *hMSH2* gene, the alteration in *EPCAM* created a "heritable somatic inactivation" of *hMSH2* in all tissues that expressed *EPCAM* [51]. By finding this mutation in a large kindred, it was found that at least some types of these deletions create a CRC-predominant form of Lynch Syndrome, reminiscent of Lynch Syndrome I predicted some twenty-five years earlier [18].

Adjuvant chemotherapy and Lynch Syndrome

Shortly after the discovery of the *hMSH2* and *hMLH1* genes in 1993-94, Minoru Koi, PhD created the first laboratory model to study the biology of DNA mismatch repair-deficient cells *in vitro* by stably transferring a copy of human chromosome 3 into HCT116 colorectal cancer cells, correcting the loss of *hMLH1* [52] (*Figure 34*).

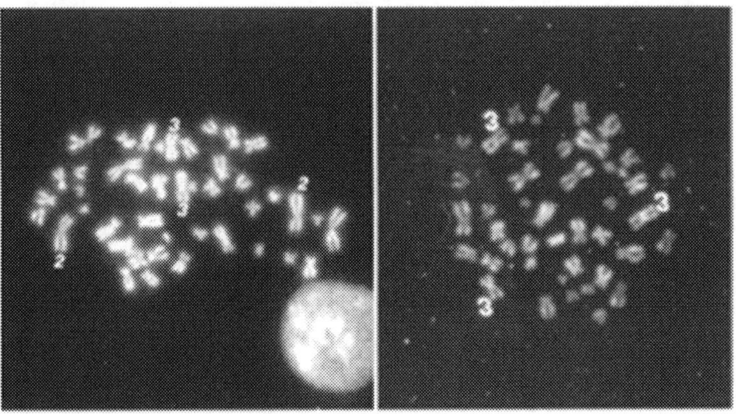

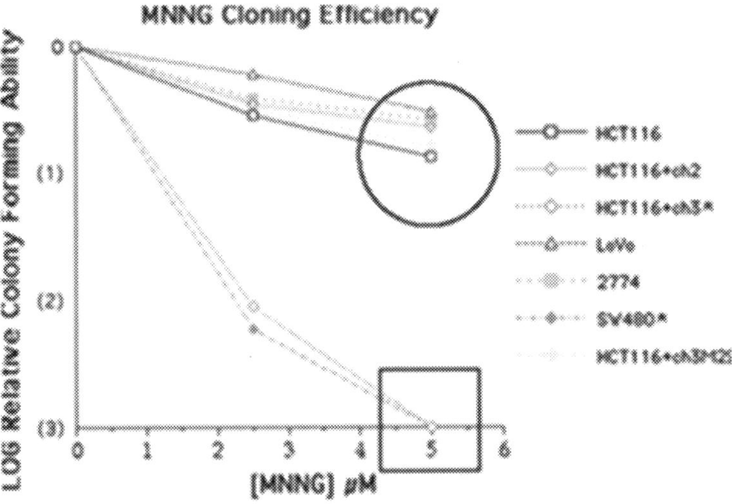

Figure 34: DNA mismatch repair deficiency and response to chemotherapeutic agents. Minoru Koi, PhD created a DNA mismatch repair-corrected cell model by stably transferring a copy of human chromosome 3 into the *hMLH1*-deficient CRC cell line HCT116, which is diploid. At the top on the left is a karyotype of the uncorrected cell line, with two copies of both chromosomes 2 and 3. This cell line is DNA mismatch repair deficient and has MSI. On the right is HCT116+chr3, which has three copies of chromosome 3. In these cells, the MSI has been corrected, and the cell line is mismatch repair proficient. In the bottom figure, the CRC cell lines that are mismatch repair deficient (as shown in the circle) can tolerate increasing doses of the alkylating agent MNNG, which damages DNA, as shown in the cells that continue to have high cloning efficiency (HCT116, HCT116+chr2, LoVo, 2774,

and HCT116+chr3M2). However, the cell lines that are DNA mismatch repair proficient (shown in the square) are sensitive to DNA damage, and cannot be grown in 5 micromolar MNNG (HCT116+chr3 and SW480).

Subsequent experiments led to the conclusion that DNA mismatch repair-deficient cells were intrinsically more resistant to DNA damage, similar to microbial cells with inactivating mutations in these genes [53, 54]. The implications were that certain chemotherapeutic drugs might not be fully effective against microsatellite unstable cancers. Additional experiments showed that mismatch repair-deficient cells were resistant to 5-fluorouracil (5-FU), the mainstay of adjuvant chemotherapy for Stage III colorectal cancer [55]. Resistance was found for other chemotherapeutic drugs [56, 57], and identical drug resistance was found in CRC cells with acquired methylation-induced silencing of *hMLH1* [58].

It was therefore necessary to determine whether patients with microsatellite instability colorectal cancers were refractory to conventional chemotherapy in clinical studies. The first published report on the subject suggested that patients with microsatellite unstable colorectal cancers had a "striking survival benefit" when given adjuvant chemotherapy [59]. However, a serious design flaw had led to this erroneous conclusion. The study was retrospective, and the patients had not been randomized to receive chemotherapy. Rather, they had been selected by their oncologists to either receive treatment or not, presumably on the basis of their age and/or performance status. Patients who were younger and healthier were more likely to be treated with the drugs. In fact, the group of the patients selected for chemotherapy had a better five year survival whether they were treated or not. However, 64% of the CRC patients <68 years old had been selected for treatment versus. only 19% of those ≥68. None the less, this report created a problem in which the empirical observations were at odds with what had been predicted from the *in vitro* biology of the tumors.

This initial finding of a beneficial effect of treatment was not confirmed in eleven subsequent studies on the subject [60]. The first contrary paper was a multicenter collaboration of patients enrolled in randomized trials, and they found that patients with tumors showing microsatellite instability had substantially better overall five year survivals, and this was particularly so *if they did not* receive adjuvant chemotherapy. Even worse, there were non-significant trends towards increased cancer-related mortalities in the Stage II and Stage III groups given adjuvant drug treatment [61].

Subsequent studies have raised the possibility that the improved survival in CRC patients with microsatellite instability may not be a sole consequence of the intrinsic resistance to chemotherapy. CRCs with microsatellite instability contain substantially more tumor-infiltrating lymphocytes, and it has been proposed that this brisk immune response may be responsible for limiting the spread of these tumors [62, 63]. Thus, the actual mechanism responsible for the poor response to chemotherapy may be related to the immune response to the hypermutated tumor cells, rather than—or in addition to—intrinsic resistance to the therapy.

Aspirin and Lynch Syndrome

A new chapter on managing cancer risk in Lynch Syndrome was provided by Sir John Burn, MD, of Newcastle, United Kingdom, who designed a prospective, randomized, placebo-controlled, multicenter study of the impact of aspirin and fiber on the development of neoplasia in Lynch Syndrome. The initial study design was to determine whether 600 mg of aspirin, 30 grams of a fermentable dietary fiber ("resistant starch"), or both, might suppress the formation of adenomatous polyps in the colon over a period of four years. Neither intervention had any effect on polyp recurrence; in fact, the relative risk [RR] for subsequent adenomatous polyps was exactly 1.0 [64].

Although a less persistent man might have been deterred, Burn was not. He conducted a follow-up analysis of outcomes after another four years, and discovered a significant reduction in the risk of CRC in those randomized to aspirin (RR for colorectal cancer=0.63, by intention to treat), and in those who actually took the aspirin for at least two years (RR for colorectal cancer=0.41, per protocol) [65]. No beneficial effect was derived from supplemental dietary fiber. No excess of adverse events was seen in the aspirin-treated patients. This remains to be confirmed, and the optimal dose of aspirin has not yet been determined. However, this represents a game-changing event in the history of hereditary cancer, and we will undoubtedly hear more about the role of aspirin in this disease.

Conclusions

Lynch Syndrome was initially recognized by the University of Michigan pathologist A.S. Warthin in 1913, who listened to his seamstress, gathered an extensive family history, constructed a pedigree, and proposed a familial, and perhaps genetic, explanation for this "cancerous fraternity". He followed up his own work, and others followed his, finding numerous similar families in a variety of communities and countries. The coordinated identification of rigorously defined families led to the linkage of the cancer-prone phenotype to a single locus on chromosome 2p in 1993. A serendipitous experiment permitted the prepared investigators to recognize that some familial colorectal cancers were associated with a novel cancer "pathway" that had been independently discovered by two other groups who did not suspect that there might be a familial form of this pathway. A focused (and furious) race ensued that led to the discovery of the four genes responsible for Lynch Syndrome. Informed by knowledge of the genetic basis of the disease, and propelled by the development and validation of two powerful clinical identifiers (microsatellite instability and immunohistochemistry), clinicians currently have an extraordinary body of useful information about Lynch Syndrome, which has permitted progress in the diagnosis and treatment of this disease. As indicated, it required the work of many investigators to reach these conclusions, and a few of these are shown in *Figure 35*.

Figure 35: A few selected contributors to the understanding of familial CRC are shown. A. Hans Vasen, MD (Leiden University, The Netherlands). Essential clinical contributor to the understanding of Lynch Syndrome in Europe. B. Manuel Perucho, PhD (Sanford-Burnham Medical Research Unit, La Jolla, CA). Discovered MSI, and proposed a novel pathway for CRC development. C. Stephen Thibodeau, PhD (Mayo Clinic, Minnesota). Independently discovered MSI, and suggested that these tumors evolved through a unique mechanism that did not involve LOH events. D. Bert Vogelstein, MD (Johns Hopkins University). Linked MSI to hereditary colorectal cancer; identified several of the DNA MMR genes, and linked mutant MMR genes to Lynch Syndrome. E. Albert de la Chapelle, MD, PhD (The Ohio State University). Together with Vogelstein and others, linked MSI to hereditary colorectal cancer; identified several of the DNA MMR genes, and linked mutant MMR genes to Lynch Syndrome. F. Lauri Aaltonen, MD, PhD (University of Helsinki, Finland). Together with Vogelstein and de la Chapelle, made the critical observation that hereditary CRC was linked to a locus on chromosome 2p, and that there was MSI in the linkage marker. G. Richard Kolodner, PhD (University of California San Diego). Cloned the human homologs of *MSH2* and *MLH1* and found germline mutations in families with Lynch Syndrome. H. Minoru Koi, PhD (Baylor University Medical Center, Dallas, TX). Created the first *in vitro* models of Lynch Syndrome from the HCT116

cell line using stable chromosome transfer to correct the DNA MMR defect. I. C. Richard Boland, MD (Baylor University Medical Center, Dallas, TX). Studied hereditary colon cancer as a medical student, coined the term "Lynch Syndrome", used the cell model developed by Koi in a series of studies on the response of DNA MMR deficient cells to chemotherapeutic drugs. J. Sir John Burn, MD, reported the first effective medical intervention for Lynch Syndrome—aspirin.

Reference List

1. Warthin AS. Heredity with reference to carcinoma as shown by the study of the cases examined in the Pathological Laboratory of the University of Michigan, 1895-1912. Arch Int Med 1913;12:546-555.
2. Warthin AS. The further study of a cancer family. J Cancer Research 1925;9:279-286.
3. Hauser IJ, Weller CV. A further report on the cancer family of Warthin. American Journal of Cancer 1936;27:434-449.
4. Bargen JA, Mayo CW, Giffin LA. Familial trends in human cancer. J Heredity 1941;32:7.
5. Savage D. A family history of uterine and gastro-intestinal cancer. Br Med J 1956;2(4988):341-343.
6. Aure JC, Nilsson S. Familial disposition of cancer of the gastrointestinal tract. Acta Chir Scand 1964;129:644-648.
7. Bieler VV, Heim U. Double cancer in siblings. Familial association of cancer of the genitaliia and intestines. Schweiz Med Wochenschr 1965;95:496-497.
8. Glidzic V, Petrovic G. [Hereditary nature of cancers of the colon]. Bull Cancer 1968;55(4):511-516.
9. Kartagener M, Wyler J. [Familial incidence of double malignancies]. Schweiz Med Wochenschr 1966;96(7):218-219.
10. Kluge T. Familial cancer of the colon. Acta Chir Scand 1964;127:392-398.
11. Heinzelmann F. [On a cancer family. A contribution to the problem of the hereditary aspects of colonic carcinoma]. Helv Chir Acta 1964;31:316-324.
12. Lynch HT, Shaw MW, Magnuson CW, Larsen AL, Krush AJ. Hereditary factors in cancer. Study of two large midwestern kindreds. Arch Intern Med 1966;117(2):206-212.
13. Lynch HT, Krush AJ. Heredity and adenocarcinoma of the colon. Gastroenterology 1967;53(4):517-527.
14. Lynch HT, Krush AJ, Larsen AL. Heredity and multiple primary malignant neoplasms: six cancer families. Am J Med Sci 1967;254(3):322-329.
15. Lynch HT, Krush AJ. Cancer family "G" revisited: 1895-1970. Cancer 1971;27(6):1505-1511.
16. Douglas JA, Gruber SB, Meister KA et al. History and molecular genetics of Lynch syndrome in family G: a century later. JAMA 2005;294(17):2195-2202.

17. Boland CR. Cancer Family Syndrome. A case report and literature review. Am J Dig Dis 1978;23(5):25s-27s.
18. Boland CR, Troncale FJ. Familial colonic cancer without antecedent polyposis. Ann Intern Med 1984;100(5):700-701.
19. Lynch HT, Riegert-Johnson DL, Snyder C et al. Lynch syndrome-associated extracolonic tumors are rare in two extended families with the same EPCAM deletion. Am J Gastroenterol 2011;106(10):1829-1836.
20. Lynch HT, Kimberling W, Albano WA et al. Hereditary nonpolyposis colorectal cancer (Lynch syndromes I and II). I. Clinical description of resource. Cancer 1985;56(4):934-938.
21. Lynch HT, Schuelke GS, Kimberling WJ et al. Hereditary nonpolyposis colorectal cancer (Lynch syndromes I and II). II. Biomarker studies. Cancer 1985;56(4):939-951.
22. Boland CR. Evolution of the nomenclature for the hereditary colorectal cancer syndromes. Fam Cancer 2005;4(3):211-218.
23. Lynch HT, Cristofaro G, Rozen P et al. History of the International Collaborative Group on Hereditary Non Polyposis Colorectal Cancer. Fam Cancer 2003;2(Suppl 1):3-5.
24. Vasen HF, Mecklin JP, Khan PM, Lynch HT. The International Collaborative Group on Hereditary Non-Polyposis Colorectal Cancer (ICG-HNPCC). Dis Colon Rectum 1991;34(5):424-425.
25. Vasen HF, Watson P, Mecklin JP, Lynch HT. New clinical criteria for hereditary nonpolyposis colorectal cancer (HNPCC, Lynch syndrome) proposed by the International Collaborative group on HNPCC. Gastroenterology 1999;116(6):1453-1456.
26. Marra G, Boland CR. Hereditary nonpolyposis colorectal cancer: the syndrome, the genes, and historical perspectives. J Natl Cancer Inst 1995;87(15):1114-1125.
27. Neale K, Bulow S. Origins of the Leeds Castle Polyposis Group. Fam Cancer 2003;2(Suppl 1):1-2.
28. Peinado MA, Malkhosyan S, Velazquez A, Perucho M. Isolation and characterization of allelic losses and gains in colorectal tumors by arbitrarily primed polymerase chain reaction. Proc Natl Acad Sci U S A 1992;89(21):10065-10069.
29. Ionov Y, Peinado MA, Malkhosyan S, Shibata D, Perucho M. Ubiquitous somatic mutations in simple repeated sequences reveal a new mechanism for colonic carcinogenesis. Nature 1993;363(6429):558-561.
30. Thibodeau SN, Bren G, Schaid D. Microsatellite instability in cancer of the proximal colon. Science 1993;260(5109):816-819.
31. Peltomaki P, Aaltonen LA, Sistonen P et al. Genetic mapping of a locus predisposing to human colorectal cancer. Science 1993;260(5109):810-812.
32. Aaltonen LA, Peltomaki P, Leach FS et al. Clues to the pathogenesis of familial colorectal cancer. Science 1993;260(5109):812-816.

33. Fishel R, Lescoe MK, Rao MR et al. The human mutator gene homolog MSH2 and its association with hereditary nonpolyposis colon cancer. Cell 1993;75(5):1027-1038.
34. Leach FS, Nicolaides NC, Papadopoulos N et al. Mutations of a mutS homolog in hereditary nonpolyposis colorectal cancer. Cell 1993;75(6):1215-1225.
35. Parsons R, Li GM, Longley MJ et al. Hypermutability and mismatch repair deficiency in RER+ tumor cells. Cell 1993;75(6):1227-1236.
36. Lindblom A, Tannergard P, Werelius B, Nordenskjold M. Genetic mapping of a second locus predisposing to hereditary non-polyposis colon cancer. Nat Genet 1993;5(3):279-282.
37. Bronner CE, Baker SM, Morrison PT et al. Mutation in the DNA mismatch repair gene homologue hMLH1 is associated with hereditary non-polyposis colon cancer. Nature 1994;368(6468):258-261.
38. Papadopoulos N, Nicolaides NC, Wei YF et al. Mutation of a mutL homolog in hereditary colon cancer. Science 1994;263(5153):1625-1629.
39. Nicolaides NC, Papadopoulos N, Liu B et al. Mutations of two PMS homologues in hereditary nonpolyposis colon cancer. Nature 1994;371(6492):75-80.
40. Palombo F, Gallinari P, Iaccarino I et al. GTBP, a 160-kilodalton protein essential for mismatch-binding activity in human cells. Science 1995;268(5219):1912-1914.
41. Papadopoulos N, Nicolaides NC, Liu B et al. Mutations of GTBP in genetically unstable cells. Science 1995;268(5219):1915-1917.
42. Miyaki M, Konishi M, Tanaka K et al. Germline mutation of MSH6 as the cause of hereditary nonpolyposis colorectal cancer. Nat Genet 1997;17(3):271-272.
43. Boland CR, Thibodeau SN, Hamilton SR et al. A National Cancer Institute Workshop on Microsatellite Instability for cancer detection and familial predisposition: development of international criteria for the determination of microsatellite instability in colorectal cancer. Cancer Res 1998;58(22):5248-5257.
44. Umar A, Boland CR, Terdiman JP et al. Revised Bethesda Guidelines for hereditary nonpolyposis colorectal cancer (Lynch syndrome) and microsatellite instability. J Natl Cancer Inst 2004;96(4):261-268.
45. Lindor NM, Rabe K, Petersen GM et al. Lower cancer incidence in Amsterdam-I criteria families without mismatch repair deficiency: familial colorectal cancer type X. JAMA 2005;293(16):1979-1985.
46. Boland CR, Shike M. Report from the Jerusalem workshop on Lynch syndrome-hereditary nonpolyposis colorectal cancer. Gastroenterology 2010;138(7):2197.
47. Goel A, Xicola RM, Nguyen TP et al. Aberrant DNA methylation in hereditary nonpolyposis colorectal cancer without mismatch repair deficiency. Gastroenterology 2010;138(5):1854-1862.
48. Palomaki GE, McClain MR, Melillo S, Hampel HL, Thibodeau SN. EGAPP supplementary evidence review: DNA testing strategies aimed at reducing morbidity and mortality from Lynch syndrome. Genet Med 2009;11(1):42-65.

49. Wijnen J, van der KH, Vasen H et al. MSH2 genomic deletions are a frequent cause of HNPCC. Nat Genet 1998;20(4):326-328.
50. Yan H, Papadopoulos N, Marra G et al. Conversion of diploidy to haploidy. Nature 2000;403(6771):723-724.
51. Ligtenberg MJ, Kuiper RP, Chan TL et al. Heritable somatic methylation and inactivation of MSH2 in families with Lynch syndrome due to deletion of the 3' exons of TACSTD1. Nat Genet 2009;41(1):112-117.
52. Koi M, Umar A, Chauhan DP et al. Human chromosome 3 corrects mismatch repair deficiency and microsatellite instability and reduces N-methyl-N'-nitro-N-nitrosoguanidine tolerance in colon tumor cells with homozygous hMLH1 mutation. Cancer Res 1994;54(16):4308-4312.
53. Hawn MT, Umar A, Carethers JM et al. Evidence for a connection between the mismatch repair system and the G2 cell cycle checkpoint. Cancer Res 1995;55(17):3721-3725.
54. Carethers JM, Hawn MT, Chauhan DP et al. Competency in mismatch repair prohibits clonal expansion of cancer cells treated with N-methyl-N'-nitro-N-nitrosoguanidine. J Clin Invest 1996;98(1):199-206.
55. Carethers JM, Chauhan DP, Fink D et al. Mismatch repair proficiency and in vitro response to 5-fluorouracil. Gastroenterology 1999;117(1):123-131.
56. Aebi S, Kurdi-Haidar B, Gordon R et al. Loss of DNA mismatch repair in acquired resistance to cisplatin. Cancer Res 1996;56(13):3087-3090.
57. Fink D, Nebel S, Aebi S et al. The role of DNA mismatch repair in platinum drug resistance. Cancer Res 1996;56(21):4881-4886.
58. Arnold CN, Goel A, Boland CR. Role of hMLH1 promoter hypermethylation in drug resistance to 5-fluorouracil in colorectal cancer cell lines. Int J Cancer 2003;106(1):66-73.
59. Elsaleh H, Joseph D, Grieu F, Zeps N, Spry N, Iacopetta B. Association of tumour site and sex with survival benefit from adjuvant chemotherapy in colorectal cancer. Lancet 2000;355(9217):1745-1750.
60. Boland CR, Goel A. Microsatellite instability in colorectal cancer. Gastroenterology 2010;138(6):2073-2087.
61. Ribic CM, Sargent DJ, Moore MJ et al. Tumor microsatellite-instability status as a predictor of benefit from fluorouracil-based adjuvant chemotherapy for colon cancer. N Engl J Med 2003;349(3):247-257.
62. Galon J, Costes A, Sanchez-Cabo F et al. Type, density, and location of immune cells within human colorectal tumors predict clinical outcome. Science 2006;313(5795):1960-1964.
63. Fridman WH, Pages F, Sautes-Fridman C, Galon J. The immune contexture in human tumours: impact on clinical outcome. Nat Rev Cancer 2012;12(4):298-306.

64. Burn J, Bishop DT, Mecklin JP et al. Effect of aspirin or resistant starch on colorectal neoplasia in the Lynch syndrome. N Engl J Med 2008;359(24):2567-2578.
65. Burn J, Gerdes AM, Macrae F et al. Long-term effect of aspirin on cancer risk in carriers of hereditary colorectal cancer: an analysis from the CAPP2 randomised controlled trial. Lancet 2011;378(9809):2081-2087.

Acknowledgements

Thanks to my cousin Leslie McCann for providing photos and helping with all of the identities of the people in the photos.

Thanks to my cousins Ed and Lynda Kuhn, Michael Boland, Steven Boland, Brian Boland and others for fact-checking the family history and proving details about the family history.

Thanks to Millie Arnold, RN, Research Nurse at Baylor University Medical Center at Dallas who worked so passionately with our hereditary colorectal cancer patients, and prepared some of the pedigree data on the Boland family.

Thanks to Sheryl Walker and Ebony Harris, of the Genetic Counseling Program at Baylor University Medical Center at Dallas for drawing pedigrees.

Thanks to Jennifer Rhees for the depiction of panhandle PCR and for her guidance of Matt Yurgelun in the cloning of the *MSH2* breakpoint sequence that ultimately led to control of the colorectal cancer problem in the Boland family.

Thanks to many colleagues who have sat down for interviews and shared private exchanges and recollections of their roles in the discoveries that contributed to the solution of the hereditary colorectal cancer problem. In particular, Bert Vogelstein has exchanged information generously for many years, and provided insight and corrections for portions of the book in which his work was cited. Thanks to Manuel Perucho and Steve Thibodeau for many conversations and specifically providing willing interviews at the time of this writing. Thanks to Richard Kolodner for being a generous collaborator and openly discussing many of the details of the competitions that were part of these discoveries. Also, Lauri Aaltonen,

Annika Lindblom, Rick Fishel and Albert de la Chapelle provided essential details of their contributions, for which I am grateful.

The entire Boland family gives thanks to Matt Yurgelun, Jennifer Rhees, Koi, and the critical input and assistance from the Vogelstein laboratory in the development of the test that has saved many lives.

Printed in the United States
By Bookmasters